TAGUCHI METHODS FOR ROBUST DESIGN

TAGUCHI METHODS FOR ROBUST DESIGN

YUIN WU
ALAN WU

FOREWORD BY
DR. GENICHI TAGUCHI

2000

Additional copies may be obtained by contacting:

The American Society of Mechanical Engineers
Customer Service
22 Law Drive, P. O. Box 2900
Fairfield, New Jersey 07007-2900
1-800-843-2763
www.asme.org

The American Supplier Institute
38701 Seven Mile Road, Suite 355
Livonia, Michigan 48152
1-800-462-4500
www.amsup.com

Library of Congress Cataloging-in-Publication Data

Wu, Yuin.
   Taguchi Methods for robust design/by Yuin Wu & Alan Wu.
      p. cm.
   Includes bibliographical references and index.
   ISBN 0-7918-0157-8
      1. Taguchi methods (Quality control) 2. Design, Industrial. 3. New products. I. Wu, Alan, 1960- II. Title.

   TS156.W85 2000
   658.5'62—dc21   00-042105

Table of Contents

List of Figures

List of Tables

Foreword

Quality Engineering (Taguchi Methods®) is a technology to forecast and prevent quality problems at the early stages of product development and product design, including the troubles associated with a product's function, pollution, and other costs that occur downstream in manufacturing and in the marketplace.

The English language publications that are available in the market today, including books and computer software, are mostly fragmentary. That is to say, their coverage of various fields of application is narrow.

This is the type of book I am delighted to see published because it provides the following unique benefits:

1. This book focuses on dynamic characteristics, explained in full detail, followed by a minor section on nondynamic characteristics. The signal-to-noise ratio (SN ratio) for dynamic characteristics, especially for the generic function of a product, is the most important measure for product development for all aspects of technology readiness, flexibility, and reproducibility. However, the SN ratio for nondynamic characteristics is also necessary for product design by simulation.

2. The book illustrates the methods of data collection and use of the SN ratio for evaluating the functionality of products in various fields of engineering. This is important because there are no books that parallel *Taguchi Methods for Robust Design*. For example, whereas in the chemical or biological fields, data such as yield or the rate of survival are used for molecules that inherently generate strong interactions, here, dynamic SN ratios such as reaction speed are introduced instead. In the design of electronic circuits, a new, complex number SN ratio is introduced to evaluate the relationships between the input and the

output. Examples are introduced with numerical values. These approaches to data collection and SN ratio use are new and are just recently being applied.

3. In the process of actually practicing Parameter Design, missing data or off-scale data often occur. The analyses for these cases are plainly illustrated in this book, and solutions are obtained by using available software.

4. The *STN for Windows* software, which includes most of the SN ratios introduced in the book, is available from American Supplier Institute (ASI). In the cases of chemical, biological, or electronics applications, for example, the software performs the calculations once data are available. Of course, it is important to know how to utilize the conclusions after the analysis is completed. The user focuses on issues of functionality and sensitivity, and the software takes care of all the calculations and provides reports as well.

Based on the above four reasons, I strongly recommend this bundle package for engineers in all fields as the best English version in Quality Engineering (see Glossary for boldface terms). I am very pleased to see this book and computer software published.

Dr. Genichi Taguchi
Executive Director
American Supplier Institute

Preface

In the beginning, quality control activities focused on inspection. In doing so, the final products were screened to prevent shipping defective products to the market. Later, the realization came that it was more efficient to monitor a manufacturing process in order to minimize the production of defectives, and thus, statistical process control was born. These experiences suggested that the further upstream quality engineering activities were implemented, the more efficient and more economical the results would be.

However, once drawings and specifications are completed and production processes are selected, product quality is almost fully determined: there is little the production engineers can do to further improve quality. Today, Quality Engineering (Taguchi Methods®), starts in the research-and-development stage. Quality optimization activities must begin before any actual product is planned and before any physical product drawings are available. The question then is, how can we evaluate the robustness of future product functions?

Here, we come to the point where we must shift our paradigms on how a quality focus can be initiated in R&D. Quality Engineering pioneer Dr. Genichi Taguchi emphasizes the following key points:

1. Do not use customer-based quality measures (such as fraction of defects or reliability) as the upstream measure of quality in R&D.
2. Use the dynamic signal-to-noise (SN) ratio as the performance index to evaluate the robustness of a product's function.

For decades, the SN ratio has been used to evaluate the performance of communication systems. This index represents the ratio of the power of a signal to the power of noise, or the ratio of desirable effects to harmful effects.

In the 1950s, Dr. Taguchi started utilizing this concept to evaluate the quality of measurement systems. His logic was that all communication systems could be considered measuring devices. Later, he pointed out that the SN ratio concept and approach could be used to evaluate the quality of product functions. This innovative concept was described in his book, *Experimental Design*, published by Maruzen in 1958. In 1972, *Signal-to-Noise Ratio Manual for Test and Measurement Methods Comparison* was published by the Japanese Standards Association.

The application of this concept has since spread beyond the original area of measurement and has penetrated into various industries for the measurement of product quality and performance. In 1980, the Japanese Standards Association and the American Supplier Institute collaborated and published the seven-volume Quality Engineering series. *Signal-to-Noise Ratio for Quality Evaluation* is the third volume of the series, introducing applications for measurement and product function evaluations.

While maintaining the original concept and philosophy, the applications of SN ratio have become more and more versatile. When the SN ratio is used to evaluate the robustness of a product's function, it represents "functionality." When applied to evaluate the robustness of a product and a process, it is referred to as "transformability." Recently, the applications have explored new frontiers: SN ratio with complex numbers for circuit design, and dynamic operating window for chemical reactions.

As the applications have become more diverse and the SN ratio equations have become more complicated, there is a strong need to elaborate on these newly developed SN ratios. This book provides detailed illustrations of these various applications.

Hundreds of successful case studies have been published, some of them are introduced in Chapter 11. It is interesting to see that the vast majority of these case studies used the zero-point proportional equation, the simplest but the most important calculation among various cases. For quick applications without knowing various cases, the beginners may skip Chapters 4, 6, 7, 8, and 9.

Although the application of the zero-point proportional equation is simple, the establishment of the ideal function that describes the behavior of a product, a process, or a system is not easy often. The ideal function differs from case to case, a reality that must be discussed by the engineers of product design, process design, or research and development. The case studies in Chapter 11 will assist in figuring out how to define the ideal function.

The authors would like to express their gratitude to Dr. Genichi Taguchi for his patient and inspirational teaching and guidance. They would also like to thank the authors who generously granted permission for the use of their case studies, the invaluable editorial assistance from Dr. William Bellows, Ms. Marilyn Hwan, and the superb efforts on manuscript preparation from David Wu and Bettina Wu.

The authors would like to thank ASME Press Editor Ms. Mary Grace Stefanchik for her dedication and Ms. Lynn Rosenfeld of ASME Press for her efforts for the book's timely appearance.

Finally, our enormous gratitude goes to Subir Chowdhury, Executive Vice President at the American Supplier Institute for his constant encouragement, editing, and support from day one.

Yuin Wu

Alan Wu

1

Introduction

1.1 WHAT IS QUALITY ENGINEERING?

Quality engineering (see Glossary) is a generic term. Its meaning can be perceived differently by different professionals. In the context of this book, however, Quality Engineering is used in the sense defined by Dr. Genichi Taguchi. (To make this distinction, we capitalize the term.) The body of knowledge of Dr. Taguchi's work, popularly known as Taguchi Methods [R], includes the following practices:

▶ Quality Engineering
▶ Experimental Design
▶ Business Data Analysis
▶ Management by Total Results
▶ Pattern Recognition

Among those methods, as described by Dr. Taguchi, only Quality Engineering and Experimental Design are available in English. See References (1) and (2).

Quality engineering is a series of approaches to predict and prevent the troubles or problems that might occur in the market after a product is sold and used by the customer under various environmental and applying conditions for the duration of designed product life.

There are two areas in Quality Engineering:

1. **Off-line:** applied in research, product, and process development.
2. **On-line:** applied during production.

In the early days of quality control, it was widely believed that poor quality was the problem of the production department. In reality, once the drawings of a product are made, its specifications are determined, and the manufacturing process is given, there is very little room for quality improvement. Drawings and specifications must be determined after Parameter Design, the approach in off-line Quality Engineering. Parameter Design is a means of selecting the best control factor level combination for the optimization of the robustness of product function against noise factors. Noise factors affect product function and include customer-usage conditions, internal deterioration, and the piece-to-piece variability of the parts that comprise a product. Of course, Parameter Design can be applied for manufacturing process optimization; but at that late stage it can be used to reduce only one type of noise: piece-to-piece variability. Parameter Design for a manufacturing process cannot reduce the problems caused by customer-usage conditions such as the operating environment. It cannot reduce deterioration either. In other words, manufacturing process optimization through Parameter Design can deal only with one of the three noise factors. In contrast, using Parameter Design for off-line Quality Engineering can reduce the impacts caused by all sources of noise. In this book, only the applications to off-line Quality Engineering are explained.

Historically, quality control activities during production rely on the use of control charts. However, control charts are basically a monitoring tool for maintaining existing quality levels; the charts do not reveal how to improve quality. Another important issue is that in the control-chart method, the economic viewpoint is vague. There are no guidelines for determining the optimum sampling frequency or how many samples should be taken. These actions directly relate to the quality and cost of a product.

In on-line Quality Engineering, the stress is on improving productivity, rather than improving quality. For example, we should diagnose the health of a manufacturing process to minimize the production of defective parts. Appropriate actions would include determining the optimum inspection interval and control limits to adjust the process, establishing preventative maintenance systems, designing the process connection systems toward the goal of full automation, and rationalizing inspection systems. All of these activities are evaluated through quality loss function considerations. Monetary evaluation is mandatory throughout all methods. For additional insight on on-line Quality Engineering, see Volume 2 of Reference 1.

There are some misunderstandings about Taguchi Methods in the Western countries. Some of them are:

1. Taguchi Method is experimental design.
2. Taguchi Method is the use of orthogonal arrays.
3. In Taguchi Method, interactions are not considered to be important, so they are neglected.

These will be discussed in the next sections.

1.2 QUALITY ENGINEERING AND EXPERIMENTAL DESIGN

The foundations of experimental design were developed by Sir R. A. Fisher in the 1920s, some 20 to 30 years before Quality Engineering was developed by Dr. Taguchi. Essentially, experimental design is a method for efficiently designing experiments and analyzing the results. It is the search for *cause-and-effect* relationships. It has been and continues to be used in areas of research that include biology, medicine, agriculture, and social sciences, etc.

When experimental design is used for science, there should be only one cause-and-effect relationship. In other words, only one equation should describe a particular natural phenomenon. In engineering, however, there are numerous equations that can describe the relationship between an object and its function, meaning that there are numerous ways of designing a product for a particular objective or function. Engineers must find the very best design, the one whose function is the most robust against all kinds of noise at the lowest cost.

From the above comparison, it is clear that Quality Engineering and experimental design differ in their objectives. Experimental design may be used for quality engineering, but in a different way than the traditional experimental design developed by Fisher. Dr. Taguchi has developed his own experimental design approaches, and they are unique in comparison to traditional applications.

In the traditional approach, nothing is mentioned about the role of any relationships among independent factors (variables)—i.e., relationships referred to as interactions. In scientific applications, interactions are commonly studied to explain a natural phenomenon.

By definition, two factors are said to interact when changes in one factor affect the influence of the second. For example, two levels of factor A, A_1 and A_2, are compared under a certain level of another factor, B_1. The result show that A_1 is better than A_2 by a certain magnitude. But when A_1 and A_2 are compared at another level of factor B, B_2, the magnitude of the effect of A is different. Therefore, ***an interaction can be expressed as the inconsistency, or nonreproducibility of* factorial effects.**

Traditionally, a product is designed, manufactured, and sold, and quality is improved based on customer feedback from the market. Any future problems that may occur in the market are not likely to be predicted or prevented during the product-design stage. However, at the very least it would be fair to say that there is a need for a systematic and effective way to do so. This need is addressed by Quality Engineering, a method in which a product is designed after optimizing the robustness of its function. The best stage of applying Quality Engineering is during the R & D stage; therefore, the conclusions obtained from even a small-scale research laboratory are well-reproduced downstream, in the large-scale manufacturing of the product as well as in the market place.

The existence of interactions suggests the existence of inconsistency and nonreproducibility of conclusions; therefore, we must try to avoid **interactions among control factors** by all means. That is the best way to improve the efficiency of research work, as will be discussed later in this chapter.

Another important issue in traditional experimental design is that the significance of a factorial effect is statistically tested against random error, as defined by the error variance. Random error is similar to **chance causes** in a statistical process control chart. In contrast, in Quality Engineering, the error includes all sources of variation: environmental disturbances, deterioration, and piece-to-piece variability. Each source is much larger than random error. In Parameter Design, noise factors are intentionally introduced and exaggerated, to purposely introduce error into an experiment.

Moreover, significance testing in experimental design is based on the validity of two key assumptions:

1. Error follows the normal distribution.
2. There is equal variability between errors.

In Quality Engineering, the distributions of noise factors are not expected to follow normal distributions. For example, product deterioration over time does not follow a normal distribution. But most importantly, there are no cases of equal variability in Quality Engineering. Instead what we want to accomplish is to find if there is a difference between the magnitude of the errors of two control factor levels. If there is a significant difference in magnitude, we can select the control factor level with a smaller error, so that a robust condition may be determined. In other words, if there is equal variability, the ability of Parameter Design to minimize error becomes impossible. The paradigm of equal variability assumption cannot coexist with Parameter Design.

Taguchi Methods is not experimental design. The philosophy and approach in traditional experimental design should not be confused with the one used in Quality Engineering.

1.3 INTERACTIONS AND ORTHOGONAL ARRAYS _____

Another common misunderstanding about Taguchi Methods is that Dr. Taguchi does not value the importance of interactions. This concern is completely wrong, and contrary to Taguchi Methods. To explain this misconception, we must understand that there are two kinds of interactions:

1. Interactions between a control factor and a noise factor
2. Interactions among control factors

Such a distinction does not exist in traditional experimental design. From a Quality Engineering viewpoint, the former is **useful** and the latter is *harmful*.

A control factor is a factor that can be selected and fixed to a certain level after Parameter Design. A **noise factor** is a factor that cannot be controlled, due to either practical or economic reasons.

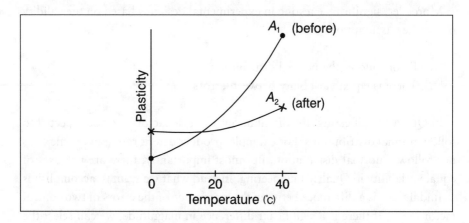

Figure 1.1   Effect of room temperature on plasticity of caramels

To explain the first type of interaction, let's use an experiment on the deterioration for two materials. Material type is a control factor, and deterioration is a noise factor. The results of this experiment show that material A_1 deteriorated significantly, but material A_2 deteriorated very little. In this case, the effect of deterioration was different when the type of material was changed from A_1 to A_2.

Right after World War II, Dr. Taguchi assisted with an experiment on the manufacturing of caramels for M Company in Japan. In Fig. 1.1, curve A_1 shows the chewing plasticity of caramels before the experiment. The plasticity varied greatly by temperature. The purpose of the experiment was to produce caramels with a plasticity that would not be affected by temperature. In the experiment, control factors such as raw materials and their contents were varied. As a result, quality (more consistent plasticity) was improved. The effect of temperature on plasticity after quality improvement was much like the A_2 curve in Fig. 1.1. The two curves show a significant interaction between the control factor (caramel formulation) and the noise factor (room temperature).

By discovering the interaction between a control factor and a noise factor, we have an opportunity to find a robust condition (e.g.) by selecting formula A_2. Such a discovery is absolutely necessary in Parameter Design, or in robust design.

In order to discover such interactions, signal-to-noise ratios (SN ratios) are calculated and compared. As described in later chapters, SN ratio is the best index for quality. The higher the SN ratio, the less deterioration. As a result, it is simple and easy for engineers to analyze. We just need to compare the SN ratio of two control factor levels.

SN ratios have been used in the communications industry for nearly a century and were introduced in Quality Engineering in the late 1950s. However, the concept of robust design had existed before SN ratios were introduced in Quality Engineering, in the form of discovering the interactions between control and noise factors under the name **direct product design** (Reference 2). Since the calculation of the interactions is very tedious, a lot of time was spent on such calculations. SN ratios were introduced to simplify data analysis.

The second type of interaction, the one among control factors, is harmful in Quality Engineering. It must be avoided by all means. One might think that since an interaction is a fact, how can we avoid or eliminate it? The answer is that the existence of an interaction depends on what kind of measurement is used for analysis. In other words, it depends on the type of quality characteristic selected for analysis. This concept has never been recognized in traditional experimental design.

As stated before, interaction is synonymous with *inconsistency* and *nonreproducibility*. The objective of Quality Engineering is to predict the problems that could occur in the market and conduct research or design a product before production—that is, the aim is to design a product based on the conclusions made in the laboratory. Conclusions must be interaction-free and reproducible later, in either a large-scale manufacturing process or in the customer's hands.

How can we select a good quality characteristic to avoid interactions? The answer is to use SN ratio, especially dynamic SN ratio. A great many case studies have proven that when such SN ratios have been used, the conclusions made in the laboratories were well-reproduced downstream.

However, it is not easy to assure that the SN ratio selected for a study will show no, or insignificant, interactions between a noise and a control factor. As a result, we need to *inspect the existence of such interactions* during the stage of laboratory research. For this purpose, orthogonal arrays are used.

Table 1.1 is an example of an orthogonal array, called the L_{12} array. In the table, control factors A, B, ..., K are assigned to columns 1, 2,..., 11, respectively. We see that in each pair of columns, the combinations (11),

Table 1.1   Orthogonal array L_{12} (2^{11})

	A	B	C	D	E	F	G	H	I	J	K	
No.	1	2	3	4	5	6	7	8	9	10	11	Result
1	1	1	1	1	1	1	1	1	1	1	1	y_1
2	1	1	1	1	1	2	2	2	2	2	2	y_2
3	1	1	2	2	2	1	1	1	2	2	2	y_3
4	1	2	1	2	2	1	2	2	1	1	2	y_4
5	1	2	2	1	2	2	1	2	1	2	1	y_5
6	1	2	2	2	1	2	2	1	2	1	1	y_6
7	2	1	2	2	1	1	2	2	1	2	1	y_7
8	2	1	2	1	2	2	2	1	1	1	2	y_8
9	2	1	1	2	2	2	1	2	2	1	1	y_9
10	2	2	2	1	1	1	1	2	2	1	2	y_{10}
11	2	2	1	2	1	2	1	1	1	2	2	y_{11}
12	2	2	1	1	2	1	2	1	2	2	1	y_{12}

(12), (21), and (22) occur the same number of times. When this happens, the array is called orthogonal, indicating that a fair comparison of any factor can be made.

To compare the effect of A, we calculate the average of the results under A_1 and A_2, respectively. The average of A_1 is calculated from run No. 1 through 6, and that of A_2, from No. 7 through 12. We can see that in the six runs under A_1, all of the other factor conditions change. The same is true for A_2. The comparison of the averages between A_1 and A_2 is made while all other factor conditions are changed. Therefore, if the difference between the averages of A_1 and A_2 becomes significantly large compared with the differences of other factors, a conclusion that A_2 is better than A_1 is probably consistent. On the other hand, if the effects of all factors are almost similar, those factorial effects are probably confounded with many interactions, and the conclusions are probably unreliable. To make sure, the optimum condition selected from such orthogonal array experimentation must be verified by conducting a confirmatory experiment. This is a requirement when orthogonal arrays are used for Quality Engineering.

Under conditions when factors are fully assigned to all columns of an orthogonal array without assigning any interactions and the conclusion is verified by a confirmatory experiment, the conclusion is said to be **robust**. That is, there is a strong possibility that the conclusion will be reproduced when conditions of other factors, not studied in the experiment (such as the conditions under which customers use the product), change in the market.

Traditionally, experimentation is conducted in a one-factor-at-a-time fashion—that is, only one factor is varied while the conditions of other factors are held constant. This seems to be a very efficient and simple method to use, and is easy to understand. If there were no interactions, a one-factor-type experiment is the best method to use.

If interactions exist, there is no way to detect them using this type of experimentation. Also, this method cannot be used to determine what any existing interactions are significant. Consequently, the best condition determined from this type of experiment could be the worst condition, due to the existence of interactions.

The following strategies regarding interactions are recommended in Quality Engineering:

▶ Selection of quality characteristic to be used for analysis
▶ Use of dynamic SN ratio
▶ Use of fully saturated orthogonal arrays
▶ Use of confirmation experiments and prediction equations

1.4   ROBUST TECHNOLOGY DEVELOPMENT

In the early days of the development of Quality Engineering, the objective was to reduce the **variability** of a product caused by environmental conditions, deterioration, and piece-to-piece variability. The aim was to reduce variability by adjusting the mean to a *specific target*. These specific targets included zero, infinity, or a singular nominal value. In today's terminology, such an objective is called nondynamic. *Nondynamic refers to having a fixed target.* Such fixed-target-type quality is evaluated by nondynamic SN ratios.

In the mid-1960s, new concepts led to improvements in measurement systems. Since then, the objective when performing a measurement, such as with a testing device or an analysis method, is not limited to measuring the sample for only one specific true value. A measuring system is designed to measure the samples for a certain range of true values. The error must be small not only for measuring a certain value but for the whole range of operation. This leads to a need for an index to evaluate the error for the full range of the output, a purpose for which dynamic SN ratio was developed.

In the 1970s, besides their application in measurement, SN ratios were widely applied to the optimization of products and processes. Interestingly, non-dynamic SN ratios were used more often than dynamic type in this period. Nondynamic SN ratios include the following categories:

▶ Nominal is best (target = nominal)
▶ Smaller is better (target = zero)
▶ Larger is better (target = infinity)
▶ Operating window (target = infinity)

Some dynamic applications for product function were reported in the same period, for example, an experiment on the driveability of trucks. There were new applications of the SN ratio to digital systems, with an example being an experiment involving a function for separating tobacco leaves from stems. Many applications were reported using SN ratio for computer simulations in electrical and mechanical areas.

In the 1980s, SN ratios were applied to a new area: evaluation of the **functionality** of products. The meaning of the term is to optimize the function for a group of products, not just a particular product. In the nondynamic approach, a product has a particular target. In parameter design, two-step optimization is used: first, the robustness of a product is improved by maximizing the SN ratio; next, the mean of the product output is adjusted to the target. In this way, products are developed sequentially. Product development is necessary every time a new product with a new target output is planned. By using the dynamic approach, it is possible to develop a broader group of products in one study. The two-step optimization strategy of the dynamic approach is also utilized to maximize the SN ratio first. As described in Chapter 3, the dynamic SN ratio includes the linear relationship between the input and output; in other words, the sensitivity and variability of the response between the input and the output are included. As defined, when the SN ratio is maximized, both linearity and sensitivity between the input and the output are improved. The implication is that the output can be easily adjusted by changing the input. In terms of robust design, the function of a group of products is improved. Therefore, the development of a new product that belongs to a group can be completed in a very short time cycle. As a result, the application started to penetrate into the basic research and development area. Today, this approach is called **robust technology development**.

The use of robust technology development provides the following benefits:

▶ **Technology readiness**

Research and developmental activities are initiated before products are planned. Studies can be conducted using small-scale laboratory experiments on test pieces to optimize the basic or generic function of a group of products.

▶ **Flexibility**

A group of products can be improved rather than just individual products. Once the robustness of the product function is optimized, newly planned products within the same family can be designed and manufactured by straightforward adjustments. In this manner, the output of the new product can be achieved in a short time at a low product-development cost.

▶ **Reproducibility**

The conclusions from far upstream—for instance, laboratory research— can be reproduced downstream, in production as well as in the market place.

All of these benefits bring about a short product-development cycle time. A new product can be put on the market before competition exists, and the company can enjoy a healthy profit until similar products from competitors appear.

In order to be successful in robust technology development, an engineer must take the following three key steps:

1. Identify the generic function of a product, system, or subsystem.
2. Use SN ratio, especially dynamic SN ratio, as the index for the robustness of function.
3. Use orthogonal arrays to predict whether the conclusions from the research can be reproduced downstream (in manufacturing as well as in the market).

Traditionally, there are common approaches in product development or product design. They try to: design a product to solve problems; analyze the root causes of troubles or variation; and measure or observe the symptoms and use them for data analysis.

All of those approaches result in selecting wrong quality characteristics. As described in Chapter 10, there are four levels in quality: Downstream quality, Midstream quality, Upstream quality, and Origin quality.

The approaches described above lead engineers to select downstream or midstream quality characteristics; therefore, the conclusions from the study cannot be well-reproduced, for the following reasons.

Downstream quality is called customer quality and includes such examples as car noise, gasoline mileage, vibration, etc. Midstream quality is called specified quality, with examples being dimensions or specifications, etc. Upstream quality is called robust quality and relies on the use of nondynamic **SN ratios**. Origin quality is called functional quality and relies on on the use of dynamic SN ratios. For the details of those characteristics, see later chapters.

Of the four quality levels, the interactions related to downstream quality tend to occur very frequently, and the ones related to midstream quality occur less significantly but still frequently. The ones associated with upstream quality occur much less often, and the ones related to origin quality occur minimally. Since an interaction is synonymous with inconsistency, poor **additivity**, or nonreproducibility, it is very important to understand that the selection of quality characteristics is the key to avoiding interactions. Once interactions can be avoided, the research from a small-scale laboratory can be well-reproduced downstream.

The first step, identification of generic function, is the most important as well as the most difficult task. Considerations of the generic function of a product or a system must be thoroughly discussed and be based on knowledge in relevant specialized fields, such as mechanical, electrical, or chemical engineering.

Once the generic function is correctly identified, the SN ratio that expresses the input and output relationship must be selected, it will be used for data analysis. However, the generic function of a certain product or a system is different from any other one. Even for the same generic function, the SN ratio equation could be different under different experimental setup due to some restricted conditions. That is why it is not easy to pick up a correct SN ratio; it is not like placing an order from a menu in a restaurant. Quite often, one has to custom-write a specific SN-ratio equation.

However, there are many ready-to-use SN ratios already developed for various cases. A quick way to understand their use and application especially for beginners, is to be exposed to those SN ratios already published for various industries. Consequently, one of the objectives of this book is to introduce a wide variety of cases through numerical examples.

1.5   WHAT IS A SIGNAL-TO-NOISE RATIO?

SN ratio is a quality index that has been historically used in the communications industry for the evaluation of communications systems. In Quality Engineering, the concept of SN ratio has been adapted by Dr. Genichi Taguchi to evaluating the quality of a product or a manufacturing process.

Conceptually, SN ratio is the ratio of signal to noise in terms of power. For example, a radio is one of the receiving systems in communication. SN ratio indicates the ratio of intended signal (useful part) to noise (harmful part) and is used to evaluate quality when a product such as a radio is functioning. For instance, an inexpensive portable radio generally is noisy when played loudly, whereas at the more expensive end of the price scale, a hi-fi receiver would be expected to have a low noise level, even at high volume. The quality of these radios is normally defined in the product specifications by using SN ratio. Of course, the SN ratio of the former is low, and of the latter, high.

From another viewpoint, SN ratio represents the ratio of sensitivity (or "average" in nondynamic terminology to variability). Traditionally, the research for a product or a manufacturing process aims for a target, a fixed target, in the first place. For example, to design an electric circuit is to generate a certain output voltage, or to design a system is to maintain a certain temperature. Variability is typically not taken into consideration until a problem occurs in the market. Fixed target translates as "average" or "sensitivity." In the current higher education system, variability is discussed very little in fields such as mechanical, electrical, or chemical engineering, but it is discussed in industrial engineering.

One idea suggested by some quality experts is to study mean and variability separately. If a study were conducted under such a paradigm, then the best condition for minimizing variability might be the condition at which the mean is minimized. In the case of a radio, if variability is separately studied, the best condition for minimizing variability is attained by turning the volume to zero. But since the sensitivity, the music, or the mean then becomes zero, too, a radio at zero variability is useless. Each hardware has a certain SN ratio showing the quality of the product. Parameter Design tries to maximize the SN ratio by changing parameter levels of the control factors associated with the product's design.

1.6   WHERE CAN SN RATIOS BE USED?

In the 1960s, SN ratio was used for the evaluation and improvement of measuring systems, such as test or analysis methods. It was the earliest application of SN ratio for Quality Engineering. Traditionally, the evaluation of a measuring system was conducted by calculating two aspects: bias (deviation) and variability. However, these two elements cannot always be distinguished. In the case of a watch, for example, it is impossible to separate them, since time changes from moment to moment.

For example, a sample with a true value of 5.0 was measured three times to have results of 7.2, 7.0, and 6.8 (see Fig. 1.2). The average is 7.0, and there is a **bias** of 7.0 - 5.0 = 2.0. **Variation** is calculated from the three results to be around 7.0.

In the case of a watch, we can measure the error between the watch time and the standard time. Since there is no way to repeat measurements, there is no way to decompose "error" into the contributions of both *bias* and *variation*.

In the automobile industry, a measuring system is evaluated from three aspects: repeatability, reproducibility, and stability. **Repeatability** is the variation in measurements performed by the same person on the same sample. **Reproducibility** is the variation in measurements resulting from different persons measuring the same sample. And **stability** is the variation caused by making measurements at different times. However, these three aspects are nothing but the variation caused by noise in Quality Engineering.

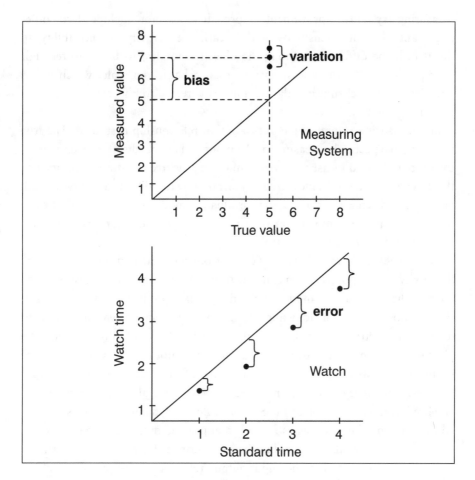

Figure 1.2   Input and output of a measuring system and of a watch

Traditionally, improvements in the quality of a measuring system are achieved by allocating the causes of variation into contributions from repeatability, reproducibility, and stability. Once the sources of variation are identified, efforts are made to remove or reduce the causes of variation. In Quality Engineering, this activity is considered to be Tolerance Design since it deals with noise. The preferred sequence of activity in Quality Engineering is for Parameter Design to precede Tolerance Design, so that the effects of noise may be reduced in a more cost-effective manner. In addition, the traditional measuring system improvement approach does not include two other important elements: **sensitivity** and **linearity**. Sensitivity is the ability to distinguish the differences among the objects (samples) to be measured. For example, a truck scale is less sensitive than a bathroom scale, which is less sensitive than a chemical balance. Linearity refers to the calibration of a measuring system.

In a measuring system, the input-to-output relationship is studied. The true value of the object to be measured is the input and the results of measurement is the output. A good measuring system must be sensitive to different inputs, i.e., the different objects to be measured. It must be easy to calibrate and have a small variability. When SN ratio is used to evaluate a measuring system, all of these three elements are combined in one index. As a result, engineers can easily evaluate and improve the system.

In the 1980s, SN ratio was considered from the viewpoint of adjustability. Sensitivity corresponds to mean in static mode, but it corresponds to adjustability in dynamic mode. In the design of a product for a fixed target, there is no necessity of adjusting the target. For example, we may want to design an electric circuit having an output voltage of 110V. Once the product is designed and put into production, it is not necessary to change the output voltage as long as we continue to manufacture and sell this particular product. Therefore, mean is considered as being equivalent to sensitivity and is placed in the numerator of the SN ratio. But in dynamic systems, such as a control system, there is always a need to adjust the output to target by using a certain input signal. Adjustability becomes critical for the design. In such a case, it is important that the input/output relationship be proportional, or linear. In other words, linearity becomes critical for adjusting systems. The greater the linearity and the steeper the input/output relationship, the better the adjustability. Therefore, the slope is used as being equivalent to sensitivity and is placed in the numerator of the SN ratio. In a dynamic system, therefore, there are three requirements: sensitivity, linearity, and variability.

The concept of dynamic-type SN ratio evolved further in the 1980s in the area of technology development. This activity is defined by the development of technology for a group of future products so as to avoid redundant research work and thereby reduce research and development cycle time. For details, see Chapter 10.

1.7   CONCEPT OF SN RATIOS

As described in the previous section, SN ratios were first used for making measurements, and later their use was expanded to expressing the quality of products in the areas of product and process design. In Quality Engineering, both applications are called dynamic-type SN ratios. But specifically, the former is called **passive type** and the latter, **active type**. The SN ratio for measurement is called passive type because the result (output) is used to estimate the true value of the sample (input). In a control system on the other hand, the SN ratio it is called active type because the intent is to change the output. These patterns may be illustrated as follows:

Measurement System (passive):

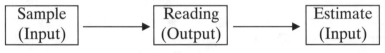

Control System (active):

As an example for the passive type, a receiver is a measurement system that receives the information of a signal sent from a transmitter. Since the quality of a communication system is effectively the same as the quality of a measuring system, the concept of the SN ratio can be applied to measuring systems.

Essentially, the basic requirements for a measuring system are:

1. From the same sample, results of measurement must be the same no matter where or when the sample is measured.
2. From two different samples, a small difference in measurement must be detected with high sensitivity.
3. A measurement system must be easy to calibrate.

Both in a communication and a measurement system, the indicator or measured values can be amplified either mechanically or electronically. However, if the measured value is amplified by ten times; the variation of measured values from the same sample also becomes greater by ten times;

the quality of the measuring system is not improved. The quality of a particular piece of hardware is constant and is captured by a SN ratio. To improve quality, it is necessary to make some changes in the hardware of the system.

The SN ratio of a measurement system is defined as follows:

$$\text{SN ratio} = \frac{\text{Power of signal}}{\text{Power of noise}} = \frac{(\text{Sensitivity per unit input})^2}{(\text{Error per measurement})^2}$$

This equation is related to the three requirements as follows: When a measuring system is sensitive to the difference between samples, the SN ratio becomes greater. When measurement error decreases, the SN ratio increases. About the third requirement, ease of calibration is shown by the input and output relationship being proportional, in other words, by the input/output relationship being linear. The more linear the relationship, the greater the SN ratio. Thus, the SN ratio equation takes care of all three aspects of a measuring system, which makes it easy for engineers to efficiently evaluate and improve the quality of a measurement system.

The SN ratio is calculated by the decomposition of data. The question of which part of the variation is considered to be the signal and which part (or parts) is considered to be the noise will differ from case to case. In the active-type dynamic characteristic, a system exhibits the following pattern:

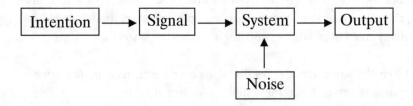

Such a pattern can be found in sport activities. In golf, for example, when a player wants to hit the ball the longest distance possible, there is an intention. The golfer then considers a signal by selecting the driver. His or her body is the system. In swinging and hitting the ball, the expected output is the ball flying a long distance. An example of noise might be wind.

The same pattern can be found in driving a car. If the intention is to drive faster, the signal is the accelerator. If the intention is to change direction, the signal is the steering angle. If the intention is to stop, the signal is the brake. An example of noise might be the driving speed.

In manufacturing processes, it is always necessary to change something, such as a dimension of a component part or a setting for a machine. In a stamping process, for example, the hardness or the thickness of steel coil varies from batch to batch. As a result, the dimension of the stamped piece varies. Using an adaptive control system, the dimension must be adjusted, based on the hardness and thickness change in the steel. In a stamping process, the dimension may be adjusted using either pressure or hold time. The important issue in such a case is which of these methods should be used for the adjustment.

Such a selection can be made based on the following criteria:

1. Which method has the higher sensitivity of adjustment? When the sensitivity is high, adjustment can be made with a small input change.
2. Which method has the better adjustability? Or which method has the better linearity? Linearity means the output is linearly proportional to the input. It is easier to adjust a system when input and output are proportional.
3. Which method has the smaller error of adjustment? Or which is less affected by noise factors?

Comparing the cases of passive-type and active-type SN ratios, we see that the three requirements are identical: sensitivity, linearity, and variability. Engineers can use the same index to evaluate or improve control systems.

1.8   BENEFITS OF USING SN RATIOS

There are many reason for using SN ratios in Quality Engineering, including the possibility of monetary evaluations, simplification of direct product design and of Robust design, easily determined adjustments and calibrations, assessment of measuring systems, enhancement of product-development cycles, and broad applicability of research. The benefits are discussed below.

1.8.1 Inverse Proportionality to the Loss Function

As seen from the equation such as Eq. (3.10), SN ratio is the ratio of sensitivity to variability squared. Therefore, its inverse is the **variance** *per unit* **input** and monetary evaluation is thus possible. In the Loss Function, the loss is proportional to **variance**.

1.8.2 Simplification of Direct Product Design

In the early 1950s, research for robustness was conducted by investigating the interactions between control and noise factors. When there is an interaction between a control factor and a noise factor, then there is a possibility that robustness can be improved. From the response table or response graph, we can select a control factor level that minimizes the variation caused by the noise factor. Such a study method was called **direct product design**. At that time, SN ratios were not utilized, but the principle was identical to that of the SN ratio. Today, such tedious calculation and observation using direct product design is no longer necessary. Instead, a comparison of SN ratios between control factor levels is made, and the one with a higher SN ratio is selected as the robust condition.

1.8.3 Simplifies Attainment of Robust Design

When using traditional methodology, engineers tend to design a product or a process by meeting the target first. However, this is a very inefficient way of designing for the following reasons. If the engineer wants to deal with a noise factor—for example, temperature, one of the environmental conditions under which the product is going to be used—the engineer has to change or adjust the design parameters to meet the target, so that the product works at a certain temperature. But while studying the effects of temperature, the engineer needs to keep other noise factors fixed at certain levels. Next, the engineer might consider another noise factor, such as humidity. He or she then tries to vary parameter levels under different humidity conditions and changes design parameters again to meet the target for humidity. In the first trial in which the aim was to meet the target at a certain temperature, the control factor levels selected were probably different from the control factor levels selected in the second trial, in which the aim was to meet the target at a certain humidity condition. In order to meet the target under a certain temperature as well as a certain humidity condition, the study must be started again from the beginning. The engineer has to do the same for any other noise factors that ought to be considered, and generally, there are a lot of noise factors. Not only is this kind of approach is tedious and time-consuming, but it cannot always be successful. Designing in this fashion is similar to solving many simultaneous equations through experimentation. If the engineer is good enough to consider as many as ten noise factors, what he or she does is similar to solving ten simultaneous equations by trial and error.

In contrast, the use of SN ratio enables the engineer to maximize robustness by simply selecting the levels of control factors that give the largest SN ratio. The next step is to adjust the mean to the target. In this way, *the efficiency of research can be improved by a factor of ten, a hundred, or a thousand.*

1.8.4   Simplification of Adjustments or Calibrations

One of the key elements in SN ratio is linearity. When the input/output relationship is not linear, the deviation from linearity is evaluated as the error after the decomposition of variation. Therefore, the SN ratio becomes smaller. When linearity is improved, the ratio becomes greater. Because the relationship between the value of an SN ratio and linearity is so simple and clear, adjusting of control systems and calibration of measurement systems becomes easier than when traditional methods are used.

1.8.5   Efficient Evaluation for Measuring Systems

In a measuring system, calibration is made to make the output equal to the input. After calibration, the slope of the input/output relationship is equal to one. When we take the inverse of an SN ratio, the value shows the variability when the slope is equal to one, suggesting that the estimation of the variance after calibration is possible without conducting physical calibration. This greatly improves the efficiency of measurement system optimization.

1.8.6   Reduction of Product-Development Cycle Time

A dynamic-type SN ratio is written based on the ideal function of a product or process. When sensitivity (the numerator of an SN ratio) increases, the product functions better, contributing to the robustness. If we can describe the input/output relationship of a dynamic system by the energy input and energy output of the system, then the effects of control factors are cumulative (additive).

While the interaction between a control factor and a noise factors enables us to find a robust condition, the interaction between control factors shows the inconsistency of conclusions: the conclusion might be different when the conditions of other control factors change. How to deal with or avoid interactions between control factors is one of the most important issues in Quality Engineering.

Facts from various case studies in the past have proven that the use of SN ratios based on the ideal function, and related with input/output energy transformation, enables us to avoid interactions between control factors. The consistency of conclusions obtained in a small-scale laboratory study can be reproduced in a large-scale manufacturing process and in the marketplace, where the customer uses the product. That is why the use of dynamic-type SN ratios can reduce product-development cycle time.

1.8.7   Research Applies to a Group of Products (Robust Technology Development)

An individual product has its own output target value. Traditionally, product research is conducted every time a new product is planned. But for a group of products of the same function within a certain output range, it would be wasteful to conduct research for each individual product, since doing so would be redundant. Instead, if we could establish an appropriate SN ratio based on the ideal function of a group of products and maximize it, the design of a specific product with a certain output target would be easily obtained by adjusting the input signal. This approach is called robust technology development, and is a breakthrough in Quality Engineering. It is believed that such an approach will soon become the core of Quality Engineering.

1.9   SIMPLE EXAMPLES

1.9.1   An Example of a Measurement System

To understand why the three aspects (linearity, sensitivity, and variability) are required to evaluate the quality of a measurement system, consider the following simple example.

In order to evaluate four weighing scales of different design (A_1, A_2, A_3, and A_4), three samples (M_1, M_2, and M_3) were used. The true values of the three samples are known to be 100, 200, and 300 pounds, respectively. A noise factor N, with two levels was used. Table 1.2 shows the results.

Table 1.2   Results of measurement (in pounds)

		Samples		
		$M_1 = 100$	$M_2 = 200$	$M_3 = 300$
Design	Noise	(lbs)	(lbs)	(lbs)
A_1	N_1	92	197	302
	N_2	98	203	308
	Total	190	400	610
	Average	95	200	305
A_2	N_1	87	207	297
	N_2	93	213	303
	Total	180	420	600
	Average	90	210	300
A_3	N_1	102	197	292
	N_2	108	203	298
	Total	210	400	590
	Average	105	200	295
A_3	N_1	90	195	300
	N_2	100	205	310
	Total	190	400	610
	Average	95	200	305

The results of Table 1.2 are plotted in Fig. 1.3.

The results were made up to give the following situations:

A_1:   Input/output relationship is linear. Variability is ± 3.

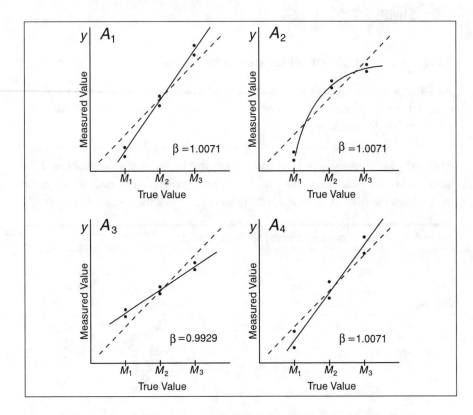

Figure 1.3 Graphs showing the results of the weighing scale experiment

A_2: Input/output relationship is not linear. Variability is ± 3.

A_3: Input/output relationship is linear. The slope is smaller than A_1.
Variability is ± 3.

A_4: Input/output relationship is linear. The slope is the same as A_1.
Variability is ± 5.

Compared with A_1

A_2 is not as linear as A_1.

A_3 has a smaller slope than A_1.

A_4 has a larger variability than A_1.

Table 1.3 shows the results of calculating the SN ratios, denoted by η, for A_1, A_2, A_3, and A_4. For the calculation, see Chapter 3.

Table 1.3   Results of calculating the SN ratios (η)

	S_T	S_β	S_e	V_e	β	η (db)
A_1	284154	284014.286	139.7	27.94	1.0071	-14.4013
A_2	284454	284014.286	439.7	87.94	1.0071	-19.3815
A_3	276154	276014.286	139.7	27.94	0.9929	-14.5254
A_4	284250	284104.286	235.7	47.14	1.0071	-16.6700

Comparing A_1 and A_2, the only difference is linearity. When the response becomes nonlinear, the deviation from linearity results in an increase of the error, or variability.

Comparing A_1 with A_3, the difference is in the slope of the response. When the response becomes less sensitive, the variation due to sensitivity, denoted by S_β, becomes smaller. The slope, β also becomes smaller.

Comparing A_1 with A_4, the difference is variability. When variability becomes worse, the error variance becomes greater.

In any comparison, the SN ratio becomes smaller when quality drops. This simple example illustrates the reason why the SN ratio is a good and effective evaluator of the quality of a measurement system.

In this example, A is a control factor with four levels. M is called a signal factor with three levels. N is a noise factor with two levels. When there are many control factors, these factors are assigned to an orthogonal array, called the inner array. The signal factors and noise factors are assigned to another array, called the outer array. These applications are discussed in Chapter 3 for dynamic-type SN ratios and Chapter 5 for nondynamic-type ones.

1.9.2   An Example of an Extrusion Process

In an extrusion process for thermoplastic tubing, the outside diameter of the tubing is adjusted by the rpm of an extruder screw.

Four screw types—A_1, A_2, A_3, and A_4—were investigated to select the one giving the best adjustability varied at four levels: $M_1 = 32$ rpm, $M_2 = 33$ rpm, $M_3 = 34$ rpm, and $M_4 = 35$ rpm.

Noise factors were compounded to be one with two levels, N_1 and N_2: Table 1.4 shows the results of the experiment.

	N_1	N_2
Time	1 hr	48 hrs
Moisture	Dry	0.2%

Compounding noise factors is an important and efficient technique in robust design. It is done to provide extreme conditions of the noise factors. In this example, both time and moisture condition are at two levels, so there are four combinations. Instead of conducting the experiment with four conditions, we need to pick up only two extreme conditions out of the four. If we can reduce the output variation caused by these two extreme conditions, any variation caused by the other two conditions should be even smaller. In this way, the scale of the experiment is halved.

Table 1.4 Experiment on best adjustability among extruder screws

Screw Type	Noise	Outside diameter (cm) Input (rpm)			
		$M_1=32$	$M_2=33$	$M_3=34$	$M_4=35$
A_1	N_1	1.596	1.646	1.696	1.746
	N_2	1.604	1.654	1.704	1.754
	Total	3.200	3.300	3.400	3.500
	Average	1.600	1.650	1.700	1.750
A_2	N_1	1.586	1.656	1.706	1.736
	N_2	1.594	1.664	1.714	1.744
	Total	3.180	3.320	3.420	3.480
	Average	1.590	1.660	1.710	1.740
A_3	N_1	1.916	1.976	2.036	2.096
	N_2	1.924	1.984	2.044	2.104
	Total	3.840	3.960	4.080	4.200
	Average	1.920	1.980	2.040	2.100
A_1	N_1	1.598	1.648	1.698	1.748
	N_2	1.602	1.652	1.702	1.752
	Total	3.200	3.300	3.400	3.500
	Average	1.600	1.650	1.700	1.750

The compounded noise factor conditions are:

N_1:   1 hr, dry condition. Both tend to make the output response a higher value.

N_2:   48 hr, wet condition. Both tend to make the output response a lower value.

Figure 1.4 shows the trends indicated by the experimental results listed in Table 1.4.

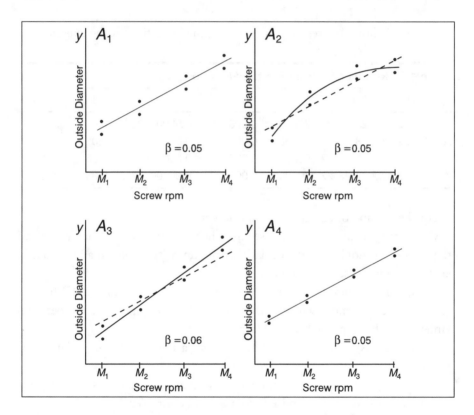

Figure 1.4   Trends of injection molding machine experiment

The four screw types exhibit the following situations:

A_1:   Linear; $\beta = 0.05$. Variability is ± 0.004 around the average.

A_2:   Not linear; $\beta = 0.05$. Variability is ± 0.004 around the average.

A_3:   Linear; the slope, $\beta = 0.06$. Variability is ± 0.004 around the average.

A_4:   Linear; the slope, $\beta = 0.05$. Variability is ± 0.002 around the average.

Compared with A_1,

A_2 is not as linear as A_1.

A_3 has a larger slope than A_1.

A_4 has a smaller variability than A_1.

Table 1.5 shows the results of calculating the SN ratios for the experiment.

Table 1.5   Results of calculating the SN ratios (η)

	S_T	S_β	S_e	V_e	β	η (db)
A_1	22.470128	22.470000	0.000128	0.000018285	0.05	21.36
A_2	22.470928	22.470000	0.000928	0.000132571	0.05	12.75
A_3	32.356928	32.356800	0.000128	0.000018285	0.06	22.94
A_4	22.470032	22.470000	0.000032	0.000004571	0.05	27.38

For the method of calculation, see Chapter 3.

Comparing A_1 and A_2, we can see that the only difference is linearity. When the response is nonlinear, the deviation from linearity results in an increase in error, or an increase in variability.

Comparing A_1 and A_3, the difference is in the slope of the response. When the response becomes more sensitive, the variation due to sensitivity, S_β, becomes larger. Also the slope, β, becomes larger.

Comparing A_1 and A_4, the difference is variability. When variability is improved, the error variance is decreased.

In all of these cases, the SN ratio worsens when the response is less desirable and increases when the response becomes more desirable.

1.10   PARAMETER DESIGN

In this section, the procedures of Parameter Design are explained. For a numerical example, see Section 3.6.

Parameter Design is also called robust design. There are three steps in product or process optimization: System Design, Parameter Design, and Tolerance Design

System design refers to creating a new system, one that has never existed before. For example, one might create a new electric circuit, a new air-bag system, or a new plastic material. System design requires creativity. It can be protected by patents. Once a new system is invented and it works after being tested at a certain condition, the system design is done.

In order to make the system robust against various manufacturing and user conditions, Parameter Design must be conducted. After Parameter Design is completed, the last step is tolerance design, which involves trade-offs between quality and cost. The Loss Function is used to convert quality into cost, in order to determine if the quality level of a certain raw material or a component part should be upgraded. It must be noted that quality improvement by tolerance design results in cost increase.

Many product-design engineers are not aware of the existence of Parameter Design, the step to improve the robustness of product function without cost increase in most cases. Therefore, after a system design is completed and the engineer is asked to improve quality, generally tolerance design is conducted without first implementing Parameter Design. The result is a limited improvement in robustness and a higher cost.

To understand the concept of Parameter Design, we must define different types of factors in experimentation or in simulation.

1. Control factor: This is a factor we can change in our design, such as the nominal values of component parts in an electric circuit or the conditions of a processing machine.
2. Noise factor: The cause of variation is called noise. There are three sources:

   ▶ Outer noise results from environmental conditions, such as temperature, humidity, etc.
   ▶ Inner noise results from deterioration, such as wear, fatigue, oxidation, etc.
   ▶ Between-product variation is a consequence of manufacturing imperfection, i.e., piece-to-piece variability.

3. Signal factor: This is a factor that is used to change the output, such as an accelerator to increase the speed or a brake to reduce the speed of a car.

Typically, control factors are assigned to an orthogonal array, called the **inner array**. Signal and noise factors are assigned to another array called the **outer array**. An experiment or a simulation is conducted for all combinations between the inner and the outer arrays.

From each run of the inner array, an SN ratio is calculated for all combinations between signal and noise factors. For example, when an L_{18} array is used, there will be 18 SN ratios. From these SN ratios, a response table is constructed to show the level averages of the control factors based on SN ratio. Also, a response table for sensitivity is constructed to show the level averages of control factors based on sensitivity. In dynamic-type SN ratios, sensitivity equates with the steepness of the slope, i.e., the slope of the regression line between the input and the output. In nondynamic-type SN ratios, sensitivity means where the average is.

From the two response tables, we want to find two types of control factors: (1) the control factors that affect the SN ratio; as the first type, and (2) the control factors that do not affect the SN ratio but affect sensitivity as the second type.

For example, the SN ratios of control factors A, B, and C were calculated as follows:

$$A_1 = \frac{6^2}{3^2} = 4 \qquad A_2 = \frac{9^2}{3^2} = 9$$

$$B_1 = \frac{6^2}{3^2} = 4 \qquad B_2 = \frac{6^2}{2^2} = 9$$

$$C_1 = \frac{6^2}{3^2} = 4 \qquad C_2 = \frac{3^2}{1.5^2} = 4$$

Recall that SN ratio is the ratio of sensitivity (numerator) to variability (denominator). When A_1 was changed to A_2, the SN ratio increased due to the increase of sensitivity. When B_1 was changed to B_2, the SN ratio increased due to the decrease of variability. Both factors belong to the first type. When C_1 was changed to C_2, both sensitivity and variability decreased, but the SN ratio was unchanged. Factor C belongs to the second type.

Parameter design is also called two-step optimization. It must be noted that in two-step optimization, we must improve robustness first and adjust sensitivity afterward, because improving robustness is difficult but adjusting sensitivity is easy in most cases. After the SN ratio is maximized by selecting appropriate control factor levels of the first type, sensitivity is adjusted, or tuned, to the right level by selecting other control factors of the second type. Thus, the optimim condition is set.

The last step is to conduct a confirmatory experiment or simulation to determine whether the conclusion we obtained can be reproduced downstream. First, the SN ratio under the optimum condition is estimated and compared with the one before Parameter Design, and their difference, called **the gain**, is calculated. This estimated gain is compared with the actual gain obtained from the confirmation. If the two gains closely agree, the conclusion is probably reproducible.

The followings are the steps of Parameter Design:

1. **Define the ideal function.**

   The ideal function is different from case to case and is the most important step. It is not always easy to appropriately define the ideal function. Usually, it requires considerable thought and discussion.

2. **Select noise factors and forecast their ranges.**

   In many cases, there are many noise factors; however, we cannot afford to consider a great number of noise factors in the research phase. Therefore, only a few of the noise factors that are considered to be the most stringent are used to provide noise effects.

3. **Compound noise factors.**

   It is very effective and efficient to compound noise factors. Compounding noise factors means to find two extreme conditions among the following noise factor combinations:

N_1 =negative-side extreme condition
N_2 =positive-side extreme condition

Sometimes three conditions are set, as follows:

N_1 = negative-side extreme condition
N_2 = standard condition
N_3 = positive-side extreme condition

4. **Select the quality characteristic and its SN ratio.**
   In Quality Engineering is recommended the use of an SN ratio—especially dynamic SN ratio—as the index for evaluating the robustness of the function. The SN ratio is selected based on the ideal function.

5. **Select control factors and levels.**
   Experimentation ought to be conducted with a fully saturated inner orthorgonal array (for control factors). The levels of control factors should cover most of the range, so that a significant improvement may be expected.

6. **Assign control, signal, and noise factors to their proper place in the array.**
   Control factors are assigned to the inner array. Signal and noise factors are assigned to the outer array. For noise factors, compounding is recommended.

7. **Conduct the experiment or simulation.**

8. **Calculate the SN ratios.**

9. **Do the first step of optimization.**
   Maximize the SN ratio by selecting all control factor levels that give the highest SN ratio.

10. **Do the second step of optimization.**
    Select the control factors whose level changes do not affect SN ratio but do affect sensitivity. Use these factors to adjust the sensitivity at a desired level. (Sensitivity means the slope for dynamic-type SN ratio and the mean for nondynamic-type SN ratio).

11. **Forecast the optimum condition.**
    This forecast is made based on the data in the response table. To estimate the SN ratio under the optimum condition, use about half of the control factors that are significant to SN ratio to arithmetically add the effects together. To estimate the sensitivity under the optimum condition, use about half of the control factors that are insignificant to SN ratio but significant to sensitivity to add the effects together. Compare these

figures with the SN ratio and the sensitivity under current conditions or the benchmark, which can be estimated in the same way from the response table.

12. **Run a confirmatory experiment.**
Use the optimum condition to physically run a confirmatory experiment, and from the results, calculate the gains and compare them to the estimated gains in order to make sure that the conclusion is reproducible.

For complete examples of Parameter Design, see Chapter 3 for dynamic-type SN ratios and Chapter 5 for nondynamic-type SN ratios.

1.11 LAYOUT OF ORTHOGONAL ARRAYS FOR PARAMETER DESIGN

To conduct Parameter Design, the use of orthogonal arrays such as L_{12} and L_{18} for the inner array is recommended. L_{12} is used for 2-level factors and L_{18} for 3-level factors. For simulation, L_{36} may be used.

For the outer array, either a simple orthogonal array such as L_4 or L_9 can be used to assign both signal and noise factors. But it is better to compound noise factors into one and assign them with signal factor(s).

Table 1.6 shows an example of the layout for a nondynamic type Parameter Design and Table 1.7 shows the same for a dynamic-type Parameter Design.

Table 1.8 illustrates the case of a dynamic-type Parameter Design with two signal factors. Fig. 1.5 shows response tables for the average SN ratios and sensitivities of control factors.

Table 1.6 Layout of an orthogonal array for nondynamic-type Parameter Design*

Test No.	A 1	B 2	C 3	D 4	E 5	F 6	G 7	H 8	I 9	J 10	K 11	N₁	N₂	N₃	η	$\bar{y}$
						Control Factor							Noise Factor			
1	1	1	1	1	1	1	1	1	1	1	1	oo	oo	oo	η_1	$\bar{y}_1$
2	1	1	1	1	1	2	2	2	2	2	2	oo	oo	oo		
3	1	1	2	2	2	1	1	1	2	2	2	.				
4	1	2	1	2	2	1	2	2	1	1	2	.				
5	1	2	2	1	2	2	1	2	1	2	1	.				
6	1	2	2	2	1	2	2	1	2	1	1	.				
7	2	1	2	2	1	1	2	2	1	2	1					
8	2	1	2	1	2	2	2	1	1	1	2					
9	2	1	1	2	2	2	1	2	2	1	1					
10	2	2	2	2	1	1	1	2	2	1	2					
11	2	2	1	1	1	2	1	1	1	2	2					
12	2	2	1	1	2	1	2	1	2	2	1	oo	oo	oo		

*SN ratio = $\eta = 10 \log \frac{\bar{y}^2}{\sigma^2}$, where $\bar{y}$ = average and σ^2 = variance around the average.

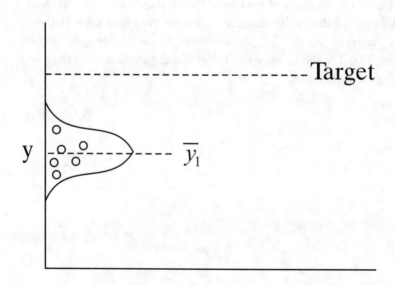

Table 1.7   Layout of an orthogonal array for dynamic-type Parameter Design[*]

Test			Control Factor						M_1		M_2		M_3		M_4		M_4		η	β
Test No.	A	B	C	D	E	F	G	H	M_1 N_1	N_2	M_2 N_1	N_2	M_3 N_1	N_2	M_4 N_1	N_2	M_4 N_1	N_2	η	β
	1	2	3	4	5	6	7	8												
1	1	1	1	1	1	1	1	1	o	o	o	o	o	o	o	o	o	o	η_1	β_1
2	1	1	2	2	2	2	2	2	o	o	o	o	o	o	o	o	o	o		
3	1	1	3	3	3	3	3	3												
4	1	2	1	1	2	2	3	3												
5	1	2	2	2	3	3	1	1												
6	1	2	3	2	1	1	2	2												
7	1	3	1	3	1	3	2	3												
8	1	3	2	1	2	1	3	1												
9	1	3	3	1	3	2	1	2												
10	2	1	1	3	3	2	2	1												
11	2	1	2	1	1	3	3	2												
12	2	1	3	2	2	1	1	3												
13	2	2	1	2	3	1	3	2												
14	2	2	2	3	1	2	1	3												
15	2	2	3	1	2	3	2	1												
16	2	3	1	3	2	3	1	2												
17	2	3	2	1	3	1	2	3												
18	2	3	3	2	1	2	3	1	o	o	o	o	o	o	o	o	o	o		

[*]SN ratio $= \eta = 10 \log \dfrac{\bar{\beta}^2}{\sigma^2}$, where β = slope of the best-fit line (sensitivity) and σ^2 = variability around the best-fit line.

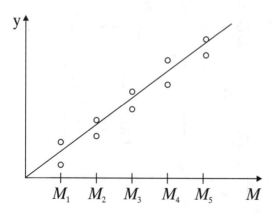

Table 1.8   Layout of an orthogonal array for dynamic-type design with two signals

	Control Factor								M_1						M_2						M_3						M_4					
									M_1^*		M_2^*		M_3^*		M_1^*		M_2^*		M_3^*		M_1^*		M_2^*		M_3^*		M_1^*		M_2^*		M_3^*	
L_{18}	A	B	C	D	E	F	G	H	N_1 N_2		N_1 N_2		N_1 N_2		N_1 N_2		N_1 N_2		N_1 N_2		N_1 N_2		N_1 N_2		N_1 N_2		N_1 N_2		N_1 N_2		N_1 N_2	
	1	2	3	4	5	6	7	8																								
1				** **	** **	** **	** **	** **	** **		** **		** **		** **		** **		** **		** **		** **		** **		** **		** **		** **	
.				** **	** **	** **	** **	** **	** **		** **		** **		** **		** **		** **		** **		** **		** **		** **		** **		** **		** **	
18				** **	** **	** **	** **	** **	** **		** **		** **		** **		** **		** **		** **		** **		** **		** **		** **		** **		** **	

Orthogonal Array y = Output response

For each controllable factor condition from an orthogonal array, the output response y is measured as signal factor M, adjustment signal factor M^* and noise factor(s) N are varied. For each condition of orthogonal array, we have:

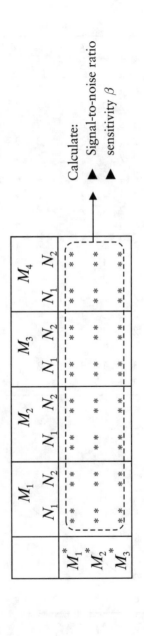

Calculate:
▲ Signal-to-noise ratio
▲ sensitivity β

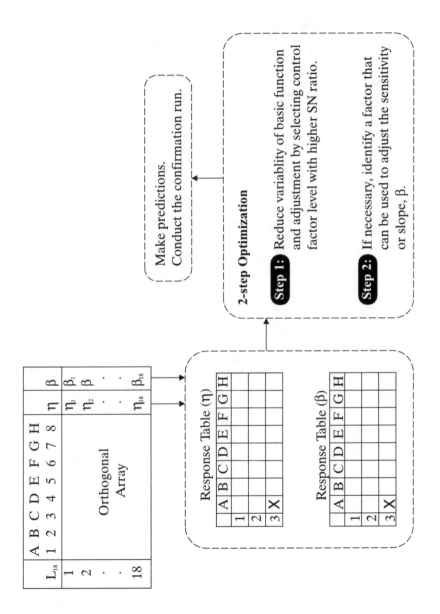

Figure 1.5 Response tables and optimization for the array shown in Table 1.8

2

Types of SN Ratios

2.1 INTRODUCTION

There are various types of SN ratios, based on different ways of classifying them. The equations for the SN ratios to be used are different for different purposes and cases. The following sections illustrate the different viewpoints on which these classifications are based.

2.2 CLASSIFICATION BASED ON THE TYPE OF DATA

Data are classified into: continuous variables, and **classified attributes**. Continuous variables include such data as dimension, strength, and voltage. **Classified attributes** are discrete values, such as the number of defects or the rate of defects or percentage of grade 1, 2, and 3. The rate of defects may seem like a continuous-variable type, but it is actually the number of defects divided by the total number of products observed, and the number of defects is a discrete value, since a defective product can be expressed as a "one" and a nondefective product can be expressed as "zero."

In Quality Engineering, it is essential that *we should avoid using attribute-type data* whenever possible. The reasons for this strategy are that this type of data may hide information, is inefficient, and may lead to interactions.

2.2.1 Attribute-Type Data is not Fully Informative

As an example, consider the case in which there are 25 students who passed an examination and 5 who failed. In this case, there are 25 "zeros" and 5 "ones." (Of course, we can define the categories differently by saying there are 25 "ones" and 5 "zeros.") The data may include a student who passed with a grade of 60 and another who scored 95. These students are classified into the zero category and considered as equal, although there is a significant difference between the two. Such important information disappears once "zero–one" type of data is used.

2.2.2 Attribute-Type Data is Inefficient

The use of classified attributes requires collecting a great deal of data. Here's why. Suppose two baseball teams, A and B, played once and A won. The winning percentage for team A is 100%, and the rate for team B is zero. But nobody would believe such a rate is reasonable. The teams must play many times before a reliable rate can be estimated. That is why a large number of data points are necessary for attribute-type data.

2.2.3 Using Attribute-Type Data may Lead to Interactions

The most serious problem of using attribute-type data is that there is a high chance of getting interactions. This indicates inconsistency or poor additivity, as briefly described in the previous chapter. For example, in a sensory test for food the following results were obtained:

$A_1 B_1$:   not tasty
$A_2 B_1$:   tastes better
$A_1 B_1$:   not tasty
$A_1 B_2$:   tastes better

Based on the above results, A_2 is better than A_1 and B_2 is better than B_1; therefore, the best condition would be estimated as $A_2 B_2$. If a test for condition $A_2 B_2$ were conducted and the result were worse, then the existence of an interaction would be indicated. This would mean that the positive effect of A and B cannot be added; there is no **additivity**. As a result, we do not believe the conclusion from such an experiment. In this situation, the source of the interaction stems from the definition of the quality characteristic: "taste" is classified into two categories: zero and one.

When, instead, a continuous output variable, such as amount of salt, was used to run the experiment, the following results were obtained:

$A_1 B_1$:   less salt 5%
$A_2 B_1$:   more salt 10% (5% more)
$A_1 B_1$:   less salt 5%
$A_1 B_2$:   more salt 12% (7% more)

In such a case, we would not conclude that $A_2 B_2$ is the best condition. Rather, we would conclude that $A_2 B_2$ may have a salt content as high as 17%, which is too salty, or not tasty.

From past experience, many engineers working in such areas as production do not believe the results from a small-scale laboratory experiment just because of the existence of interactions. In their experience, the conclusions from the laboratory were not reproducible in the large-scale production environment. There are various cases of using SN ratios for classified attributes. However, because they are prone to the sorts of problems evident in the preceding examples, we should try *to avoid using such quality characteristics as much as possible.*

2.3   CLASSIFICATION BASED ON INTENTION

Classification based on intention refers to whether the SN ratio is dynamic or nondynamic. As mentioned in Chapter 1, the earliest application of SN ratios in quality engineering was for the evaluation and improvement of measurement systems in the late 60s. In a measurement system, there is an input signal (the true value of a sample to be measured) and the output response (the measured result). Therefore, it is a dynamic-type ratio.

In the 1970s, different forms of SN ratios — called nondynamic SN ratios — were developed for the purpose of robust design of products or processes.

Table 2.1   Classification of dynamic SN ratios

Type	Application
Passive	Measurement system
Active	Product design
	Process design
	Feed-forward control
	Feedback control
	Manufacturing: transformability
	Research and development: technology development

Nondynamic-type SN ratios are applied to quality characteristics — such as nominal-is-best, smaller-is-better, larger-is-better, and operating window — when the input/output relationship is not considered.

Nominal-is-best is the case when there is a finite target, such as when designing an electric circuit with a fixed output voltage. Smaller-is-better is the case when the minimum output (zero) is desirable, an example being the carbon monoxide content in the exhaust gas from a car. Larger-is-better is the case when the maximum output (infinite) is desirable, such as strength or power.

The objective of using nondynamic type SN ratios is to improve the robustness of a product or a process. More precisely, it is to improve the robustness of the objective function of a product or a process. After robustness is accomplished, there is no additional intention of adjusting the output value. This contrasts with the dynamic-type SN ratios where the output value is known to be different from time to time. In a passive type of example, the sample to be measured differs at every input, so the output or the measured result is different each time. In an active type of example, such as a control system, the output must be adjusted from time to time.

In the 1980s, applications of the active-type dynamic SN ratios were applied to improve the "basic function" of a group of products or processes, instead of an individual product or process. Such an approach is generally called robust technology development.

2.4   CLASSIFICATION BASED ON INPUT AND OUTPUT _____

As described before, quality characteristics are classified into continuous variables and discrete, or classified, attributes. The latter is also referred to as digital type. In this aspect, SN ratios can be classified into the following cases:

Case	Input	Output
1	Continuous variables	Continuous variables
2	Continuous variables	Digital
3	Digital	Continuous variables
4	Digital	Digital

In Case 1, which occurs most frequently, both input and output are continuous variables. When driving a car, for example, steering-wheel angle is the input and turning radius is the output. Case 2 occurs in digital function, such as an on/off control system using temperature as the signal. It also occurs in alarm systems or indicators. For Case 3, such as a transmitter in a communications system, the input is digital (mark and space) and the output is voltage. Case 4 occurs often in chemical processes, such as separation, purification, refining, or filtration. For those applications see References (1) and (2).

2.5   OTHER WAYS OF CLASSIFYING SN RATIOS _____

SN ratios can also be classified based on the number of signal factors: single signal factors, double signal factors, multiple signal factors, and no signal factors. SN ratios with single-signal factor occur most frequently. In some cases, there are two or multiple signal factors. In an integrated-circuit (IC) fabrication process study, two signal factors — dimension and input voltage — were used to measure the output current. In the research of a certain material, cross-sectional dimension and the load added to a test piece are considered as the two signals to measure deformation. The case without signal factors belongs to nondynamic type, as described before.

SN ratios may also be classified by the following **noise factors**: multiple noise factors, compounded noise factors, and no noise factors. When multiple **noise factors** are studied, they are either assigned to an outside orthogonal array or assigned in full factorial fashion. However, the most efficient way to deal with multiple **noise factors** is to have them compounded for three levels, such as N_1 = negative-side extreme condition, N_2 = standard condition, and N_3 = positive-side extreme condition;
Or compound them for two levels, such as N_1 = positive-side worst condition and N_2 = negative-side worst condition.

By compounding, the number of runs in the experiment can be reduced to a fraction, so that the experiment can be very efficiently conducted.

Often, no noise factors occur in chemical experimentation. In a chemical reaction, two repetitions for one run (condition) of an experiment are equivalent to two experiments, since they double the time and cost of the study. However, the existence of noise factors is imperative for the determination of SN ratios. For such cases, the so called "split-type analysis" is used to calculate SN ratios. See **Chapter 4** for more details.

As seen from the above classification, there are many SN ratio equations. To a novice, it may be puzzling to know which is the right or appropriate one for use. Quite often, we cannot find the one which exactly fits our need. In such a situation, a custom-written SN ratio must be developed. To select the proper SN ratio, we need to be exposed to the application of existing SN ratio cases and the discussions about the basic functions of the subject to be optimized.

2.6 HOW TO SELECT SN RATIOS

Quite often, the conclusions of a study under a certain environmental condition can not be reproduced in other environments. In such a case, the conclusions are useless; the time and money spent on the research were wasted.

The most important consequence of research is that the conclusions obtained from a small, laboratory-scale study be reproducible down-stream — in manufacturing, in the market, or under customers' various usage conditions.

Nonreproducibility of conclusions results from the existence of interactions between control factors. The word **interaction** is synonymous with the inconsistency, non**reproducibility**, or non**additivity** of **factorial effects**. Therefore, the key to avoiding interactions is to carefully select quality characteristics; i.e., to carefully select what to measure or what to analyze. This was the reasoning behind the theme for the 1988 American Supplier Institute's Taguchi Methods Symposium: *"To get quality, don't measure quality."* It means that in order to improve quality, the existing quality items, such as vibration, defects, or audible noise — termed downstream quality — do not provide valuable data for determining reproducible conclusions.

The strategies to avoid interactions are:

1. Use dynamic SN ratios.
2. Relate input and output to energy transformation.
3. Based on the input and the output, find an appropriate SN ratio for the analysis.
4. Use orthogonal arrays to assign control factors, and analyze them to check for interactions.

The reasons to use the above strategies are:

1. Energy has addivity. When input and output are energy related, the amount of output is proportional to the amount of input.
2. If such an output is used to construct a dynamic SN ratio for analysis, the additivity of main effects can be expected.
3. If there is additivity, there are no interactions. With no interactions, reproducible conclusions can be expected.

There are various types of SN ratios, as described in this chapter, and it is critical to carefully select an appropriate one. Numerous case studies (see **Chapter 11**) have shown that when an appropriate SN ratio was used, the predicted conclusions were well reproduced in the confirmatory experiments.

Of all types of SN ratios, the most import, as well as the most frequently used and the simplest, type is called the **zero-point proportional equation**. The reason for its name stems from the fact that when the input/output relationship is energy related, the output becomes zero when the input is zero. In such a case, the input/output equation is written as

$$y = \beta M$$

where

y = output
β = constant, slope, or sensitivity
M = input (signal)

However, there are many cases in many engineering fields when this type of SN ratio cannot be used. For example, when the input or the output cannot be measured due to lack of technology, or when the input or the output is digital, such as 0 and 1. It is therefore necessary to become familiar with various cases of SN ratios and to be able to select the right one. Learning from successful case studies helps to do so. It must be noted that over 90% of the case studies recently published used the zero-point proportional equation.

Based on this fact, the reader may not have to understand — at least in the beginning — cases that rely on SN ratios other than the zero-point proportional equation described in **Chapters 4 and 6**. However, those cases do happen, and when they do, it is important to determine which published case should be used as a model and to understand how to decompose the data so that the useful portion and harmful portion may be separated to construct an appropriate SN ratio.

2.7   IDEAL FUNCTION

From the engineering viewpoint, everything is dynamic; everything is energy related: there is always an input and an output. For example,

	Input	Output
Resistor	voltage	current
Measurement	true value	measured value
Welding	load	deflection
Injection molding	mold dimension	product dimension

Traditionally, the objective for quality improvement has been to "solve problems." These problems arise either in manufacturing or from the customer's use. Such an approach to quality is reactive, rather than proactive — which entails trying to avoid future problems by improving quality at the basic research or product-design state. In the world of quality,

First, there was a problem.

The role of problem solving is to find the root causes; therefore, cause-and-effect relationships are important. Establishing cause-and-effect relationships is the role of experimental design, not the role of Quality Engineering. It would be very hard to think about the ideal function of a product when *root cause analysis is always on the engineer's mind*. That is why the traditional quality paradigm must be shifted, from reacting to poor quality to "proacting" to improve quality.

Indeed, the correct identification of an ideal function is difficult, and the ideal function differs from case to case. There are no generic answers. The ideal function for each case must be thoroughly explored and discussed. Adding to the difficulty is that many design engineers working in a specific field, such as electric circuits or engines, are not familiar with Quality Engineering, and quality engineers are not familiar with the specific field. Nevertheless, identification of an ideal function requires the knowledge of both fields; therefore, design and quality must be discussed together.

As mentioned above, the ideal function is different from case to case, and a *paradigm shift* is extremely difficult to make solely on one's own. The best way of overcoming this difficulty is to learn from published, successful case studies in the field in which the engineer is involved.

Basic Dynamic-Type SN Ratios for Continuous Variables

3.1 INTRODUCTION

In this chapter, some basic dynamic-type SN ratios for continuous variables are introduced. As described before, the equation to be used will differ from case to case. The selection of the right case for a study is based on engineering objectives and viewpoints. It is important for an engineer to understand the function of a product or process and his or her objectives for the study. Once a proper SN ratio is selected, the calculations can be made by using the equations in this chapter or by inputting data to the software. In order to simplify the explanations, only one control factor and, usually, only one level of the factor are used in the examples.

3.2 ZERO-POINT PROPORTIONAL EQUATION

Table 3.1 shows the inputs and the outputs of a measurement experiment. The inputs are the samples whose true values are known; these are the levels of the signal factors. The outputs are the results measured.

An explanation of symbols used is as follows:

$M_1, M_2, \ldots, M_k$ = true values of samples
$y_{11}, y_{12}, \ldots, y_{1r_0}$ = results of measuring M_1
$y_{21}, y_{22}, \ldots, y_{2r_0}$ = results of measuring M_2
$y_1, y_2, \ldots, y_k$ = totals of measurements at M_i
r_0 = number of data points in each signal level

Table 3.1 Readings from a measurement system

Signal Factor	M_1	M_2	...	M_k
	y_{11}	y_{21}	...	y_{k1}
Reading	y_{12}	y_{22}	...	y_{k2}
	...	...	...	...
	y_{1r_0}	y_{2r_0}	...	y_{kr_0}
Total	y_1	y_2	...	y_k

There are kr_0 pieces of observations in the table. The readings from y_{11} to y_{1r_0} show the results of measuring sample M_1. The variation among kr_0 pieces of data is caused by the following sources: different samples and repetitions.

The variation caused by different samples includes the following components: linear portion, quadratic portion, and higher-order portion.

The variation caused by repetitions is a kind of noise factor. In many studies, a compounded noise factor is set and observed, rather than just observing simple repetitions.

Since a SN ratio is determined from the two parts: desirable portion and harmful portion.

The data must be decomposed as follows:

$$\text{Total variation } = \text{Variation caused by the linear portion} + \text{Variations caused by other portions}$$

In the case of a proportional equation, when the signal is zero, the output must be zero. In a measurement system, if a sample to be measured contains no ingredient, the measured result must read zero. Here, the ideal function is expressed as

$$y = \beta M \qquad (3.1)$$

where

M = signal

y = output

β = the slope of the response line or the regression coefficient

In reality, there are errors in observations, and the data in Table 3.1 are expressed by the following equation:

$$y_{ij} = \beta M_i + e_{ij} \tag{3.2}$$

where

$$i = 1, 2, \ldots, k$$

$$j = 1, 2, \ldots, r_0$$

Equation (3.2) is expressed as simultaneous equations with one unknown, β. The value of β is selected so as to minimize the total of the squares of differences between the right side and the left side of the equation (the least-squares method).

$$S_e = \left(y_{11} - \beta M_1\right)^2 + \left(y_{12} - \beta M_1\right)^2 + \ldots + \left(y_{kr_0} - \beta M_k\right)^2 \tag{3.3}$$

The value of β that minimizes S_e is given by

$$\beta = \frac{1}{r_0 r}\left(M_1 y_1 + M_2 y_2 + \ldots + M_k y_k\right) \tag{3.4}$$

where

$$r = M_1^2 + M_2^2 + \ldots + M_k^2 \tag{3.5}$$

and r_0 is the total number of measurements under M_i.

To decompose the data in Table 3.1, S_T, the total variation of the squares of kr_0 pieces of data is first calculated. The symbol f denotes the degree of freedom.

$$S_T = y_{11}^2 + y_{12}^2 + \ldots + y_{kr_0}^2 \quad \text{and} \quad f = kr_0 \tag{3.6}$$

The variation caused by the linear effect, denoted by S_β, is given by

$$S_\beta = \frac{1}{r_0 r}\left(M_1 y_1 + M_2 y_2 + \ldots + M_k y_k\right)^2 \quad \text{and} \quad f = 1 \tag{3.7}$$

The error variation (S_e), including the deviation from linearity, V_e, is

$$S_e = S_T - S_\beta \quad \text{and} \quad f = kr_0 - 1 \quad (3.8)$$

The error variance (V_e) is the error variation divided by its degree of freedom.

$$V_e = \frac{S_e}{kr_o - 1} \quad (3.9)$$

The definition of this SN ration is

$$\eta \rightarrow 10 \log \frac{\beta^2}{\sigma^2} \quad (3.10)$$

To calculate the SN ratio of Eq. (3.10), the error variance, V_e, calculated in Eq. (3.9) is used to estimate the σ^2 in equation (3.10). To estimate the β^2, a correction is necessary. Statistically, S_β, the variation caused by the linear effect, has the following contents:

$$E(S_\beta) = r_0 r \beta^2 + \sigma^2 \quad (3.11)$$

where E is the "expected value," as defined in statistics.

When data are repeatedly collected in the same way for an infinite number of times and their S_β is calculated each time, the average of an infinite number of S_β's is denoted by $E(S_\beta)$. The term σ^2 designates the error contained in the data, such as experimental error or measurement error. What is needed to calculate the SN ratio is the use of β^2 as the numerator. Therefore, the SN ratio in decibel (db) units is calculated as

$$\eta = 10 \log \frac{\frac{1}{r_0 r}(S_\beta - V_e)}{V_e} \quad \text{(db)} \quad (3.12)$$

Example

Two measurement systems, A_1 and A_2, are compared in order to measure displacement in a process. Three standards, M_1, M_2, and M_3 are used to evaluate the two systems. Their true values are

$M_1 = 30 \ \mu\text{m}$

$M_2 = 60 \ \mu\text{m}$

$M_3 = 90 \ \mu\text{m}$

Two people, R_1 and R_2, measure the standards once each, to obtain the results shown in Table 3.2.

Table 3.2 Displacement measurement

Signal Factor		$M_1 = 30$	$M_2 = 60$	$M_3 = 90$
	R_1	65	136	208
A_1	R_2	74	147	197
	Total	139	283	405
	R_1	61	135	201
A_2	R_2	71	145	208
	Total	132	280	409

The calculation of the SN ratio for A_1 is shown below.

$$S_T = 65^2 + 74^2 + \ldots + 197^2 = 131,879 \quad \text{and} \quad f = 6 \quad (3.13)$$

$$r_0 r = 2 \times \left(30^2 + 60^2 + 90^2\right) = 25,200 \quad (3.14)$$

$$S_\beta = \frac{(M_1 y_1 + M_2 y_2 + M_3 y_3)^2}{r_0 r} = \frac{(30 \times 139 + 60 \times 283 + 90 \times 405)^2}{25,200}$$

$$= \frac{57,600^2}{25,200} = 131,657.14 \quad \text{and} \quad f = 1 \quad (3.15)$$

$$S_e = S_T - S_\beta = 131,879 - 131,657.14 = 221.86 \quad \text{and} \quad f = 5 \quad (3.16)$$

$$V_e = \frac{S_e}{5} = \frac{221.86}{5} = 44.37 \quad (3.17)$$

$$\eta = 10 \log \left[\frac{\left(\dfrac{1}{25,200} \right)(131,657.14 - 44.37)}{44.37} \right] \qquad (3.18)$$

$$= 10 \log 0.1177 = -9.29 \text{ (db)}$$

The SN ratio of A_2 is calculated similarly, with the following result:

$$\eta(A_1) = -9.29 \text{ (db)} \qquad (3.19)$$

$$\eta(A_2) = -7.79 \text{ (db)} \qquad (3.20)$$

The SN ratio of A_2 is higher than that of A_1 by 1.5 db.

Recall from Eq. (3.10) that an SN ratio is the ratio of sensitivity (slope) to variability in quadratic form. In a measuring system, slope is calibrated to 1, called slope calibration. The gain of 1.5 db is equivalent to 1.41 in anti-log scale. It means that after slope calibration, (the slopes of A_1 and A_2 are adjusted equally), the error variance of A_2 will become smaller than A_1 by a factor of 1.41.

3.3 REFERENCE-POINT PROPORTIONAL EQUATION

In a measuring system, there are two kinds of calibration: point calibration and slope calibration.

For example, a watch is a measuring system of time. When we correct our watches by the standard time signal, this is **point calibration**. In old-style (mechanical and nonquartz type) watches, there is a pace-adjusting slide inside the watch. If the watch runs about 5 minutes faster a day, an adjustment is made by moving the slide toward the slower side. This is called **slope calibration**.

In a control system, both kinds of calibration are made. For example, in a dyeing process, the amount of dye to be used is determined by comparison with a standard sample. This is point calibration. SN ratio can be used to improve the dyeing process. Recall that an SN ratio may be improved by increasing β, the slope in the equation. In one case of a dyeing process, β was increased (and the SN ratio was improved) by finding a strong dye. Now, one could say that when β is too large, adjustment of the color may be difficult, since a small measuring error affects the amount of dye added to the process and results in excess amount of color variation in the product (cloth). But generally, there is no worry about β being too sensitive. We only need to add filler to dilute the dye to reduce its sensitivity (β). Also recall that through the defining equation for η,

$$\eta = \frac{\beta^2}{\sigma^2}$$

if η is unchanged and β becomes smaller (in this case by dilution), σ becomes smaller. This relationship is an important advantage of using the SN ratio. Thus, if the effect of the measuring error of the dye is reduced (smaller β), σ, the variation of product color after dyeing becomes smaller. The reason is that *increasing* **sensitivity** *has the same effect as reducing* **variability**. As mentioned before, this is called the slope calibration.

In point calibration, the reference point could be either the zero point or some other point. However, it is common for only a small section in the entire range of measurement to be used for a particular application, and that range is quite often far from zero point. In such a case, it would be better to select a reference point within the range rather than using a zero point, because in doing so, the error due to calibration becomes smaller.

In reference-point calibration, a standard, M_s, is used as the reference point. Measurements are conducted, and the average is calculated to be $\bar{y}_s$. The ideal relationship between the readings and the signals is:

$$y - \bar{y}_s = \beta(M - M_s) \tag{3.21}$$

Table 3.3   Data after reference-point calibration

Signal	$M_1 - M_s$	$M_2 - M_s$	...	$M_k - M_s$
Reading	$y_{11} - \bar{y}_s$	$y_{21} - \bar{y}_s$	...	$y_{k1} - \bar{y}_s$
	$y_{12} - \bar{y}_s$	$y_{22} - \bar{y}_s$	...	$y_{k2} - \bar{y}_s$
	...	...	...	...
	$y_{1r_0} - \bar{y}_s$	$y_{2r_0} - \bar{y}_s$	...	$y_{kr_0} - \bar{y}_s$
Total	y_1	y_2	...	y_k

Table 3.3 shows the data after reference-point calibration.

As noted above, first, the average of the r_0 readings at the reference point, y_{s1}, y_{s2}, ..., y_{sr_0} is calculated.

$$\bar{y}_s = \frac{(y_{s1} + y_{s2} + \ldots + y_{sr_0})}{r_0} \qquad (3.22)$$

Results after reference-point calibration are shown in Table 3.3.

The slope, or the linear coefficient, β, is also called the **sensitivity coefficient**. It is given by the following equation:

$$\beta = \frac{1}{r_0 r}[y_1(M_1 - M_s) + y_2(M_2 - M_s) + \ldots + y_k(M_k - M_s)] \qquad (3.23)$$

where

$$r = (M_1 - M_s)^2 + (M_2 - M_s)^2 + \ldots + (M_k - M_s)^2 \qquad (3.24)$$

The proportional equation is

$$(y - \bar{y}_s) = \beta(M - M_s) \qquad (3.25)$$

For the calculation of SN ratio, the total variation, S_T, is

$$S_T = \text{Total of squares of}(y_{ij} - \bar{y}_s) = \sum_{i=1}^{k}\sum_{j=1}^{r_0}(y_{ij} - \bar{y}_s)^2 \qquad \text{and} \qquad f = kr_0 \qquad (3.26)$$

The linear effect of the signal, S_β, is

$$S_\beta = \frac{1}{r_0 r}[y_1(M_1 - M_s) + y_2(M_2 - M_s) + \ldots + y_k(M_k - M_s)]^2 \qquad \text{and}$$

$$f = 1 \qquad (3.27)$$

The error variation, S_e, is

$$S_e = S_T - S_\beta \qquad \text{and} \qquad f = kr_0 - 1 \qquad (3.28)$$

The error variance, V_e, is:

$$V_e = \frac{1}{kr_0 - 1} S_e \tag{3.29}$$

The SN ratio, η, is

$$\eta = 10 \log \frac{\frac{1}{r_0 r}(S_\beta - V_e)}{V_e} \tag{3.30}$$

Example

The quality of two ammeters, A_1 and A_2, used in spot welding were compared using six samples, $M_1, M_2, ..., M_6$, measured by three operators, R_1, R_2, and R_3. The control and signal factors are as follows:

Control factor (ammeter): A_1, A_2
Signal factor (sample): $M_1 = 6.425$
$M_2 = 8.015$
$M_3 = 9.557$
$M_4 = 11.195$
$M_5 = 12.785$
$M_6 = 14.375$

Table 3.4 shows the results of the experiment.

Table 3.4 Experiment about ammeters

		M_1 6.425	M_2 8.015	M_3 9.557	M_4 11.195	M_5 12.785	M_6 14.375
A_1	R_1	6.80	8.60	10.35	12.00	13.70	15.40
	R_2	6.90	8.65	10.40	12.15	14.00	15.65
	R_3	7.15	9.00	10.45	12.10	13.85	15.55
A_2	R_1	6.40	8.10	9.75	11.30	13.00	14.60
	R_2	6.40	8.05	9.70	11.35	13.00	14.55
	R_3	6.35	8.10	9.65	11.30	12.95	14.55

First, the results are pretreated. In this example, M_1 is used as the reference point or reference signal, so that

$$M_1 = M_s = 6.425$$

The average of the readings at A_1 and M_1 is calculated to be $\bar{y}_s$, which is called the reference data for A_1.

$$\bar{y}_s(A_1) = \frac{6.80 + 6.90 + 7.15}{3} = 6.95 \tag{3.31}$$

Similarly, the reference data for A_2 is calculated as

$$\bar{y}_s(A_2) = \frac{(6.40 + 6.40 + 6.35)}{3} = 6.38 \tag{3.32}$$

Next, the data are adjusted by subtracting 6.425 (M_1) from each value of M, 6.95 from each data point for A_1, and 6.38 for each data point for A_2. Table 3.5 shows the results after reference-point calibration.

Table 3.5 Results after reference-point adjustment

		$M_1 - M_s$	$M_2 - M_s$	$M_3 - M_s$	$M_4 - M_s$	$M_5 - M_s$	$M_6 - M_s$
		0	1.590	3.132	4.770	6.360	7.950
	R_1	-0.15	1.65	3.40	5.05	6.75	8.45
A_1	R_2	-0.05	1.70	3.45	5.20	7.05	8.70
	R_3	0.20	2.05	3.50	5.15	6.90	8.60
	Total	0.00	5.40	10.35	15.40	20.70	25.75
	R_1	0.02	1.72	3.37	4.92	6.62	8.22
A_2	R_2	0.02	1.67	3.32	4.97	6.62	8.17
	R_3	-0.03	1.72	3.27	4.92	6.57	8.17
	Total	0.01	5.11	9.96	14.81	19.81	24.56

The SN ratio of A_1 is calculated as follows:

$$S_T = (-0.15)^2 + (-0.05)^2 + \ldots + 8.60^2 = 488.58500 \qquad \text{and} \qquad f = 18$$

$$\text{(3.33)}$$

$$S_\beta = \frac{(0 \times 0 + 1.590 \times 5.40 + 3.132 \times 10.35 + \ldots + 7.950 \times 25.75)^2}{3\left(0^2 + 1.590^2 + 3.132^2 + \ldots + 7.950^2\right)}$$

$$= \frac{450.8247^2}{3 \times 138.74252} = 488.29757 \qquad \text{and} \qquad f = 1 \qquad \text{(3.34)}$$

$$S_e = 488.58500 - 488.29757 = 0.28743 \qquad \text{and} \qquad f = 17 \qquad \text{(3.35)}$$

$$V_e = \frac{0.28743}{17} = 0.01691 \qquad \text{(3.36)}$$

$$\eta = 10 \log \left[\frac{\left(\frac{1}{3 \times 138.74252}\right)(488.29757 - 0.01691)}{0.01691} \right] \qquad \text{(3.37)}$$

$$= 10 \log 69.38 = 18.41 \text{ (db)}$$

The SN ratio of A_2 is calculated similarly:

$$\eta(A_1) = 18.41 \text{ (db)}$$

$$\eta(A_2) = 25.81 \text{ (db)}$$

A_2 is better than A_1 by 7.40 db.

3.4   LINEAR EQUATION

In the previous section, two cases of SN ratios were discussed. The selection of the right case depends on the objective of the study, or the ideal function of the

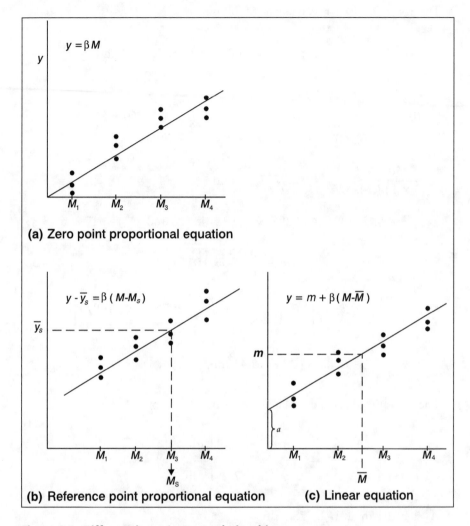

Figure 3.1 Different input/output relationships

product or process to be studied. The zero-point proportional equation is used when the input is zero and the output should be zero, as shown in Fig. 3.1(a). In other words, the regression line should pass through the origin. The reference-point proportional equation is used if the reference sample is measured, and here, the output should be equal to the reference data, as shown in Fig. 3.1(b).

Another situation is the case when there is no specific restriction on the input/output relationship shown by a regression line. This is called the linear equation.

In a study of a sphygmomanometer, we are not interested in the area that the blood pressure is equal to zero, and whether the regression line passes through the origin also is not our concern. In such a case, a linear equation may be used.

From the results in Table 3.1, a linear equation is given as:

$$y = m + \beta(M - \overline{M}) + e \tag{3.38}$$

where m is the average and e is the error.

Parameters m and β are estimated by

$$m = \overline{y} \tag{3.39}$$

$$\beta = \frac{1}{r_0 r}\left[y_1\left(M_1 - \overline{M}\right) + y_2\left(M_2 - \overline{M}\right) + \ldots + y_k\left(M_k - \overline{M}\right)\right] \tag{3.40}$$

where

$$\overline{M} = \frac{\left(M_1 + M_2 + \ldots + M_k\right)}{k} \tag{3.41}$$

$$r = \left(M_1 - \overline{M}\right)^2 + \left(M_2 - \overline{M}\right)^2 + \ldots + \left(M_k - \overline{M}\right)^2 \tag{3.42}$$

and r_0 is the number of repetitions under each signal-factor level.

It must be noted that in the case of the linear equation, the total variation, S_T, is calculated by subtracting S_m from the total of the squares of individual data. In this case, S_T shows the variation around the mean.

$$S_T = y_{11}^2 + y_{12}^2 + \ldots + y_{kr_0}^2 - S_m \quad \text{and} \quad f = kr_0 - 1 \tag{3.43}$$

$$S_m = \frac{\left(\sum y_{ij}\right)^2}{kr_0} \tag{3.44}$$

$$S_\beta = \frac{1}{r_0 r}\left[y_1\left(M_1 - \overline{M}\right) + y_2\left(M_2 - \overline{M}\right) + \ldots + y_k\left(M_k - \overline{M}\right)\right]^2 \quad \text{and}$$

$$f = 1 \tag{3.45}$$

$$S_e = S_T - S_\beta \quad \text{and} \quad f = kr_0 - 2 \tag{3.46}$$

$$V_e = \frac{1}{kr_0 - 2} S_e \tag{3.47}$$

The SN ratio is

$$\eta = 10 \log \frac{\frac{1}{r_0 r}(S_\beta - V_e)}{V_e} \tag{3.48}$$

Example

In an injection-molded product, injection pressure, M, was used as the signal factor to adjust the product dimension. Control factor A is the type of material. Assume that this is a case for using a linear equation.

Table 3.6 Results of injection-molding experiment

		$M_1 = 30$ $M_1 - \overline{M}$ -15	$M_2 = 40$ $M_2 - \overline{M}$ -5	$M_3 = 50$ $M_3 - \overline{M}$ 5	$M_4 = 60$ $M_4 - \overline{M}$ 15
A_1	R_1	4.608	4.640	4.682	4.718
	R_2	4.590	4.650	4.670	4.702
	Total	9.198	9.290	9.352	9.420
A_2	R_1	4.584	4.631	4.693	4.737
	R_2	4.602	4.643	4.681	4.728
	Total	9.186	9.274	9.374	9.465

The following definitions apply:

$$\overline{M} = \frac{M_1 + M_2 + M_3 + M_4}{4} = \frac{30 + 40 + 50 + 60}{4} = 45$$

$$M_1 - \overline{M} = 30 - 45 = -15$$

$$M_2 - \overline{M} = 40 - 45 = -5$$

$$M_3 - \overline{M} = 50 - 45 = 5$$

$$M_4 - \overline{M} = 60 - 45 = 15$$

The SN ratio of A_1 is calculated as follows:

$$S_m = \frac{(4.608 + 4.640 + \ldots + 4.670 + 4.702)^2}{8} \tag{3.49}$$

$$= 173.538450 \qquad \text{and} \qquad f = 1$$

$$S_T = (4.608)^2 + (4.590)^2 + \ldots + 4.702^2 - 173.538450 \tag{3.50}$$

$$= 0.013766 \qquad \text{and} \qquad f = 7$$

$$r = \left(M_1 - \overline{M}\right)^2 + \left(M_2 - \overline{M}\right)^2 + \left(M_3 - \overline{M}\right)^2 + \left(M_4 - \overline{M}\right)^2 \tag{3.51}$$

$$r_0 r = 2 \times \left[(-15)^2 + (-5)^2 + 5^2 + 15^2\right] = 1000 \tag{3.52}$$

$$S_\beta = \frac{1}{1000}[(-15) \times 9.198 + \ldots + 15 \times 9.420]^2 = \frac{(3.64)^2}{1000} \tag{3.53}$$

$$= 0.0132496 \qquad \text{and} \qquad f = 1$$

$$S_e = S_T - S_\beta \tag{3.54}$$

$$= 0.013766 - 0.0132496 = 0.0005164 \qquad \text{and} \qquad f = 6$$

$$V_e = \frac{S_e}{6} = \frac{0.0005164}{6} = 0.0000861 \tag{3.55}$$

$$\eta = 10 \log \frac{\frac{1}{r_0 r}\left(S_\beta - V_e\right)}{V_e}$$

$$= 10 \log \left[\frac{\frac{1}{1000}(0.0132496 - 0.0000861)}{0.0000861}\right] \tag{3.56}$$

$$= 10 \log 0.1529 = -8.156 (\text{db})$$

The SN ratio of A_2 is calculated similarly and gives the result of

$$\eta(A_2) = -4.363 \text{ (db)} \tag{3.57}$$

Therefore, material A_2 is better than A_1 by

$$\text{gain} = -4.363 - (-8.156) = 3.79 \text{ (db)} \tag{3.58}$$

It must be noted that the selection of an SN ratio is not based on "how a response looks." For instance, Fig. 3.2(a) is an example of the voltage/current relationship of a DC motor study in a company. Since the regression line does not pass through the origin, as can be seen from Fig. 3.2(b), to improve quality, the engineers tried to use a linear equation. The engineers said that based on their design, there is no current until the voltage reaches 1.5 volts. However, this conclusion is misleading because ideally,

Even when voltage is as low as 0.1 volt, current is flowing no matter how small that flow may be.

Therefore, the zero-point proportional equation must be used for this case, as shown in Fig. 3.2(c). Any deviation from the regression line in the figure then becomes error.

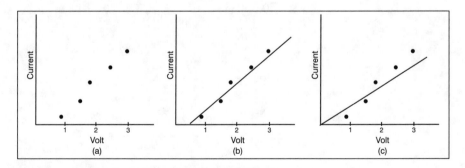

Figure 3.2   Voltage and current relationship

3.5   LINEAR EQUATION USING A TABULAR DISPLAY OF THE ORTHOGONAL POLYNOMIAL EQUATION _____

When the intervals for signal-factor level are set equal, the SN ratios can be easily calculated. Table 3.7 is part of a tabular display of Chevyshev's orthogonal polynomial equation. Although the table can be used to calculate linear, quadratic, or higher-order terms, only the linear term is used in SN-ratio calculation. *Note:* this table is used only when the level intervals are equal.

In the table,

b_1 = linear term

b_2 = quadratic term

$$b_i = \frac{W_1 A_1 + \ldots + W_k A_k}{r_0 \lambda S h^i}$$

h = level interval

n_e of $b_i = r_0 \times S \times h^{2i}$

$$S_{bi} = \frac{(W_1 A_1 + \ldots + W_k A_k)^2}{r_0 \lambda^2 S}$$

From Table 3.1, the SN ratio and the linear coefficient are calculated as follows:

$$S_T = y_{11}^2 + y_{12}^2 + \ldots + y_{kr_0}^2 - S_m \quad \text{and} \quad f = k r_0 - 1 \qquad (3.59)$$

$$S_m = \frac{\left(y_{11} + y_{12} + \ldots + y_{kr_0}\right)^2}{k r_0} \quad \text{and} \quad f = 1 \qquad (3.60)$$

$$S_\beta = \frac{(W_1 y_1 + W_2 y_2 + \ldots + W_k y_k)^2}{r_0 \lambda^2 S} \quad \text{and} \quad f = 1 \qquad (3.61)$$

$$\beta = \frac{W_1 y_1 + W_2 y_2 + \ldots + W_k y_k}{r_0 \lambda S h} \qquad (3.62)$$

$$S_e = S_T - S_\beta \quad \text{and} \quad f = k r_0 - 2 \qquad (3.63)$$

$$V_e = \frac{S_e}{k r_0 - 2} \qquad (3.64)$$

$$\eta = 10 \log \dfrac{\dfrac{1}{r_0 \lambda^2 Sh^2}(S_\beta - V_e)}{V_e} \tag{3.65}$$

To calculate S_β and β, the values of $W_1, W_2, ..., W_k$ are found from Table 3.7 under column b_1 corresponding to the signal factor level, k. h is the level interval of the signal factor. $A_1, A_2, ..., A_k$ in Table 3.7 correspond to $y_1, y_1, ..., y_k$ in Table 3.1.

Table 3.7 Orthogonal polynomial equation (level intervals must be equal)

# of Levels Coefficients	$k=2$	$k=3$		$k=4$			$k=5$			
	b_1	b_1	b_2	b_1	b_2	b_3	b_1	b_2	b_3	b_4
W_1	-1	-1	1	-3	1	-1	-2	2	-1	1
W_2	1	0	-2	-1	-1	3	-1	-1	2	-4
W_3		1	1	1	-1	-3	0	-2	0	6
W_4				3	1	1	1	-1	-2	-4
W_5							2	2	1	1
$\lambda^2 S$	2	2	6	20	4	20	10	14	10	70
λS	1	2	2	10	4	6	10	14	12	24
S	1/2	2	2/3	5	4	9/5	10	14	72/5	288/35
λ	2	1	3	2	1	10/3	1	1	5/6	35/12

# of Levels Coefficients	$k=6$					$k=7$				
	b_1	b_2	b_3	b_4	b_5	b_1	b_2	b_3	b_4	b_5
W_1	-5	5	-5	1	-1	-3	5	-1	3	-1
W_2	-3	-1	7	-3	5	-2	0	1	-7	4
W_3	-1	-4	4	2	-10	-1	-3	1	1	-5
W_4	1	-4	-4	2	10	0	-4	0	6	0
W_5	3	-1	-7	-3	-5	1	-3	-1	1	5
W_6	5	5	5	1	1	2	0	-1	-7	-4
W_7						3	5	1	3	1
$\lambda^2 S$	70	84	180	28	252	28	84	6	154	80
λS	35	56	108	48	120	28	84	36	264	240
S	35/2	112/3	324/5	576/7	400/7	28	84	216	3168/7	4800/7
λ	2	3/2	5/3	7/12	21/10	1	1	1/6	7/12	7/20

Table 3.8   Results of experiment

Signal	$M_1 = 3.7$	$M_2 = 3.9$	$M_3 = 4.1$
	635.1	610.4	599.3
Reading	633.5	616.7	598.6
	631.5	612.5	593.2
	629.2	610.5	596.7
Total	2529.3	2450.1	2387.8

Example

In an experimental study of piston processing, the finish cavity depth was considered as the signal factor, M, and the reading was in grams. Table 3.8 shows the results. Since the level intervals of M are equal, Table 3.7 can be used.

$$S_T = 635.1^2 + 633.5^2 + \ldots + 596.7^2 - S_m$$

$$= 2582.6267 \quad \text{and} \quad f = 11 \tag{3.66}$$

$$S_m = \frac{(635.1 + 633.5 + \ldots + 596.7)^2}{12} = 4522969.6530 \tag{3.67}$$

From Table 3.7,

$$W_1 = -1$$

$$W_2 = 0$$

$$W_3 = +1$$

$$\lambda^2 S = 2$$

$$r_0 = 4$$

$$S_\beta = \frac{(W_1 y_1 + W_2 y_2 + W_3 y_3)^2}{r_0 \lambda^2 S}$$

$$= \frac{[(-1) \times 2529.3 + 0 \times 2450.1 + 1 \times 2387.8]^2}{4 \times 2} \quad (3.68)$$

$$= 2502.7813 \quad \text{and} \quad f = 1$$

From Table 3.7,

$$\lambda S = 2$$

The signal-factor level interval is

$$h = 0.2$$

The linear coefficient, β, is calculated as

$$\beta = \frac{W_1 y_1 + W_2 y_2 + W_3 y_3}{r_0 \lambda S h}$$

$$\quad (3.69)$$

$$= \frac{(-1) \times 2529.3 + 0 \times 2450.1 + 1 \times 2387.8}{4 \times 2 \times 0.2} = -88.44$$

$$S_e = S_T - S_\beta = 2582.6267 - 2502.7813$$

$$\quad (3.70)$$

$$= 79.8454 \quad \text{and} \quad f = 10$$

$$V_e = \frac{S_e}{10} = \frac{79.8454}{10} = 7.98454 \quad (3.71)$$

The SN ratio is given by

$$\eta = 10\log\frac{\dfrac{1}{r_0\lambda^2 S h^2}\left(S_\beta - V_e\right)}{V_e}$$

$$= 10\log\frac{\dfrac{1}{4\times2\times0.2^2}\left(2502.7813 - 7.98454\right)}{7.98454} \qquad (3.72)$$

$$= 29.90(\text{db})$$

3.6   NUMERICALLY CONTROLLED (NC) MACHINE PROCESSING

3.6.1 Introduction

In order to optimize the performance of a numerically controlled (NC) machine used to process a hard steel material, the following experiment was conducted (see Reference 3). According to the principle of robust technology development described in Chapter 10, the ideal function of this process was defined as follows:

$$y = \beta M \qquad (3.73)$$

where

M (input) = programmed dimension
y (output) = part dimension after machining

In order for the machine to perform well for all component parts that it was to process, the input dimensions had to cover a wide range of expected values.

Since this study was conducted before product planning, a special test piece (Fig. 3.3) was designed. The test piece was designed in such a simple shape that measurement error was minimized.

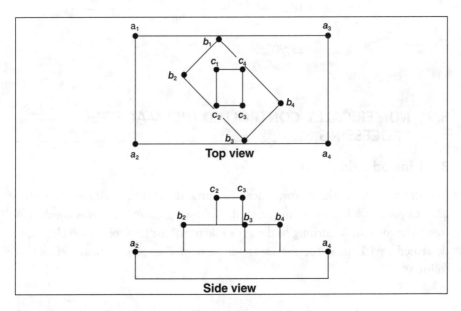

Figure 3.3 Test-piece design and signal-factor levels

From the 12 reference points shown in Fig. 3.3, $(a_1, a_2, ..., c_3, c_4)$, 66 dimensions were selected as the signal-factor levels, as follows:

Signal Level	M_1	M_2	M_3	M_4	...	M_{66}
Dimension	$a_1 - a_2$	$a_1 - a_3$	$a_1 - a_4$	$a_1 - b_1$	...	$c_3 - c_4$

The control factors and the noise factor are shown in Table 3.9.

Table 3.9   Control and noise factors and their levels

Control Factors	Level 1	Level 2	Level 3
A: Tool travel direction	Up	Down	
B: Speed (m/min)	Slower	Standard	Faster
C: Feed rate (m/min)	Slower	Standard	Faster
D: Tool material	Softer	Standard	Harder
E: Tool stiffness	Lower	Standard	Higher
F: Tool angle 1	Smaller	Standard	Larger
G: Tool angle 2	Smaller	Standard	Larger
H: Depth (mm)	Lower	Standard	Higher
Noise Factor		Level 1	Level 2
Variability of Material Hardness		Softer	Harder

3.6.2   Experiment and Analysis Using Signal-to-Noise Ratio

Control factors were assigned to an L_{18} arrays as shown on the left side of Table 3.10. The product dimensions of experiment no. 1 are shown in Table 3.11.

The SN ratio for experiment no. 1 is calculated as follows.

Total sum of the squares is

$$S_T = 70.992^2 + 84.607^2 + \ldots + 10.955^2$$

$$= 250021.740385 \quad \text{and} \quad f = 132 \tag{3.74}$$

The variation due to proportionality, S_β, is

$$S_\beta = \frac{1}{r_0 r}(M_1 y_1 + M_2 y_2 + \ldots + M_{66} y_{66})^2 \quad \text{and} \quad f = 1 \tag{3.75}$$

where

$$r_0 r = 2\left(M_1^2 + M_2^2 + \ldots + M_{66}^2\right)$$

$$= 2\left(71.000^2 + 84.599^2 + \ldots + 11.000^2\right) \tag{3.76}$$

$$= 250146.969846$$

Table 3.10   Layout and results

No.	A	B	C	D	E	F	G	H	SN Ratio (db)	Sensitivity (β)
1	1	1	1	1	1	1	1	1	31.41	-0.0022
2	1	1	2	2	2	2	2	2	39.70	0.0058
3	1	1	3	3	3	3	3	3	39.68	0.0028
4	1	2	1	1	2	2	3	3	9.25	0.0730
5	1	2	2	2	3	3	1	1	44.56	-0.0001
6	1	2	3	3	1	1	2	2	42.02	0.0020
7	1	3	1	2	1	3	2	3	33.75	0.0057
8	1	3	2	3	2	1	3	1	44.59	0.0003
9	1	3	3	1	3	2	1	2	19.18	0.0114
10	2	1	1	3	3	2	2	1	42.80	0.0011
11	2	1	2	1	1	3	3	2	30.55	0.0145
12	2	1	3	2	2	1	1	3	26.41	0.0166
13	2	2	1	2	3	1	3	2	25.86	0.0148
14	2	2	2	3	1	2	1	3	35.24	0.0056
15	2	2	3	1	2	3	2	1	42.52	0.0022
16	2	3	1	3	2	3	1	2	41.01	-0.0009
17	2	3	2	1	3	1	2	3	2.63	0.1801
18	2	3	3	2	1	2	3	1	39.30	0.0025

Table 3.11   Results of experiment no. 1

	M_1	M_2	...	M_{66}
Signal	$(a_1 - a_2)$	$(a_1 - a_3)$	...	$(c_3 - c_4)$
	71.000	84.599	...	11.000
N_1	70.992	84.607	...	10.958
N_2	70.991	84.607	...	10.995
Total	141.983	169.214	...	21.913

so that

$$S_\beta = \frac{1}{250146.969846}(71.000 \times 141.983 + 84.599 \times 169.214 + \dots$$

$$+ 11.000 \times 21.913)^2 \qquad (3.77)$$

$$= 250021.645747 \quad \text{and} \quad f = 1$$

The error variation, S_e, is

$$S_e = S_T - S_\beta$$

$$= 250021.740385 - 250021.645747 \qquad (3.78)$$

$$= 0.094638 \quad \text{and} \quad f = 131$$

The error variance, V_e, is

$$V_e = \frac{S_e}{131} = \frac{0.094638}{131} = 0.0007224 \qquad (3.79)$$

The SN ratio is calculated as

$$\eta = 10 \log \frac{\frac{1}{r_0 r}(S_\beta - V_e)}{V_e}$$

$$= 10 \log \frac{\frac{1}{250146.969846}(250021.645747 - 0.0007224)}{0.0007224} \qquad (3.80)$$

$$= 10 \log 1383.581112 = 31.41(\text{db})$$

Table 3.12 Response table

Factor	SN Ratio			Sensitivity		
	Level 1	Level 2	Level 3	Level 1	Level 2	Level 3
A	33.7933	31.8133		0.0112	0.0263	
B	35.0917	33.2417	30.0767	0.0065	0.0162	0.0332
C	30.6800	32.8783	34.8517	0.0156	0.0344	0.0062
D	22.5900	34.9300	40.8900	0.0468	0.0076	0.0018
E	35.3783	33.9133	29.1183	0.0050	0.0162	0.0350
F	28.8200	30.9117	38.6783	0.0356	0.0166	0.0040
G	32.9683	33.9033	31.5383	0.0054	0.0328	0.0180
H	40.8633	33.0533	24.4933	0.0010	0.0079	0.0473

The sensitivity is calculated by

$$S = 10 \log \frac{1}{r_0 r} (S_\beta - V_e)$$

$$= 10 \log \frac{1}{250146.969846} (250021.645747 - 0.0007224) \quad (3.81)$$

$$= 10 \log 0.9994990$$

$$= -0.0022 (\mathrm{db})$$

The SN ratios of the other 17 runs are similarly calculated and one shown in Table 3.10.

From the results in Table 3.10, a response table for SN ratio and sensitivity can be created, as shown in Table 3.12.

For example, the average SN ratio for A_1 is calculated from the results in Table 3.10 as follows:

$$\eta(\overline{A_1}) = \frac{1}{9}(31.41 + 39.70 + \dots + 19.18) = 33.7933 \quad (3.82)$$

Figures 3.4 and 3.5 show the results of Table 3.12.

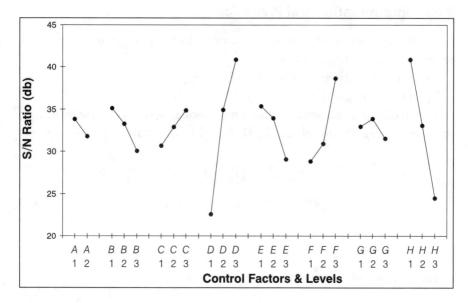

Figure 3.4 Response graph (SN)

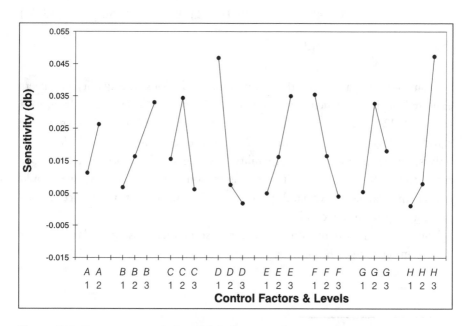

Figure 3.5 Response graph (sensitivity)

3.6.3 Interpretation and Prediction

From Fig. 3.3, we have selected the control-factor level with a higher SN response as the optimum configuration.

Initial configuration: $A_1 B_2 C_2 D_2 E_2 F_2 G_2 H_2$

Optimum configuration: $A_1 B_1 C_3 D_3 E_1 F_3 G_2 H_1$

The prediction of SN under the optimum configuration was done by adding together the larger factor effects: B, D, F, and H, as follows:

$$\eta = \left(\overline{B}_1 - \overline{T}\right) + \left(\overline{D}_3 - \overline{T}\right) + \left(\overline{F}_3 - \overline{T}\right) + \left(\overline{H}_1 - \overline{T}\right) + \overline{T}$$

$$= 35.09 + 40.89 + 38.68 + 40.86 - 3 \times 32.80 \tag{3.83}$$

$$= 57.24(\text{db})$$

The same was done for the initial configuration:

$$\eta = \overline{B}_2 + \overline{D}_2 + \overline{F}_2 + \overline{H}_2 - 3\overline{T}$$

$$= 33.24 + 34.93 + 30.91 + 33.05 - 3 \times 32.80 \tag{3.84}$$

$$= 33.73(\text{db})$$

From the comparison of the above two predictions, the quality engineers expected an improvement by more than 23 db in SN. That translates to a factor of 224 reduction in the variance or a factor of 15 reduction in the standard deviation. (Every time SN gains 6 db, the standard deviation halves). In terms of process capability, C_p, we would expect it to improve more than 10 times the initial configuration. That is to say, we would expect the range of variability of this NC machining to reduce to 10 percent of the initial condition.

The sensitivities (S) and slopes (β) were also predicted using the larger factor effects on sensitivity: B, D, E, F, and H.

Optimum configuration was

$$S = \overline{B}_1 + \overline{D}_3 + \overline{E}_1 + \overline{F}_3 + \overline{H}_1 - 4\overline{T}$$

$$= 0.0065 + 0.0018 + 0.0047 + 0.0040 + 0.0006 - 4 \times 0.0186 \qquad (3.85)$$

$$= -0.0568(\text{ db})$$

Initial configuration was

$$S = \overline{B}_2 + \overline{D}_2 + \overline{E}_2 + \overline{F}_2 + \overline{H}_2 - 4\overline{T}$$

$$= 0.0162 + 0.0076 + 0.0162 + 0.0166 + 0.0079 - 4 \times 0.0186 \qquad (3.86)$$

$$= -0.0099(\text{db})$$

Using $S = 10 \log \beta^2$, the above results translate to slopes of

$\beta = 0.9935$ for the optimum configuration

$\beta = 0.9989$ for the initial configuration

Table 3.13   Result from the confirmation run

	SN Ratio (db)		Sensitivity (slope)	
	Predicted	Actual	Predicted	Actual
Initial	33.73	34.71	0.9989	0.9992
Optimum	57.24	54.09	0.9935	0.9939
Gain	23.51	19.38		

3.6.4   The Confirmation Run

Two configurations—namely, the initial and the optimum—were tried and the output response was measured. The same signal and noise factor levels as in the experiment were used. The result is summarized in Table 3.13.

The engineers confirmed an almost 20-db gain in SN ratio. Both the absolute value and gain in SN ratio had excellent reproducibility. A gain of 19.38-db actual out of 23.51-db expected was considered to be confirmed.

Recall that the optimization in a Parameter Design study requires a two-step optimization:

Step 1: Reduce variability by maximizing SN ratio
Step 2: Adjust the sensitivity to the desired sensitivity level

Step 1 has been completed. As for Step 2, the adjustment in this case can be done easily by adjusting the input program. This is accomplishedby multiplying by a constant. Since the sensitivity at the optimum configuration was 0.9939, the input-signal level at the time of NC programming should be adjusted by:

$$M = \frac{y}{\beta} = \frac{y}{0.9939} = 1.0061y \qquad (3.87)$$

Note (3.1a): Linear Equation and Its Variation

In order to explain the derivation of the SN ratio, it is necessary to illustrate the mathematics of a linear equation and its variation.

The purpose of data analysis is to better understand the magnitude of variability within a group of data. For example, two manufacturing conditions were studied by taking five samples from each condition, and the product quality was compared with the product target value. In this case, the variability included in ten data points (called total variation), includes three sources of variation: the difference between two conditions, the variability within five samples in each condition, and the deviation of the grand overall average from the target.

Variation is the expression of variability in quadratic form. By using the quadratic form, it is possible to decompose the total of the squares of a group of data into the individual sources of change. To do so, linear equations expressing these three sources are written, and each linear equation is squared to be in quadratic form. However, when the number of data points in a linear equation are different, the calculated variation increases; therefore, it is necessary to divide the squared value by the **number of units** so that a comparison with other sources of variation can be made on the same basis.

A **linear equation** indicates a piece of information. If we want to decompose the total variation into several sources of variation, the same number of linear equations as sources must be written. The linear equations to be written depend on what kind of variation the engineer is interested in. For example, if an interaction is considered to be pooled with the error, decomposition must be made with this consideration in mind.

Equation (3.88) is called a linear equation of y.

$$L = c_1 y_1 + c_2 y_2 + \ldots + c_k y_k \tag{3.88}$$

The number of units of the linear equation, denoted by D, is defined as

$$D = c_1^2 + c_2^2 + \ldots + c_k^2 \tag{3.89}$$

The variation of L, or the linear equation L expressed in quadratic form, denoted by S, is defined as

$$S = \frac{L^2}{D} \tag{3.90}$$

The reason why the square of a linear equation is divided by the number of units is explained as follows. When data are systematically collected by using a two-way table or an orthogonal array, the data include various kinds of information. In order to decompose the total variation into individual components, the so-called quadratic form is used by calculating the square of a linear equation. By the use of squares, variation can be decomposed into the components of the sources of variation.

For example, the results of factors A and B were collected as follows:

$A_1 B_1 :\ \ y_1,\ y_2$
$A_1 B_2 :\ \ y_3$
$A_2 B_1 :\ \ y_4,\ y_5$
$A\ B\ :\ \ \ \cdots$

The linear equation of the grand average, denoted by L_m, is given by

$$L_m = \frac{1}{6}(y_1 + y_2 + \ldots + y_6) \tag{3.91}$$

The linear equation for the effect of A, denoted by L_A, is given by

$$L_A = \frac{1}{3}(y_1 + y_2 + y_3) - \frac{1}{3}(y_4 + y_5 + y_6) \tag{3.92}$$

The linear effect of B, denoted by L_B, is written by

$$L_B = \frac{1}{4}(y_1 + y_2 + y_4 + y_5) - \frac{1}{2}(y_3 + y_6) \tag{3.93}$$

These are all included in the total variation of the six data points. To evaluate the magnitude of the individual effects, a linear equation is squared. But in many cases, the amount of input for the individual equation is different. For example, there are four data points for B_1 and two for B_2 in the linear equation of B. In the linear equation for m, there are six data points. In order to make a fair comparison, we must divide the square of a linear equation by the number of units (the amount of input).

Consider the following two linear equations:

$$\left.\begin{array}{l} L_1 = c_1 y_1 + c_2 y_2 + \ldots + c_k y_k \\ L_2 = c'_1 y_1 + c'_2 y_2 + \ldots + c'_k y_k \end{array}\right\} \tag{3.94}$$

which are subject to the condition,

$$c_1 \times c'_1 + c_2 \times c'_2 + \ldots + c_k \times c'_k = 0 \tag{3.95}$$

In this situation, L_1 and L_2 are said to be orthogonal to each other, and the total variation of y, denoted by S_T, can be decomposed into the following components:

$$S_T = S_{L_1} + S_{L_2} + S_e \tag{3.96}$$

where S_{L_1}, S_{L_2}, and S_e are the variations of L_1 and L_2 and the error, respectively. S_e is the remaining part after subtracting S_{L_1} and S_{L_2} from S_T. The number of degrees of freedom for S_{L_1} and S_{L_2} is equal to 1 each.

Example

A certain quality characteristic was measured for of two kinds of materials with the following results:

$$\text{Material } A_1 : y_1 = 8 \quad y_2 = 10 \quad y_3 = 11 \quad y_4 = 11$$

$$\text{Total: } A_1 = 40 \quad \text{Average: } \overline{A}_1 = 10$$

$$\text{Material } A_2 : y_5 = 11 \quad y_6 = 13 \quad y_7 = 12$$

$$\text{Total: } A_2 = 36 \quad \text{Average : } \overline{A}_2 = 12$$

The total variation, S_T, is calculated as

$$S_T = y_1^2 + y_2^2 + \ldots + y_7^2$$

$$= 8^2 + 10^2 + \ldots + 12^2 \qquad (3.97)$$

$$= 840 \quad \text{and} \quad f_T = 7$$

where f_T is the total degrees of freedom.

In this case, we can write the following two linear equations:

The linear equation showing the average is

$$L_{1=} \frac{\sum y}{k} = \frac{1}{7}(y_1 + y_2 + \ldots + y_7) \qquad (3.98)$$

The linear equation to indicate the difference between the two averages, A_1 and A_2, is

$$L_2 = \overline{A}_1 - \overline{A}_2 = \frac{A_1}{4} - \frac{A_2}{3}$$

$$= \frac{1}{4}(y_1 + y_2 + y_3 + y_4) - \frac{1}{3}(y_5 + y_6 + y_7)$$

$$= \frac{1}{4}(8 + 10 + 11 + 11) - \frac{1}{3}(11 + 13 + 12) \tag{3.99}$$

$$= 10 - 12 = -2$$

As defined,

$$c_1 = c_2 = c_3 = c_4 = c_5 = c_6 = c_7 = \frac{1}{7}$$

$$c'_1 = c'_2 = c'_3 = c'_4 = \frac{1}{4}$$

$$c'_5 = c'_6 = c'_7 = -\frac{1}{3}$$

so that

$$c_1 \times c'_1 + c_2 \times c'_2 + \ldots + c_7 \times c'_7 = 0$$

The number of units for each linear equation is

$$D_1 = c_1^2 + c_2^2 + \ldots + c_7^2$$

$$= (1/7)^2 + (1/7)^2 + \ldots + (1/7)^2$$

$$= (1/7)^2 \times 7 = (1/7)$$

$$\tag{3.100}$$

$$D_2 = \left(c'_1\right)^2 + \left(c'_2\right)^2 + \ldots \left(c'_7\right)^2$$

$$= (1/4)^2 \times 4 + (-1/3)^2 \times 3$$

$$= (1/4) + (1/3)$$

The variation of each linear equation is

$$S_{L_1} = \frac{L_1^2}{D_1} = \frac{\left(\frac{\sum y}{7}\right)^2}{\frac{1}{7}} = \frac{(\sum y)^2}{7}$$

(3.101)

$$= \frac{(40 + 36)^2}{7} = 825.14 \quad \text{and} \quad f_{L_1} = 1$$

$$S_{L_2} = \frac{L_2^2}{D_2}$$

$$= \frac{\left(\frac{A_1}{4} - \frac{A_2}{3}\right)^2}{\frac{1}{4} + \frac{1}{3}} = \frac{(3A_1 - 4A_2)^2}{12^2\left(\frac{1}{4} + \frac{1}{3}\right)}$$

(3.102)

$$= \frac{(3 \times 40 - 4 \times 36)^2}{12(3 + 4)} = 6.86 \quad \text{and} \quad f_{L_2} = 1$$

The remaining part, S_e, called the error variation, is the total of individual deviations from its average squared;

$$S_e = \left(y_1 - \overline{A}_1\right)^2 + \left(y_2 - \overline{A}_1\right)^2 + \ldots + \left(y_4 - \overline{A}_1\right)^2$$
$$+ \left(y_5 - \overline{A}_2\right)^2 + \left(y_6 - \overline{A}_2\right)^2 + \left(y_7 - \overline{A}_2\right)^2$$
$$= (8 - 10)^2 + (10 - 10)^2 + \ldots + (12 - 12)^2$$
$$= 2^2 + 0^2 + \ldots + 0^2 = 8 \quad \text{and} \quad f_e = 5$$

(3.103)

Thus, the total variation is decomposed into

$$S_T = S_{L_1} + S_{L_2} + S_e$$

(3.104)

$$840 = 825.14 + 6.86 + 8.00 \tag{3.105}$$

The relationship between the degrees of freedom is

$$f_T = f_{L_1} + f_{L_2} + f_e \tag{3.106}$$

Note 3.1b: Decomposition of Variation for the Case of Zero-Point Proportional Equation

Inputs M_1, M_2, ..., M_k and outputs y_1, y_2, ..., y_k are shown in Table 3.14 and Fig. 3.6.

Table 3.14   Inputs and outputs

Input	M_1	M_2	. . . . .	M_k
Output	y_1	y_2	. . . . .	y_k

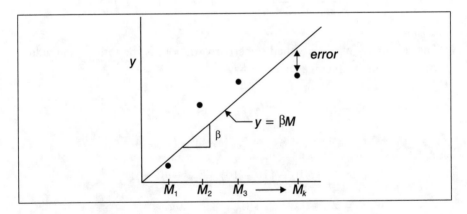

Figure 3.6   Zero-point proportional equation

First, the total variation, S_T, is calculated:

$$S_T = y_1^2 + y_2^2 + \ldots + y_k^2 \quad \text{and} \quad f_T = k \tag{3.107}$$

The ideal function is written as

$$y_i = \beta M_i \tag{3.108}$$

But, in reality, the actual relationship is

$$y_i = \beta M_i + e_i \tag{3.109}$$

where β is the slope, and e_i is the error caused by variation, or the deviation from the ideal function. For example, the error at M_k is

$$e_k = y_k - \beta M_k \tag{3.110}$$

The total error variation, S_e, is

$$
\begin{aligned}
S_e &= \sum (y_i - \beta M_i)^2 \\
&= \sum y_i^2 - 2\beta \sum M_i y_i + \beta^2 \sum M_i^2
\end{aligned}
\tag{3.111}
$$

The slope, β, which minimizes the total error variation, is determined by differentiating Eq. (3.111) with respect to β and then setting it equal to zero.

$$\frac{dS_e}{d\beta} = -2 \sum M_i y_i + 2\beta \sum M_i^2 = 0 \tag{3.112}$$

β is solved as

$$
\begin{aligned}
\beta &= \frac{\sum M_i y_i}{\sum M_i^2} \\
&= \frac{1}{\sum M_i^2} (M_i y_i + M_2 y_2 + \ldots + M_k y_k)
\end{aligned}
\tag{3.113}
$$

To derive the variation caused by β, we use the mathematics as described in Note (3.1a).

Equation (3.113) is a linear equation of y. The coefficients $c_1, c_2, ..., c_k$, in Eq. (3.88) for Equation (3.113) are:

$$c_1 = \frac{M_1}{\sum M_i^2}$$

$$c_2 = \frac{M_2}{\sum M_i^2}$$

...

$$c_k = \frac{M_k}{\sum M_i^2}$$

Therefore, the number of units of Eq. (3.113) are denoted by

$$D = \left(\frac{1}{\sum M_i^2}\right)^2 \left(M_1^2 + M_2^2 + ... + M_k^2\right)$$

$$= \frac{\sum M_i^2}{\left(\sum M_i^2\right)^2} = \frac{1}{\sum M_i^2} \tag{3.114}$$

The variation of linear equation β, denoted by S_β, is therefore

$$S_\beta = \frac{L^2}{D} = \frac{\left(\dfrac{\sum M_i y_i}{\sum M_i^2}\right)^2}{\dfrac{1}{\sum M_i^2}} = \frac{\left(\sum M_i y_i\right)^2}{\sum M_i^2} \quad \text{and} \quad f_\beta = 1 \tag{3.115}$$

Substituting Eq. (3.113) into Eq. (3.111), the error variation is rewritten as

$$S_e = \sum y_i^2 - 2\frac{\sum M_i y_i}{\sum M_i^2} \times \sum M_i y_i + \left(\frac{\sum M_i y_i}{\sum M_i^2}\right)^2 \times \sum M_i^2$$

$$= \sum y_i^2 - \frac{\left(\sum M_i y_i\right)^2}{\sum M_i^2} = S_T - S_\beta \quad \text{and} \quad f_e = k - 1 \quad (3.116)$$

or

$$S_T = S_\beta + S_e \quad (3.117)$$

The relationship between the degrees of freedom is

$$f_T = f_\beta + f_e \quad (3.118)$$

The variances of β and e, denoted by V_β and V_e, respectively, are

$$V_\beta = \frac{S_\beta}{f_\beta} = \frac{S_\beta}{1} = S_\beta \quad (3.119)$$

$$V_e = \frac{S_e}{f_e} \quad (3.120)$$

Note 3.1c: Decomposition of Variation for a Linear Equation

In the case when a linear equation is used, the regression line may not pass through the origin, as is evident in Fig. 3.7.

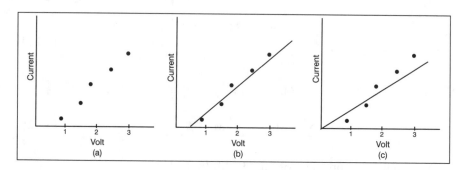

Figure 3.7 Linear equation

Table 3.15 Inputs and outputs

Input	M_1	M_2	. . . . .	M_k
Output	y_1	y_2	. . . . .	y_k

The relationship shown on Table 3.15 is written as

$$y_i = a + \beta M_i \tag{3.121}$$

$$\left. \begin{aligned} y_1 &= a + \beta M_1 \\ y_2 &= a + \beta M_2 \\ &\cdots \\ y_k &= a + \beta M_k \end{aligned} \right\} \tag{3.122}$$

$$\sum y_i = ka + \beta \sum M_i \tag{3.123}$$

To solve β and a from Eq. (3.121), first multiply M_i to both sides of Eq. (3.122).

$$\left. \begin{aligned} M_1 y_1 &= aM_1 + \beta M_1^2 \\ M_2 y_2 &= aM_2 + \beta M_2^2 \\ &\cdots \\ M_k y_k &= aM_k + \beta M_k^2 \end{aligned} \right\} \tag{3.124}$$

$$\sum y_i M_i = a \sum M_i + \beta \sum M_i^2 \tag{3.125}$$

Next, multiply both sides of Eq. (3.123) by $\sum M_i$:

$$\left(\sum M_i \right) \left(\sum y_i \right) = ka \left(\sum M_i \right) + \beta \left(\sum M_i \right)^2 \tag{3.126}$$

Multiply both sides of Eq. (3.125) by k:

$$k\left(\sum M_i y_i\right) = ka\left(\sum M_i\right) + k\beta\left(\sum M_i\right)^2 \tag{3.127}$$

Subtract Eq. (3.126) from Eq. (3.127):

$$k\left(\sum M_i y_i\right) - \left(\sum M_i\right)\left(\sum y_i\right) = \beta\left[k\left(\sum M_i^2\right) - \left(\sum M_i\right)^2\right] \tag{3.128}$$

β is solved as

$$\beta = \frac{k(\sum M_i y_i) - (\sum M_i)(\sum y_i)}{k\left(\sum M_i^2\right) - \left(\sum M_i\right)^2}$$

$$= \frac{\sum M_i y_i - \dfrac{(\sum M_i)(\sum y_i)}{k}}{\sum M_i^2 - \dfrac{(\sum M_i)^2}{k}} \tag{3.129}$$

The numerator in Eq. (3.129) can be rewritten as

$$\sum M_i y_i - \frac{(\sum M_i)(\sum y_i)}{k}$$

$$= \sum M_i y_i - 2\frac{(\sum M_i)(\sum y_i)}{k} + \frac{k(\sum M_i)(\sum y_i)}{k^2}$$

$$= \sum M_i y_i - \frac{(\sum M_i)(\sum y_i)}{k} - \frac{(\sum M_i)(\sum y_i)}{k} + \frac{k(\sum M_i)(\sum y_i)}{k^2}$$

$$= \sum M_i y_i - \overline{M}\left(\sum y_i\right) - \left(\sum M_i\right)\bar{y} + \sum \overline{M}\bar{y}$$

$$= \sum (M_i - \overline{M})(y_i - \bar{y}) \tag{3.130}$$

where

$$\overline{M} = \sum M_i / k \tag{3.131}$$

Also, the denominator of Eq. (3.129) can be rewritten as

$$\sum M_i^2 - \frac{\left(\sum M_i\right)^2}{k} = \sum M_i^2 - 2\frac{\left(\sum M_i\right)^2}{k} + \frac{\left(\sum M_i\right)^2}{k}$$

$$= \sum M_i^2 - 2\frac{\left(\sum M_i\right)^2}{k} + k\frac{\left(\sum M_i\right)^2}{k^2} \quad (3.132)$$

$$= \sum M_i^2 - 2\left(\sum M_i\right)\overline{M} + \sum \left(\overline{M}\right)^2$$

$$= \sum \left(M_i - \overline{M}\right)^2$$

From Eqs. (3.130) and (3.132), Eq. (3.130) can be rewritten as

$$\beta = \frac{\sum M_i y_i - \frac{\left(\sum M_i\right)\left(\sum y_i\right)}{k}}{\sum M_i^2 - \frac{\left(\sum M_i\right)^2}{k}}$$

$$= \frac{\sum \left(M_i - \overline{M}\right)\left(y_i - \overline{y}\right)}{\sum \left(M_i - \overline{M}\right)^2} \quad (3.133)$$

Since

$$\sum \left(M_i - \overline{M}\right) = 0 \quad (3.134)$$

Eq. (3.133) can be rewritten as

$$\beta = \frac{\sum \left(M_i - \overline{M}\right)\left(y_i - \overline{y}\right)}{\sum \left(M_i - \overline{M}\right)^2}$$

$$= \frac{\sum \left(M_i - \overline{M}\right)y_i}{\sum \left(M_i - \overline{M}\right)^2} - \frac{\sum \left(M_i - \overline{M}\right)}{\sum \left(M_i - \overline{M}\right)^2}\overline{y} \quad (3.135)$$

$$= \frac{\sum \left(M_i - \overline{M}\right)y_i}{\sum \left(M_i - \overline{M}\right)^2}$$

If the levels of M are defined so that

$$\sum M_i = 0 \tag{3.136}$$

then Eq. (3.123) can be rewritten as

$$a = \frac{1}{k}\left[\sum y_i - \beta\left(\sum M_i\right)\right]$$

$$= \frac{\sum y_i}{k} = \bar{y} \tag{3.137}$$

Next, the variation of the average, $\bar{y}$, and the slope, β, are derived as follows. Both Eqs. (3.135) and (3.137) are linear equations of y. These are denoted by L_β and L_m respectively:

$$L_m = \frac{1}{k}(y_1 + y_2 + \ldots + y_k) \tag{3.138}$$

$$L_\beta = \frac{\sum(M_i - \overline{M})y_i}{\sum(M_i - \overline{M})^2} \tag{3.139}$$

In order to observe the orthogonality of the above two equations, Eq. (3.95) is used.

$$c_1 \times c'_1 + c_2 \times c'_2 + \ldots + c_k \times c'_k = 0$$

$$\frac{1}{k} \times \frac{1}{\left(\sum M_i - \overline{M}\right)^2}\left[(M_1 - \overline{M}) + (M_2 - \overline{M}) + \ldots + (M_k - \overline{M})\right]$$

$$= \frac{1}{k \times \sum(M_i - \overline{M})^2} \times \left(\sum M_i - \overline{M}\right) = 0 \tag{3.140}$$

It is seen that the two equations (3.138 and 3.139) are orthogonal to each other. Therefore, the variation of either L_m or L_β consists of one component of the total variation.

To calculate these variations, the number of units for L_m or L_β, denoted by D_m or D_β respectively, are calculated first:

$$D_m = \left(\frac{1}{k}\right)^2 \times k = \frac{1}{k} \qquad (3.141)$$

$$D_\beta = \left[\frac{1}{\sum(M_i - \overline{M})^2}\right]^2 \left[(M_1 - \overline{M})^2 + (M_2 - \overline{M})^2 + \ldots + (M_k - \overline{M})^2\right]$$

$$= \frac{\sum(M_i - \overline{M})^2}{\left[\sum(M_i - \overline{M})^2\right]^2} = \frac{1}{\sum(M_i - \overline{M})^2}$$

$$(3.142)$$

Therefore, S_m and S_β are calculated by

$$S_m = \frac{(L_m)^2}{D_m} = \frac{\left[\frac{1}{k}(\sum y_i)\right]^2}{\frac{1}{k}} = \frac{(\sum y)^2}{k} \qquad \text{and} \qquad f_{m=1} \qquad (3.143)$$

$$S_\beta = \frac{(L_\beta)^2}{D_\beta} = \frac{\left[\dfrac{\sum(M_i - \overline{M}) \times y_i}{\sum(M_i - \overline{M})^2}\right]^2}{\dfrac{1}{\sum(M_i - \overline{M})^2}} \qquad (3.144)$$

$$= \frac{\left[\sum(M_i - \overline{M}) \times y_i\right]^2}{\sum(M_i - \overline{M})^2} \qquad \text{and} \qquad f_\beta = 1$$

Thus, the total variation, S_T, is decomposed into

$$S_T = S_m + S_\beta + S_e \qquad (3.145)$$

$$f_T = f_m + f_\beta + f_e \qquad (3.146)$$

Note 3.1d: Derivation of the SN Ratio for Zero-Point Proportional Equation

Based on the illustration in Note (3.1b), the decomposition of the total variation is summarized in Table 3.16. The table is called an **ANOVA** table (**analysis of variance** table).

Table 3.16   ANOVA table of a zero-point proportional equation

Source	Degree of freedom	Variation	Variance	$E(V)$, Expectation of variance
β	1	S_β	V_β	$r\beta^2 + \sigma^2$
e	$k-1$	S_e	V_e	σ^2
Total	k	S_T		

In the table, the expectation of variance is derived from statistics. Generally, the data collected in experimentation include experimental error. The error deviates either to the positive or the negative side from the true value. When we calculate an average from a group of data, about half of the data deviate to the positive side of the true value and half to the negative side, thereby essentially cancelling each other. As a result, the average calculated is considered to be a good estimate of the true value.

However, once a datum is squared to calculate variation, the deviation (either positive or negative) remains in the squared value without cancellation. Because of this, the variation or the variance calculated becomes an overestimate. The expectation of variance in the ANOVA table shows the contents of the average of variances, which were calculated from an infinite number of data taken from the same population.

The value r in $E(V)$ is the number of units of β.

$$r = \sum M_i^2 \qquad (3.147)$$

This is the case when there are no replications under each signal-factor level. *When there are r_0 replications under each signal-factor level, the r in the above equation become $r_0 r$.*

The SN ratio is estimated by the equation

$$\eta = 10 \log \frac{\beta^2}{\sigma^2} \tag{3.148}$$

From $E(V)$ in Table 3.16, the above equation is estimated by

$$\eta = 10 \log \frac{\frac{1}{r_0 r}(S_\beta - V_e)}{V_e} \tag{3.149}$$

Note (3.1e): Derivation of SN Ratio for a Linear Equation

From Note (3.1c), the decomposition of the total variation is summarized in Table 3.17.

Table 3.17   ANOVA table for a linear equation

Source	Degree of freedom	Variation	Variance	E(V)
m	1	S_m	V_m	$km^2 + \sigma^2$
β	1	S_β	V_β	$r\beta^2 + \sigma^2$
e	$k-2$	S_e	V_e	σ^2
Total	k	S_T		

Similar to the case of the zero-point proportional equation, the variances are calculated as follows:

$$V_m = \frac{S_m}{f_m} = S_m \tag{3.150}$$

$$V_\beta = \frac{S_\beta}{f_\beta} = S_\beta \tag{3.151}$$

$$V_e = \frac{S_e}{f_e} = \frac{S_e}{k-2} \tag{3.152}$$

The SN ratio is estimated as

$$\eta = 10 \log \frac{\beta^2}{\sigma^2} = 10 \log \frac{\frac{1}{r_0 r}(S_\beta - V_e)}{V_e} \tag{3.153}$$

where

$$r = \sum (M_i - \overline{M})^2 \tag{3.154}$$

Various Cases

4.1 ESTIMATION OF NOISE

In the determination of an SN ratio, after the ideal function is defined, decomposition of the data is conducted based on the definition of the ideal function. If the ideal function is that the input is proportional to the output, as in most cases, then the data are decomposed into the following components:

$$
\begin{aligned}
\text{Total variation} &= \text{Useful part} + \text{Harmful part} \\
&= \text{Proportional part} + \text{Remaining parts}
\end{aligned}
$$

The proportional part is the linear portion of the signal. In most cases, this is the useful or desirable part. Remaining parts include the higher-order portions of the signal factor (quadratic, cubic, etc.), the main effect of the noise factor, and the interaction between the signal and the noise factors.

Signal factor: quadratic
cubic

Noise factor: linear
quadratic
cubic

Interaction: signal factor x noise factor

Miscellaneous: experimental error

The above-noted remaining parts are considered to be the error and are used to determine the error variance in the calculation of the SN ratio.

$$\text{SN ratio} = 10 \log \frac{\frac{1}{r_0 r}(S_\beta - V_e)}{V_N} \tag{4.1}$$

It is appropriate that the remaining parts mentioned above be considered as the harmful parts and be placed, together with the error, in the denominator. But it might give an overestimate for the error variance, which is subtracted from S_β in the numerator. Therefore, it makes more sense to distinguish the harmful part in the denominator from the error part in the numerator. For this purpose, V_e is used to denote the former and V_N the latter. They are calculated from S_e and S_N, respectively.

$$S_N \text{ (harmful part)} = S_T - S_\beta$$
$$\tag{4.2}$$
$$= S_{\beta \times N} + S_e$$

Following is the illustration for the decomposition of total variation, S_T, into S_β, S_N, and S_e from the results in Table 4.1.

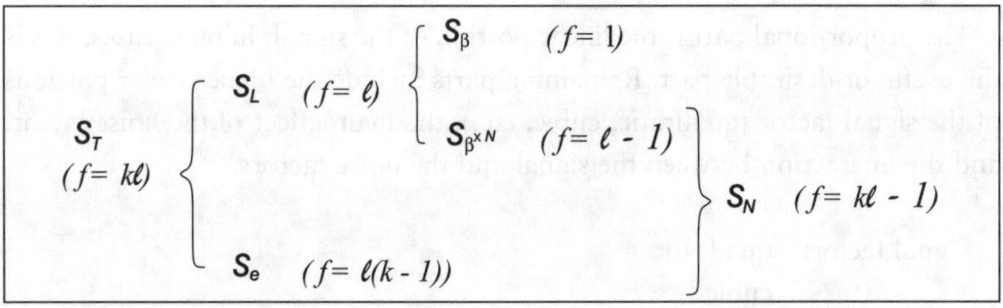

Figure 4.1 Decomposition of variation

Calculation of an SN ratio from Table 4.1 is performed as follows.

$$S_T = y_{11}^2 + y_{21}^2 + \ldots + y_{kl}^2 \quad \text{and} \quad f = kl \tag{4.3}$$

Table 4.1   Inputs and outputs

	M_1	M_2	...	M_k	L
N_1	y_{11}	y_{21}	...	y_{k1}	L_1
N_2	y_{12}	y_{22}	...	y_{k2}	L_2
...	...	...	...	...	...
N_l	y_{1l}	y_{2l}	...	y_{kl}	L_l
Total	y_1	y_2	...	y_k	

$$\left.\begin{array}{l} L_1 = M_1 y_{11} + M_2 y_{21} + \ldots + M_k y_{k1} \\[6pt] L_2 = M_1 y_{12} + M_2 y_{22} + \ldots + M_k y_{k2} \\[6pt] \ldots \\[6pt] L_l = M_1 y_{1l} + M_2 y_{2l} + \ldots + M_k y_{kl} \end{array}\right\} \tag{4.4}$$

$$S_\beta = \frac{(M_1 y_1 + M_2 y_2 + \ldots + M_k y_k)^2}{r_0 r} \quad \text{and} \quad f = 1 \tag{4.5}$$

$$r = M_1^2 + M_2^2 + \ldots + M_k^2 \quad \text{and} \quad r_0 = l \tag{4.6}$$

$$S_L = \frac{L_1^2 + L_2^2 + \ldots + L_l^2}{r} \quad \text{and} \quad f = l \tag{4.7}$$

$$S_{\beta \times N} = \frac{L_1^2 + L_2^2 + \ldots + L_l^2}{r} - S_\beta \quad \text{and} \quad f = l - 1 \tag{4.8}$$

$$S_e = S_T - S_\beta - S_{\beta \times N} \quad \text{and} \quad f = l(k - 1) \tag{4.9}$$

$$V_e = \frac{S_e}{l(k - 1)} \tag{4.10}$$

$$S_N = S_T - S_\beta \quad \text{and} \quad f = kl - 1 \tag{4.11}$$

$$V_N = \frac{S_N}{kl - 1} \tag{4.12}$$

$$\eta = 10 \log \frac{\frac{1}{r_0 r}(S_\beta - V_e)}{V_N} \tag{4.13}$$

Example

In a circuit design, the ideal function is that the output voltage is proportional to the input voltage. Table 4.2 shows the results of a simulation.

Table 4.2   Inputs and outputs

	$M_1 = 1$	$M_2 = 2$	$M_3 = 3$
N_1	168.60	505.80	843.00
N_2	108.23	324.69	541.15
Total	276.83	830.49	1384.15

In the table, M is the input voltage (the signal factor), and N is the compounded noise factor.

$$S_T = 168.60^2 + 108.23^2 + \ldots + 541.15^2$$
$$= 1,404,889.252 \quad \text{and} \quad f = 6 \tag{4.14}$$

$$r = M_1^2 + M_2^2 + M_3^2$$
$$= 1^2 + 2^2 + 3^2 = 14 \quad \text{and} \quad r_0 = 2 \tag{4.15}$$

$$S_\beta = \frac{(M_1 y_1 + M_2 y_2 + M_3 y_3)^2}{r_0 r}$$

$$= \frac{(1 \times 276.83 + 2 \times 830.49 + 3 \times 1384.15)^2}{2 \times 14} \tag{4.16}$$

$$= 1,324,688.102 \quad \text{and} \quad f = 1$$

$$\left.\begin{array}{l} L_1 = 1 \times 168.60 + 2 \times 505.80 + 3 \times 843.00 = 3.709.20 \\ L_2 = 1 \times 108.23 + 2 \times 324.69 + 3 \times 541.15 = 2,381.06 \end{array}\right\} \tag{4.17}$$

$$S_{\beta \times N} = \frac{L_1 + L_2^2}{r} - \frac{(L_1 + L_2)^2}{2r} = \frac{(L_1 - L_2)^2}{2r}$$

$$\tag{4.18}$$

$$= \frac{(3709.20 - 2381.06)^2}{2 \times 14} = 62,998.4236 \quad \text{and} \quad f = 1$$

$$S_e = S_T - S_\beta - S_{\beta \times N}$$

$$= 1,404,889.252 - 1,324,688.102 - 62,998.4236 \tag{4.19}$$

$$= 17,202.7264 \quad \text{and} \quad f = 4$$

$$V_e = \frac{S_e}{4} = \frac{17,202.7264}{4} = 4,300.6816 \tag{4.20}$$

$$V_N = \frac{S_{\beta \times N} + S_e}{1 + 4}$$

$$\tag{4.21}$$

$$= \frac{62,998.4236 + 17,202.7264}{5} = 16,040.2300$$

$$\eta = 10 \log \frac{\frac{1}{r_0 r}(S_\beta - V_e)}{V_N}$$

$$= 10 \log \frac{\frac{1}{2 \times 14}(1,324,688.102 - 4,300.6816)}{16,040.2300} \tag{4.22}$$

$$= 10 \log 2.9399$$

$$= 4.68(\text{db})$$

4.2   CASE WITH AN ADJUSTMENT FACTOR

In most cases of applying dynamic SN ratios to quality characteristics, the ideal function is expressed as an output proportional to an input. As defined, the input signal generates an output. In some cases, however, the input is not restricted to one signal factor.

In an injection-molding process, for example, the ideal function is when product dimensions are proportional to mold dimensions. This is the most frequently occurring type of ideal function in manufacturing. In an integrated-circuit fabrication process, the ideal function is when the dimension on a wafer is proportional to the mask dimension. In a machine processing, it is when the product dimension is proportional to the tool position. All of these systems have one common ideal function called **transformability**. In each case, the ideal function involves transforming the intention (mold dimension, mask dimension, or the computer input to a processing machine) to the output (product dimension).

Such systems can be optimized through the Parameter Design approach. Under the optimized condition, we expect that intended dimensions are transformed into product dimensions, despite noise factor changes. But in many cases, the effect of noise factors is so large that the process cannot produce the products within tolerance. Adjustment of the output dimensions must be made by providing either a feed-forward or a feedback system. For this purpose, an **adjusting factor** or a **tuning factor** is selected as the second signal. In the case of an injection-molding process, a signal such as mold pressure or mold temperature is used as the tuning factor.

In an injection-molding process, mold dimension is a signal factor. In a study for transformability, it is recommended that the levels of mold dimension cover a wide range so that the dimensions of future products be included. For the adjusting factor, mold pressure is used, but the level intervals are set just wide enough for tuning. For example, assume that the three levels of the tuning factor, denoted by M^*, are set as follows:

$$\left.\begin{array}{l} M_1^* = M_2^* - h \\[2mm] M_2^* = \text{Nominal} \\[2mm] M_3^* = M_2^* + h \end{array}\right\} \qquad (4.23)$$

Table 4.3 shows the dimensions of products from the combinations of the signal factor, M, adjusting factor, M^*, and noise factor, N.

Table 4.3 Results with a tuning factor

	M_1	M_2	...	M_k	L
$N_1 M_1^*$	y_{11}	y_{12}	...	y_{1k}	L_1
$N_1 M_2^*$	y_{21}	y_{22}	...	y_{2k}	L_2
$N_1 M_3^*$	y_{31}	y_{32}	...	y_{3k}	L_3
$N_2 M_1^*$	y_{41}	y_{42}	...	y_{4k}	L_4
$N_2 M_2^*$	y_{51}	y_{52}	...	y_{5k}	L_5
$N_2 M_3^*$	y_{61}	y_{62}	...	y_{6k}	L_6

In Table 4.3, L is a linear equation of the proportional part caused by the signal factor, M.

$$L_1 = M_1 y_{11} + M_2 y_{12} + \ldots + M_k y_{1k}$$
$$L_2 = M_1 y_{21} + M_2 y_{22} + \ldots + M_k y_{2k}$$
$$\ldots$$
$$L_6 = M_1 y_{61} + M_2 y_{62} + \ldots + M_k y_{6k} \tag{4.24}$$

Decomposition of $6k$ pieces of data is as follows:

$$S_T = y_{11}^2 + y_{12}^2 + \ldots + y_{6k}^2 \quad \text{and} \quad f = 6k \tag{4.25}$$

$$S_\beta = \frac{(L_1 + L_2 + \ldots + L_6)^2}{r_0 r} \quad \text{and} \quad f = 1 \tag{4.26}$$

where

$$r_0 = 6 \tag{4.27}$$

$$r = M_1^2 + M_2^2 + \ldots + M_k^2 \tag{4.28}$$

$$S_{\beta^*} = \frac{(-L_1 + L_3 - L_4 + L_6)^2}{4\left(M_1^2 + M_2^2 + \ldots + M_k^2\right)} \quad \text{and} \quad f = 1 \qquad (4.29)$$

This is a complicated calculation, as illustrated below. First, if there were only one noise-factor level, N_1, and the tuning factor level were fixed at M_1^*, the results would be

	M_1	M_2	...	M_k	Linear Equation
$N_1 M_1^*$	y_{11}	y_{12}	...	y_{1k}	L_1

The linear effect would be

$$L_1 = M_1 y_{11} + M_2 y_{12} + \ldots M_k y_{1k} \qquad (4.30)$$

Its number of units, r, would be

$$r = M_1^2 + M_2^2 + \ldots + M_k^2 \qquad (4.31)$$

The variation of its linear effect would be

$$S_\beta = \frac{L_1^2}{r} \qquad (4.32)$$

Actually, there are six conditions of N_1, N_2, M_1^*, M_2^*, and M_3^* combined, and there are six linear equations: L_1, L_2, ..., L_6.

The total linear effect is given by Eq. (4.26).

Next, the linear effect of the tuning (adjusting) factor, M^*, is discussed. Since the range of M^* is narrow and we are not interested in whether the line passes through the origin, a linear equation will be used. From Section 3.5, the table of Chebyshev's orthogonal polynomial equation is used for a simpler calculation. As described before, **the level intervals must be equal for the table to be usable.**

It is seen from Section 3.5, the level interval is equal to h. Since there are three levels, the following values are found from Table 3.7:

$$W_1 = -1$$
$$W_2 = 0$$
$$W_3 = +1$$
$$\lambda^2 S = 2$$

Also, there are two noise-factor levels, defined by two repetitions under each signal factor, M. That means $r_0 = 2$.

Summarizing the above, S_{β^*}, the linear effect of M^*, is given by Eq. (4.29).

$$S_{\beta^*} = \frac{(W_1 L_1 + W_2 L_2 + W_3 L_3 + W_1 L_4 + W_2 L_5 + W_3 L_6)^2}{r_0 \lambda^2 Sr}$$

$$= \frac{(-L_1 + L_3 - L_4 + L_6)^2}{2 \times 2 \times r} \tag{4.33}$$

$$= \frac{(-L_1 + L_3 - L_4 + L_6)^2}{4\left(M_1^2 + M_2^2 + \ldots + M_k^2\right)}$$

Equation (4.33) is the same as Eq. (4.29).

The total variation of L (linear effect of M) caused by N and M^*, denoted by S_L, is given by

$$S_L = \frac{L_1^2 + L_2^2 + \ldots + L_6^2}{M_1^2 + M_2^2 + \ldots + M_K^2} \quad \text{and} \quad f = 6 \tag{4.34}$$

The total variation of the harmful part, denoted by S_{res}, is given by

$$S_{res} = S_L - S_\beta - S_{\beta^*} \quad \text{and} \quad f = 4 \tag{4.35}$$

$$S_e = S_T - S_L \quad \text{and} \quad f = 6k - 6 \tag{4.36}$$

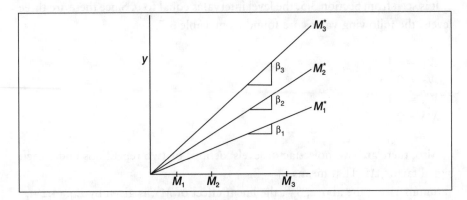

Figure 4.2 Response of y with adjusting factor

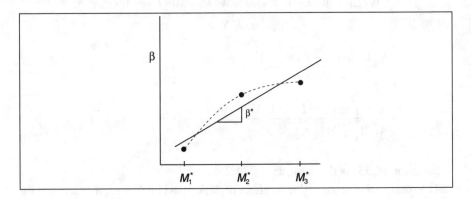

Figure 4.3 Response of slope

S_{β^*} is the amount of change (of the linear portion) of β caused by the change of the adjusting factor, M^*. From Fig. 4.2, it is evident that β changes when M^* (the level of the adjusting factor) changes. But the change of β may or may not be linear, as shown by the dotted line of Fig. 4.3. S_{β^*} is the variation of the linear portion. In this case, the ideal function is when β, the shrinkage in this injection-molding example, is ideally proportional to the change of the adjusting factor. That means the larger both β and β^* are, the better.

From the above decomposition, Table 4.4 is obtained, and two kinds of SN ratios are calculated: η, the SN ratio of transformability, and η^*, the SN ratio of adjustability.

Table 4.4   ANOVA table

Source	f	S	V
β	1	S_β	V_β
β^*	1	S_{β^*}	V_{β^*}
res	4	S_{res}	
e	$6(k-1)$	S_e	V
T	$6k$	S_T	

The SN ratio for transformability, η, is given by

$$\eta = 10 \log \frac{\frac{1}{r_0 r}(S_\beta - V_e)}{V_N} \tag{4.37}$$

where

$$V_e = \frac{S_e}{6(k-1)} \tag{4.38}$$

$$V_N = \frac{S_e + S_{\text{res}}}{6(k-1)+4} \tag{4.39}$$

$$r = M_1^2 + M_2^2 + \ldots + M_k^2 \tag{4.40}$$

$$r_0 = 6\,(\text{ the number of data points under } M) \tag{4.41}$$

The SN ratio for adjustability is η^*, using V_N as the denominator.

$$\eta^* = 10 \log \frac{\frac{1}{r^*}(S_{\beta^*} - V_e)}{V_N} \tag{4.42}$$

where

$$\begin{aligned}
r^* &= r_0 \left(\lambda^2 s\right) r h^2 \\
&= 2 \times \left(\lambda^2 s\right) \times \left(M_1^2 + M_2^2 + \ldots + M_k^2\right) \times h^2 \\
&= 4\left(M_1^2 + M_2^2 + \ldots + M_k^2\right) \times h^2
\end{aligned} \tag{4.43}$$

It must be noted that the r_0 in Eq. (4.41) is not the same as the r_0 in Eq. (4.43). The former is the number of repetitions under the level of M, which is equal to 6. But the latter is the number of repetitions under the combination of M and M^*, which is equal to 2.

In Eq. (4.43), h is the level interval of the adjusting factor, M^*. M^* has 3 levels with equal intervals.

SN ratios η and η^* are analyzed separately. As mentioned earlier, the two differ in that η is the index for good transformability; it is much more important than adjustability, η^*.

Example

In an injection-molding process, an experiment was conducted to improve transformability using an L_{18} orthogonal array. Mold dimensions and product dimensions were considered as the input and the output, respectively. Hold pressure was varied as the adjustment signal factor. Two shots were taken as a noise factor.

Signal factor: M (mm)
$\qquad M_1 = 5.012$
$\qquad M_2 = 6.225$
$\qquad M_3 = 6.890$
$\qquad M_4 = 7.116$

Adjustment signal factor: $M^* \left(\text{kgf} / \text{cm}^2 \right)$
$\qquad M_1^* = 250$
$\qquad M_2^* = 300$
$\qquad M_3^* = 350$

Noise factor: N (shot)
$\qquad N_1 = 5\text{th shot}$
$\qquad N_2 = 10\text{th shot}$

The results of experiment no. 1 are shown in Table 4.5.

Table 4.5 Results of experiment no. 1

		M_1	M_2	M_3	M_4	L
		5.012	6.225	6.890	7.116	
M_1^*	N_1	4.806	6.089	6.628	6.958	L_1
250	N_2	4.810	6.084	6.635	6.952	L_2
M_2^*	N_1	4.860	6.190	6.758	6.107	L_3
300	N_2	4.865	6.193	6.763	7.113	L_4
M_3^*	N_1	4.963	6.301	6.910	7.210	L_5
350	N_2	4.969	6.360	6.915	7.214	L_6

The SN ratio and sensitivity are calculated after the decomposition is made. Total variation, S_T, is

$$S_T = 4.806^2 + 6.089^2 + \ldots + 7.214^2$$

$$= 937.344267 \quad \text{and} \quad f = 24 \tag{4.44}$$

Linear equation, L, is used, as follows:

$$
\left.
\begin{aligned}
L_1 &= M_1 y_{11} + M_2 y_{12} + M_3 y_{13} + M_4 y_{14} \\
&= 5.012 \times 4.806 + 6.225 \times 6.089 + 6.890 \times 6.628 + 7.116 \times 6.958 \\
&= 157.171745 \\
L_2 &= 157.166202 \\
L_3 &= 152.911102 \\
L_4 &= 160.147983 \\
L_5 &= 163.014541 \\
L_6 &= 163.474802
\end{aligned}
\right\}
\tag{4.45}
$$

Magnitude of the input, $r_0 r$, is calculated as follows:

$$r = M_1^2 + M_2^2 + M_3^2 + M_4^2$$

$$= 5.012^2 + 6.225^2 + 6.890^2 + 7.116^2 = 161.980325 \qquad (4.46)$$

and since

$$r_0 = 6 \qquad (4.47)$$

then

$$r_0 r = 6 \times 161.980325 = 971.881950 \qquad (4.48)$$

$$S_L = \frac{L_1^2 + L_2^2 + \ldots + L_6^2}{r}$$

$$= \frac{157.171745^2 + 157.166202^2 + \ldots + 163.474802^2}{161.980325} \qquad (4.49)$$

$$= \frac{151731.1049}{161.980325} = 936.7255245 \qquad \text{and} \qquad f = 6$$

Variation of proportional constant, S_β, is

$$S_\beta = \frac{(L_1 + L_2 + \ldots + L_6)^2}{r_0 r}$$

$$= \frac{(157.171745 + 157.166202 + \ldots + 163.474802)^2}{971.881950} \qquad (4.50)$$

$$= \frac{953.886373^2}{971.881950} = 936.224006 \qquad \text{and} \qquad f = 1$$

In the case of adjustment, the linear equation is used, but the regression line may or may not pass through the origin. Since the adjusting factor M^* has an equal level interval, Table 3.7 may be used for easier calculation.

Variation of adjustability, S_β, is

$$S_{\beta^*} = \frac{(L_1 + L_2 - L_5 - L_6)}{4r}$$

$$= \frac{(157.171745 + 157.166202 - 163.014541 - 163.474802)^2}{4 \times 161.980325} \quad (4.51)$$

$$= 0.227893 \quad \text{and} \quad f = 1$$

It must be noted that Eq. (4.51) looks different from Eq. (4.29). This is because the layout of Table 4.5 is different from that of Table 4.3. However, the calculation is consistent: S_{β^*} is calculated from the difference between M_1^* and M_3^*.

Residual variation, S_{res}, is

$$S_{\text{res}} = S_L - S_\beta - S_{\beta^*}$$

$$= 936.7255245 - 936.224006 - 0.227893 \quad (4.52)$$

$$= 0.2736255 \quad \text{and} \quad f = 4$$

Variation for correction, S_e, is

$$S_e = S_T - S_L$$

$$= 937.344267 - 936.7255245 \quad (4.53)$$

$$= 0.6187425 \quad \text{and} \quad f = 18$$

Variance of noise, V_N, is

$$V_N = \frac{S_e + S_{\text{res}}}{f_e + f_{\text{res}}} = \frac{0.6187425 + 0.2736255}{18 + 4}$$

$$= 0.040562181 \quad (4.54)$$

Variance for correction, V_e, is

$$V_e = \frac{S_e}{f_e} = \frac{0.6187425}{18} = 0.034374583 \tag{4.55}$$

SN ratio of transformability, η, is

$$\eta = 10 \log \frac{\frac{1}{r_0 r}(S_\beta - V_e)}{V_N}$$

$$= 10 \log \frac{\frac{1}{971.881950}(936.224006 - 0.034374583)}{0.040562181} \tag{4.56}$$

$$= 10 \log 23.74 = 13.76 \,(\mathrm{db})$$

SN ratio of adjustability, η^*, is

$$\eta^* = 10 \log \frac{\frac{1}{4rh^2}\left(S_{\beta^*} - V_e\right)}{V_N}$$

$$= 10 \log \frac{\frac{1}{4 \times 161.980325 \times 50^2}(0.227893 - 0.034374583)}{0.040562181} \tag{4.57}$$

$$= 10 \log 0.000002945 = -55.31 \,(\mathrm{db})$$

where $h^2 = \left(M_1^* - \overline{M}^*\right)^2 = (350 - 300)^2 = 50^2$

Sensitivity of transformability, S, is

$$S = 10 \log \frac{1}{r_0 r}(S_\beta - V_e)$$

$$= 10 \log \frac{1}{971.881950}(950.244590 - 0.0047205) \tag{4.58}$$

$$= 10 \log 0.98 = -0.10 \,(\mathrm{db})$$

Sensitivity of adjustability, S^*, is

$$S^* = 10 \log \frac{1}{4rh^2} \left(S_{\beta^*} - V_e \right)$$

$$= 10 \log \frac{1}{4 \times 161.980325 \times 50^2} (0.227893 - 0.0047205) \qquad (4.59)$$

$$= 10 \log 0.00034 = -34.63 \, (\text{db})$$

4.3 CASE (I) WITH DOUBLE SIGNALS

Traditionally, the research for improvement of manufacturing technology is conducted using pertinent quality characteristics. For instance, a soldering experiment for a certain component part, a quality characteristic such as strength is used for analysis. Such a quality characteristic is called *response* or *objective quality characteristic*, since it directly relates to the objective.

In the research for a new product, objective quality characteristics are used also. In Quality Engineering, the use of objective quality characteristics is not recommended because this is inefficient for research.

The word *inefficient* means that the conclusions obtained from small-scale laboratory research might not be reproduced in a large-scale manufacturing environment, or the conclusion might be reversed after the product is sold to the customer. As a result, a large, manufacturing-scale experiment is necessary. Also, the same type of experiment has to be repeated every time a new product is to be introduced.

Recently, *concurrent engineering* or *simultaneous engineering* has been promoted in industry for the purpose of reducing new-product-development cycle time. However, the definitions and approaches are quite different by different promoters. One of the approaches is to conduct product development and process development at the same time. But these are conducted at different places by different groups of people, which is inefficient. In robust technology development, promoted by Dr. Taguchi, the two researches can be combined into one.

In a soldering-process improvement study, for example, two boards are used for experimentation. The two boards are prepared so that the difference between the boards produces the effect of a compounded noise factor, such as the difference in thermal capacity. Each board consists of three sets of terminals with a different cross-sectional area. The noise factor is denoted by N, and the cross-sectional area is denoted by M^*.

From the manufacturing viewpoint, it would be ideal for the current to be proportional to the cross-sectional area. Therefore, cross-sectional area is considered as the input signal, and current is the output result. From a product function viewpoint, it would be ideal for the current to be proportional to voltage. Voltage, denoted by M, is then considered as another signal. Instead of using two signal factors to maximize two SN ratios, the two signals — cross-sectional area and voltage — can be combined as one signal factor with one SN ratio for optimization. To optimize the relationship between cross-sectional area and current is to optimize transformability, the basic function in manufacturing. To optimize the voltage and current relationship is to optimize the basic function of the product. Thus, by combining the two signals into one, we can optimize the functions of the process and the product simultaneously.

This is a very efficient simultaneous engineering approach for optimizing both the **manufacture** and the **function** of a product.

In the experiment, the relationship between voltage, M, cross-sectional area, M^*, and current, y, are measured. These are shown in Table 4.6.

Table 4.6 Voltage/current relationship

		M_1	M_2	...	M_k
M_1^*	N_1	y_{11}	y_{12}	...	y_{1k}
	N_2	y_{21}	y_{22}	...	y_{2k}
M_2^*	N_1	y_{31}	y_{32}	...	y_{3k}
	N_2	y_{41}	y_{42}	...	y_{4k}
M_3^*	N_1	y_{51}	y_{52}	...	y_{5k}
	N_2	y_{61}	y_{62}	...	y_{6k}

Ideally, current, y, would be proportional to voltage, as well as to the cross-sectional area. Its ideal function is therefore

$$y = \beta M M^*$$

By considering the product of M and M^* as one signal factor, L_1 and L_2, the linear equations of the proportional term at N_1 and N_2, respectively, are calculated as follows:

$$\left. \begin{array}{l} L_1 = M_1^* M_1 y_{11} + M_1^* M_2 y_{12} + \ldots + M_3^* M_k y_{5k} \\ L_2 = M_1^* M_1 y_{21} + M_1^* M_2 y_{22} + \ldots + M_3^* M_k y_{6k} \end{array} \right\} \tag{4.60}$$

Total variation, S_T, is decomposed as shown in Fig. 4.4.

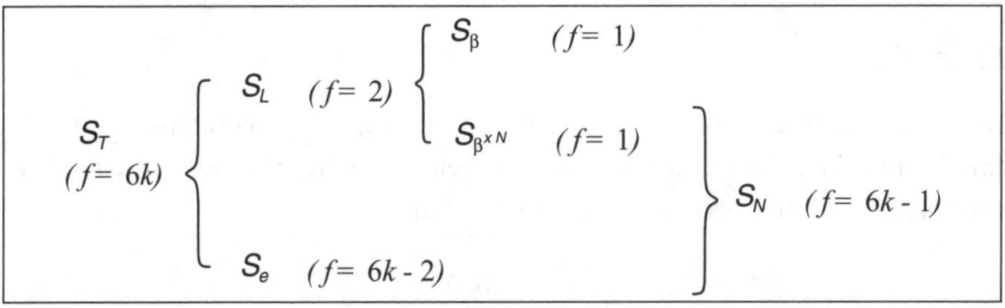

Figure 4.4   Decomposition of variation

$S_{\beta \times N}$ is the variation caused by the noise factor. S is sensitivity.

$$S_T = y_{11}^2 + y_{12}^2 + \ldots + y_{6k}^2 \quad \text{and} \quad f = 6k \tag{4.61}$$

$$S_\beta = \frac{(L_1 + L_2)^2}{2r} \quad \text{and} \quad f = 1 \tag{4.62}$$

$$r = \left(M_1^* M_1 \right)^2 + \left(M_1^* M_2 \right)^2 + \ldots + \left(M_3^* M_k \right)^2 \tag{4.63}$$

$$S_{\beta \times N} = \frac{L_1^2 + L_2^2}{r} - S_\beta \quad \text{and} \quad f = 1 \tag{4.64}$$

$$S_e = S_T - S_\beta - S_{\beta \times N} \quad \text{and} \quad f = 6k - 2 \qquad (4.65)$$

$$S_N = S_T - S_\beta \quad \text{and} \quad f = 6k - 1 \qquad (4.66)$$

$$V_e = \frac{S_e}{6k - 2} \qquad (4.67)$$

$$V_N = \frac{S_N}{6k - 1} \qquad (4.68)$$

$$\eta = 10 \log \frac{\frac{1}{2r}(S_\beta - V_e)}{V_N} \qquad (4.69)$$

$$S = 10 \log \frac{1}{2r}(S_\beta - V_e) \qquad (4.70)$$

Example

In a Parameter Design study of fine patterning for integrated-circuit (IC) fabrication (see Reference 4), the current flowing through a circuit is proportional to cross-sectional area and voltage:

$$y = \beta M M^* \qquad (4.71)$$

where

y = current
M^* = line width
M = voltage

Since the line length and height are constant, the cross-sectional area is only proportional to its width. Table 4.7 shows the results of one experimental run. In the table, noise conditions N_1 and N_2 represent the center and corner in a wafer, respectively.

In this example, the SN ratio and the sensitivity are calculated without distinguishing V_N from V_e.

$$S_T = 12.50^2 + 12.53^2 + \ldots + 40.25^2 = 162302 \quad \text{and} \quad f = 98 \quad (4.72)$$

Table 4.7   Results of experiment

M	M*	M_1^* (0.5V)	M_2^* (1.0V)	M_3^* (1.5V)	M_4^* (2.0V)	M_5^* (2.5V)	M_6^* (3.0V)	M_7^* (4.0V)
M_1	N_1	12.50	24.90	37.12	49.10	60.71	71.91	92.87
(1.2 μm)	N_2	12.53	24.99	37.28	49.30	60.97	72.23	93.32
M_2	N_1	10.74	21.41	31.95	42.28	52.34	62.07	80.41
(1.0 μm)	N_2	10.77	21.49	32.06	42.44	52.55	62.33	80.77
M_3	N_1	9.210	18.38	27.42	36.32	45.01	53.45	69.44
(0.8 μm)	N_2	9.246	18.46	27.56	36.51	45.25	53.75	69.84
M_4	N_1	8.525	17.00	25.36	33.61	41.65	49.49	64.39
(0.7 μm)	N_2	8.528	17.00	25.37	33.62	41.68	49.51	64.43
M_5	N_1	7.746	15.46	23.09	30.61	37.96	45.14	58.82
(0.6 μm)	N_2	7.762	15.48	23.11	30.63	37.99	45.18	58.88
M_6	N_1	6.864	13.71	20.48	27.15	33.70	40.11	52.36
(0.5 μm)	N_2	6.824	13.61	20.32	26.96	33.46	39.82	52.00
M_7	N_1	5.461	10.91	16.30	21.65	26.90	32.05	41.98
(0.4 μm)	N_2	5.222	10.43	15.61	20.73	25.77	30.71	40.25

$$S_\beta = \frac{(M_1 M_1^* y_{11} + M_1 M_2^* y_{12} + \ldots + M_7 M_7^* y_{77})^2}{2r}$$

$$= \frac{1}{2r}\{[(1.2 \times 0.5)(12.50 + 12.53) + (1.2 \times 1.0)(24.90 + 24.99)$$

$$+ \ldots + (0.4 \times 4.0)(41.98 + 40.25)]^2\}$$

$$= 160667 \quad \text{and} \quad f = 1 \tag{4.73}$$

$$r = (1.2 \times 0.5)^2 + (1.2 \times 1.0)^2 + \ldots + (0.4 \times 4.0)^2 = 168.175 \tag{4.74}$$

$$S_e = S_T - S_\beta$$

$$= 162302 - 160667 \tag{4.75}$$

$$= 1635 \quad \text{and} \quad f = 97$$

$$V_e = \frac{S_e}{97} = \frac{1635}{97} = 16.86 \tag{4.76}$$

$$\eta = 10 \log \frac{\frac{1}{2r}(S_\beta - V_e)}{V_e}$$

$$= 10 \log \frac{\frac{1}{2 \times 168.175}(160667 - 16.86)}{16.86} \tag{4.77}$$

$$= 10 \log 28.3 = 14.52 \, (\text{db})$$

$$S = 10 \log \frac{1}{2r}(S_\beta - V_e)$$

$$= 10 \log \frac{1}{2 \times 168.175}(160667 - 16.86) \tag{4.78}$$

$$= 10 \log 477.63 = 26.79 \, (\text{db})$$

4.4 CASE (II) WITH DOUBLE SIGNALS

In the previous section, double-signal factors were used to improve product function and manufacturing transformability. Two separate signal factors were combined into one, and its ideal function was written as

$$y = \beta M M^* \tag{4.79}$$

In another case, the ideal function could be different, such as

$$y = \frac{\beta M}{M^*} \tag{4.80}$$

where the equation may be applied to material development. Products made of plastic material are often manufactured by either an injection-molding or an extrusion process. In the case of an injection-molding process, the signal factor is mold dimension and the output is product dimension. For the research of a structural material, the cross-sectional area of the product is considered as the signal.

In the study, the following definitions apply:

Dimension: $M_1^*, M_2^*, \ldots M_k^*$
Load: M_1, M_2, M_3
Noise: N_1, N_2

Test pieces with k levels of dimension are prepared and tested at three levels of load to measure deformation, denoted by y. Two levels of a noise factor, such as temperature, are considered. Thus, the ideal function would be for the deformation to be inversely proportional to cross-sectional area and proportional to load, as shown in Eq. (4.80).

Table 4.8 shows the results of the deformation caused by different load and cross-sectional area change to improve the physical property of a plastic material.

Table 4.8 Load, cross section, and deformation

		M_1^*	M_2^*	...	M_k^*
M_1	N_1	y_{11}	y_{12}	...	y_{1k}
	N_2	y_{21}	y_{22}	...	y_{2k}
M_2	N_1	y_{31}	y_{32}	...	y_{3k}
	N_2	y_{41}	y_{42}	...	y_{4k}
M_3	N_1	y_{51}	y_{52}	...	y_{5k}
	N_2	y_{61}	y_{62}	...	y_{6k}

The linear equations at different noise-factor levels are calculated by

$$\left. \begin{array}{l} L_1 = \dfrac{M_1}{M_1^*}y_{11} + \dfrac{M_1}{M_2^*}y_{12} + \ldots + \dfrac{M_3}{M_k^*}y_{5k} \\[3mm] L_2 = \dfrac{M_1}{M_1^*}y_{21} + \dfrac{M_1}{M_2^*}y_{22} + \ldots + \dfrac{M_3}{M_k^*}y_{6k} \end{array} \right\} \qquad (4.81)$$

Total variation is

$$S_T = y_{11}^2 + y_{12}^2 + \ldots + y_{6k}^2 \quad \text{and} \quad f = 6k \qquad (4.82)$$

Total variation is decomposed as shown in Fig. 4.5.

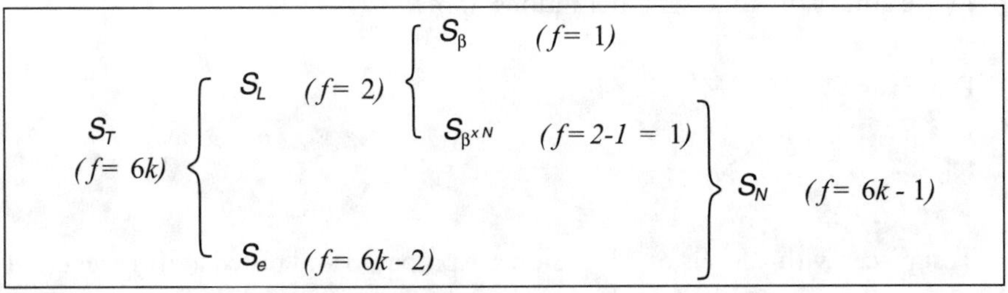

Figure 4.5 Decomposition of variation

Variation of L is

$$S_L = \frac{L_1^2 + L_2^2}{r} \quad \text{and} \quad f = 2 \qquad (4.83)$$

Variation of the proportional term is

$$S_\beta = \frac{(L_1 + L_2)^2}{2r} \quad \text{and} \quad f = 1 \qquad (4.84)$$

where

$$r = \left(\frac{M_1}{M_1^*}\right)^2 + \left(\frac{M_1}{M_2^*}\right)^2 + \ldots + \left(\frac{M_3}{M_k^*}\right)^2 \qquad (4.85)$$

Variation of L due to noise is

$$S_{\beta \times N} = S_L - S_\beta$$

$$= \frac{L_1^2 + L_2^2}{r} - \frac{(L_1 + L_2)^2}{2r} = \frac{(L_1 + L_2)^2}{2r} \quad \text{and} \quad f = 1 \qquad (4.86)$$

Variation of error is

$$S_e = S_T - S_L = S_T - S_\beta - S_{\beta \times N} \quad \text{and} \quad f = 6k - 2 \quad (4.87)$$

Variation of noise is

$$S_N = S_T - S_\beta \quad \text{and} \quad f = 6k - 1 \quad (4.88)$$

Variance of error is

$$V_e = \frac{S_e}{6k - 2} \quad (4.89)$$

Variance of noise is

$$V_N = \frac{S_N}{6k - 1} \quad (4.90)$$

The SN ratio is

$$\eta = 10 \log \frac{\frac{1}{2r}(S_\beta - V_e)}{V_N} \quad (4.91)$$

Sensitivity is

$$S = 10 \log \frac{1}{2r}(S_\beta - V_e) \quad (4.92)$$

It must be noted that the levels of signal M^* are only different in dimension (cross-sectional area), but otherwise maintain their shape. It must also be noted that varying the cross-sectional shape is important as a control factor, not as a signal or noise factor.

The objective of this experiment is to improve the stiffness of the material. This is accomplished by minimizing sensitivity, or the slope, β. Minimizing sensitivity means that minimum deformation occurs in response to the load added to test pieces. We need to find the condition which minimizes sensitivity without affecting SN ratio.

4.5 CASE WHEN SIGNAL-FACTOR LEVELS ARE DIFFERENT AT DIFFERENT RUNS OF AN ORTHOGONAL ARRAY _____

In most of the experiments, signal-factor levels are fixed at certain levels throughout the runs of an orthogonal array. But in some cases, the signal-factor levels are different at each run. Some examples follow.

In research on the improvement of luminescent material for vacuum fluorescent display (see Reference 5), the ideal function is that the brightness of luminescent material be proportional to both voltage and current. In the experiment, voltage was fixed at 20, 30, and 40 volts, and current was different each time. As a result, power — which is the product of voltage and current — was different each time. Table 4.9 shows the results of three runs from an L_{18} orthogonal array. The input is power (mW), the product of voltage and current, and the output is brightness (ad/m^2).

Table 4.9 Power and brightness

No.			M_1			M_2			M_3		
1	In	M	20	20	20	30	30	30	40	40	40
		M^*	0.386	0.397	0.420	0.545	0.564	0.597	0.668	0.693	0.734
		mW	7.72	7.94	8.40	16.35	16.92	17.91	26.72	27.72	29.36
	Out	ad/m^2	85	92	93	189	202	204	278	294	295
2	In	M	20	20	20	30	30	30	40	40	40
		M^*	0.455	0.444	0.561	0.627	0.615	0.789	0.757	0.739	0.963
		mW	9.10	8.88	11.22	18.81	18.45	23.67	30.28	29.56	38.52
	Out	ad/m^2	136	132	163	286	286	356	419	411	518
3	In	M	20	20	20	30	30	30	40	40	40
		M^*	0.392	0.402	0.367	0.588	0.637	0.570	0.727	0.799	0.706
		mW	7.84	8.04	7.34	17.64	19.11	17.10	29.08	31.96	28.24
	Out	ad/m^2	94	96	99	254	278	275	387	433	420

The ideal function is given by

$$y = \beta MM^*$$ (4.93)

where

$y =$ brightness (ad/m^2)
$M =$ voltage (mV)
$M^* =$ current (mA)

The SN ratio and sensitivity of experiment no. 1 are calculated as shown below.

$$S_T = y_1^2 + y_2^2 + \ldots + y_9^2$$ (4.94)

$$= 85^2 + 92^2 + \ldots + 295^2 = 393224 \quad \text{and} \quad f = 9$$

$$r = \left(M_1 \times M_1^*\right)^2 + \left(M_1 \times M_2^*\right)^2 + \left(M_1 \times M_3^*\right)^2 + \left(M_2 \times M_4^*\right)^2 + \ldots$$
$$+ \left(M_3 \times M_9^*\right)^2$$

$$= (20 \times 0.386)^2 + (20 \times 0.397)^2 + (20 \times 0.420)^2 + (30 \times 0.545)^2 + \ldots$$
$$+ (40 \times 0.734)^2 = 7.72^2 + 7.94^2 + \ldots + 29.36^2$$

$$= 3411.95$$ (4.95)

$$S_\beta = \frac{\left(M_1 M_1^* y_1 + M_1 M_2^* y_2 + \ldots + M_3 M_9^* y_9\right)^2}{r}$$

$$= \frac{(7.72 \times 85 - 7.94 \times 92 + \ldots + 29.36 \times 295)^2}{3411.95} = \frac{36568.55^2}{3411.95}$$ (4.96)

$$= 391934.42 \quad \text{and} \quad f = 1$$

$$S_e = S_T - S_\beta = 393224 - 391934.42 = 1289.58 \quad \text{and} \quad f = 8 \quad (4.97)$$

$$V_e = \frac{S_e}{8} = \frac{1289.58}{8} = 161.20 \quad (4.98)$$

$$\eta = 10 \log \frac{\dfrac{1}{3411.95}(391934.42 - 161.20)}{161.20} \quad (4.99)$$

$$= 10 \log 0.7123 = -1.47\,(\text{db})$$

$$S = 10 \log \frac{1}{3411.95}(391934.42 - 161.20)$$

$$= 10 \log 1148237 \quad (4.100)$$

$$= 20.60\,(\text{db})$$

As another example, an experiment to improve the robustness of a small motor is presented. The ideal function is that output torque be proportional to input voltage. Therefore, voltage is the input signal, and torque is the output. Normally, voltage is fixed at certain levels to observe torque. But, if it is more convenient to conduct the experiment by maintaining the torque level constant and observe voltage (rather than maintaining voltage and observe torque), the signal-factor level will change from observation to observation. This presents the same situation as the example of luminescent-material development.

Although signal levels are different from time to time, the SN ratio calculation and optimization procedures are exactly the same as usual, except for the tedious inputting of the signal levels each time.

4.6   SPLIT-TYPE ANALYSIS

4.6.1   What is Split-Type Analysis?

The objective of Parameter Design is to find the control-factor-level combination that is maximally robust against noise. Therefore, it is imperative that noise conditions must be properly set up in experimentation. The more noise factors considered in an experiment, the more chances are there to find a robust design. However, more noise conditions usually mean more cost and time for conducting the study, so it is an excellent practice to use a compounding noise factor with only two or three levels to achieve two objectives: exaggerate the effect of noise factors and save cost and time. In such cases, there are only two or three data points in one experimental run.

In some cases, providing one or two samples or conducting more measurements in order to get more data points is rather easy. For example, it is easy to take extra pieces of products from an injection-molding process once the molding conditions are set and the process is stabilized. In a study of the transformability of a machine, processing one more product is easy. Or may be easy to measure one sample under different customer conditions in order to get a additional data points.

On the other hand, in the study of a chemical reaction, getting extra data point means conducting one more whole chemical reaction, which doubles the time and cost of experimentation. Therefore, only one experiment is conducted for one run of an orthogonal array in many cases. That means there are no noise factors for the estimation of the error variance, which is normally used to calculate the SN ratio. The **split-type analysis** is used for this case.

Split-type analysis is a method for calculating SN ratios from the results obtained from an orthogonal-array experiment without noise factors.

4.6.2   Split-Type Analysis for Two-Level Orthogonal Arrays

In an experiment, two-level control factors $A, B, C, D, E, F,$ and G are assigned to an L_8 orthogonal array. Signal factor, M, is assigned to lie outside the L_8 array as shown in Table 4.10. The L_8 array is used just for ease of illustration. We recommend using L_{18} or L_{12} or L_{36} arrays.

From the table, it is seen that there is no noise factor, which normally is used to estimate the error variance and is in the denominator of a SN ratio. Instead, here the SN ratio of A_1 is calculated by decomposing the results under A_1 shown in the table. The zero-point proportional equation is assumed as the ideal function.

The twelve pieces of data in Table 4.10 are decomposed as shown in Fig. 4.6.

Table 4.10 Results without noise factors

	A	B	C	D	E	F	G	M_1	M_2	M_3	Total
No.	1	2	3	4	5	6	7				
1	1	1	1	1	1	1	1	y_{11}	y_{12}	y_{13}	y_1
2	1	1	1	2	2	2	2	y_{21}	y_{22}	y_{23}	y_2
3	1	2	2	1	1	2	2	y_{31}	y_{32}	y_{33}	y_3
4	1	2	2	2	2	1	1	y_{41}	y_{42}	y_{43}	y_4
								$y_{.1}$	$y_{.2}$	$y_{.3}$	
5	2	1	2	1	2	1	2	y_{51}	y_{52}	y_{53}	y_5
6	2	1	2	2	1	2	1	y_{61}	y_{62}	y_{63}	y_6
7	2	2	1	1	2	2	1	y_{71}	y_{72}	y_{73}	y_7
8	2	2	1	2	1	1	2	y_{81}	y_{82}	y_{83}	y_8

$$\left. S_T \atop (f=12) \right\{ \begin{array}{ll} S_{row} & (f=3) \\ S_\beta & (f=1) \\ S_e & (f=8) \end{array}$$

Figure 4.6 Decomposition of variation

S_{row}, the variation caused by four rows (no. 1, 2, 3, and 4), is the variation caused by control factors $B, C, D, E, F,$ and G, and this variation is separated from the SN calculation.

$$S_T = y_{11}^2 + y_{12}^2 + \ldots + y_{43}^2 \quad \text{and} \quad f = 12 \qquad (4.101)$$

$$\left. \begin{array}{l} y_{.1} = y_{11} + y_{21} + y_{31} + y_{41} \\ y_{.2} = y_{12} + y_{22} + y_{32} + y_{42} \\ y_{.3} = y_{13} + y_{23} + y_{33} + y_{43} \end{array} \right\} \qquad (4.102)$$

$$S_\beta = \frac{1}{r_0 r} (M_1 y_{.1} + M_2 y_{.2} + M_3 y_{.3})^2 \quad \text{and} \quad f = 1 \tag{4.103}$$

$$r_0 = 4 \tag{4.104}$$

where r_0 is the number of runs under A_1.

$$r = M_1^2 + M_2^2 + M_3^2 \tag{4.105}$$

Next, the variation between rows, denoted by S_{row}, is calculated. It is the variation around the average of the four rows. Therefore, the equation to calculate the variation around the mean is used as follows:

$$S_{\text{row}} = \frac{1}{k} \left(y_1^2 + y_2^2 + y_3^2 + y_4^2 \right) - \frac{(y_1 + y_2 + y_3 + y_4)^2}{r_0 k} \quad \text{and} \quad f = r_0 - 1 \tag{4.106}$$

$$k = 3 \tag{4.107}$$

where k is the number of data points in each run.

$$S_e = S_T - S_\beta - S_{\text{row}} \quad \text{and} \quad f = 8 \tag{4.108}$$

$$V_e = \frac{S_e}{8} \tag{4.109}$$

$$\eta = 10 \log \frac{\frac{1}{r_0 r} (s_\beta - V_e)}{V_e} \tag{4.110}$$

S_{row} is the variation between runs 1, 2, 3, and 4: the mixed variation caused by control factors $B, C, D, E, F,$ and G. It is neither the variation of the signal nor the variation of noise, so it is removed from the total variation, S_T. The SN ratio of A_2 is calculated similarly from the results under A_2.

The SN ratio of B_1 is calculated in the same way. The results of B_1 are shown in Table 4.11.

Table 4.11   Results of B_1

No.	M_1	M_2	M_3	Total
1	y_{11}	y_{12}	y_{13}	y_1
2	y_{21}	y_{22}	y_{23}	y_2
5	y_{51}	y_{52}	y_{53}	y_5
6	y_{61}	y_{62}	y_{63}	y_6
Total	$y_{.1}$	$y_{.2}$	$y_{.3}$	

Example

In an experiment using an L_{12} array, the results are shown in Table 4.12.

Table 4.12   Results of experiment

	Control Factor				Signal Factor			
No.	A	B	...	J	$M_1 = 3$	$M_2 = 5$	$M_3 = 8$	Result
1	1	1			6.2	9.9	16.5	$y_1 = 32.6$
2	1	1			7.5	11.0	16.9	$y_2 = 35.4$
3	1	1			5.8	9.4	15.8	$y_3 = 31.0$
4	1	2			5.9	9.5	15.7	$y_4 = 31.1$
5	1	2			7.0	11.3	16.1	$y_5 = 34.4$
6	1	2			6.9	12.1	17.0	$y_6 = 36.0$
					$y_{.1} = 39.3$	$y_{.2} = 63.2$	$y_{.3} = 98.0$	200.5
7	2	1			5.8	10.2	16.2	32.2
8	2	1			7.1	10.8	14.9	32.8
9	2	1			6.3	8.9	13.1	28.3
10	2	2			6.5	9.9	14.0	30.4
11	2	2			7.1	10.9	14.5	32.5
12	2	2			6.9	8.9	10.0	25.8
					39.7	59.6	82.7	182.0

The SN ratio of A_1 is calculated as follows:

$$S_T = 6.2^2 + 9.9^2 + \ldots + 17.0^2 = 2533.67 \qquad \text{and} \qquad f = 18 \qquad (4.111)$$

$$\left.\begin{array}{l} y_{.1} = 6.2 + 7.5 + \ldots + 6.9 = 39.3 \\[2mm] y_{.2} = 9.9 + 11.0 + \ldots + 12.1 = 63.2 \\[2mm] y_{.3} = 16.5 + 16.9 + \ldots + 17.0 = 98.0 \end{array}\right\} \qquad (4.112)$$

$$r_0 = 6 \qquad (4.113)$$

$$\begin{aligned} r &= M_1^2 + M_2^2 + M_3^2 \\ &= 3^2 + 5^2 + 8^2 = 98 \end{aligned} \qquad (4.114)$$

$$\begin{aligned} S_\beta &= \frac{(M_1 y_{.1} + M_2 y_{.2} + M_3 y_{.3})^2}{r_0 r} \\[2mm] &= \frac{(3 \times 3.93 + 5 \times 63.2 + 8 \times 98.0)^2}{6 \times 98} \end{aligned} \qquad (4.115)$$

$$= 2522.59 \qquad \text{and} \qquad f = 1$$

$$\begin{aligned} S_{\text{row}} &= \frac{1}{k}\left(y_1^2 + y_2^2 + \ldots + y_6^2\right) - \frac{(y_1 + y_2 + \ldots + y_6)^2}{r_0 k} \\[2mm] &= \frac{1}{3}\left(32.6^2 + 35.4^2 + \ldots + 36.0^2\right) - \frac{(32.6 + 35.4 + \ldots + 36.0)^2}{6 \times 3} \end{aligned}$$

$$= 7.81 \qquad \text{and} \qquad f = 5 \qquad (4.116)$$

$$S_e = S_T - S_\beta - S_{\text{row}}$$

$$= 2533.67 - 2522.59 - 7.81 \qquad (4.117)$$

$$= 3.27 \qquad \text{and} \qquad f = 12$$

$$V_e = \frac{S_e}{f_e} = \frac{3.27}{12} = 0.272 \qquad (4.118)$$

$$\eta = 10 \; \log \frac{\frac{1}{r_0 r}(S_\beta - V_e)}{V_e}$$

$$= 10 \; \log \frac{\frac{1}{6 \times 98}(2522.59 - 0.272)}{0.272} \qquad (4.119)$$

$$= 10 \; \log 15.772 = 11.98 \; (\text{db})$$

The SN ratio of A_2 is calculated as follows:

$$S_T = 5.8^2 + 10.2^2 + \ldots + 10.0^2 = 2022.24 \qquad \text{and} \qquad f = 18 \qquad (4.120)$$

$$\left. \begin{aligned} y_{.1} &= 5.8 + 7.1 + \ldots + 6.9 = 39.7 \\ y_{.2} &= 10.2 + 10.8 + \ldots + 8.9 = 59.6 \\ y_{.3} &= 16.2 + 14.9 + \ldots + 10.0 = 82.7 \end{aligned} \right\} \qquad (4.121)$$

$$r_0 = 6 \qquad (4.122)$$

$$r = 98 \qquad (4.123)$$

$$S_\beta = \frac{(3 \times 39.7 + 5 \times 59.6 + 8 \times 82.7)^2}{6 \times 98} \qquad (4.124)$$

$$= 1978.90$$

$$S_{\text{row}} = \frac{1}{3}\left(32.2^2 + 32.8^2 + \ldots + 25.8^2\right) - \frac{(32.2 + 32.8 + \ldots + 25.8)^2}{6 \times 3}$$

$$= 12.98 \qquad (4.125)$$

$$S_e = 2022.24 - 1978.90 - 12.98$$

$$= 30.36 \qquad (4.126)$$

$$V_e = \frac{30.36}{12} = 2.53 \qquad (4.127)$$

Table 4.13 Results under B_1

No.	$M_1 = 3$	$M_2 = 5$	$M_3 = 8$	Total
1	6.2	9.9	16.5	32.6
2	7.5	11.0	16.9	35.4
3	5.8	9.4	15.8	31.0
7	5.8	10.2	16.2	32.2
8	7.1	10.8	14.9	32.8
9	6.3	8.9	13.1	28.3
Total	38.7	60.2	93.4	192.3

$$\eta = 10 \log \frac{\frac{1}{6 \times 98}(1978.9 - 2.53)}{2.53} \tag{4.128}$$

$$= 10 \ \log 1.32 = 1.23 \,(\text{db})$$

The SN ratio of B_1 is calculated as follows:

$$S_T = 6.2^2 + 7.5^2 + \ldots + 13.1^2 = 2322.89 \quad \text{and} \quad f = 18 \tag{4.129}$$

$$r_0 = 6 \tag{4.130}$$

$$r = 98 \tag{4.131}$$

$$S_\beta = \frac{(3 \times 38.7 + 5 \times 60.2 + 8 \times 93.4)^2}{6 \times 98} \tag{4.132}$$

$$= 2305.54 \quad \text{and} \quad f = 1$$

$$S_{\text{row}} = \frac{1}{3}\left(32.6^2 + 35.4^2 + \ldots + 28.3^2\right) - \frac{(32.6 + 35.4 + \ldots + 28.3)^2}{6 \times 3}$$

$$= 9.09 \quad \text{and} \quad f = 5 \tag{4.133}$$

$$S_e = 2322.89 - 2305.54 - 9.09$$

$$= 8.26 \quad \text{and} \quad f = 12 \tag{4.134}$$

$$V_e = \frac{8.26}{12} = 0.688 \tag{4.135}$$

$$\eta = 10 \ \log \frac{\frac{1}{6 \times 98}(2305.54 - 0.688)}{0.688} \tag{4.136}$$

$$= 10 \ \log 5.69 = 7.56 \ (\text{db})$$

4.6.3   Split-Type Analysis for Mixed-Type Orthogonal Arrays

When a three-level **orthogonal array** is used for split-type analysis, the method of calculating SN ratios is exactly the same as the case of using a two-level series of orthogonal arrays. The following is an example of calculation using an L_{18} orthogonal array.

Table 4.14   Results without noise factors

No.	A B C D E F G H 1 2 3 4 5 6 7 8	M_1	M_2	...	M_k	Total
1	1 1 1 1 1 1 1 1	y_{11}	y_{12}	...	y_{1k}	y_1
2	1 1 2 2 2 2 2 2	y_{21}	y_{22}	...	y_{2k}	y_2
3	1 1	.	.	...	.	.
4	1 2	.	.	...	.	.
5	1 2	.	.	...	.	.
6	1 2					
7	1 3					
8	1 3					
9	1 3					
10	2 1					
11	2 1					
12	2 1					
13	2 2					
14	2 2					
15	2 2					
16	2 3					
17	2 3					
18	2 3	$y_{18.1}$	$y_{18.2}$	$y_{18.3}$	...	y_{18}

A two-level control factor, A, and seven three-level control factors, B, C, D, E, F, G, and H, were assigned to an L_{18} orthogonal array. Signal factor M was put outside the L_{18} array, as shown in Table 4.14.

Since there are no noise factors, split-type analysis is used to calculate SN ratios. First, the SN ratio of A_1 is shown as an example of a two-level factor. Next, the SN ratio of B_1 is shown as an example of a three-level factor. Table 4.15 shows the results of A_1.

Table 4.15 Results of A_1

Experiment No.	M_1	M_2	...	M_k	Total
1	y_{11}	y_{12}	...	y_{1k}	y_1
2	y_{21}	y_{22}	...	y_{2k}	y_2
...	...	...	...	...	...
9	y_{91}	y_{92}	...	y_{92}	y_{9k}
Total	$y_{.1}$	$y_{.2}$	...	$y_{.k}$	

$$S_T = y_{11}^2 + y_{12}^2 + \ldots + y_{9k}^2 \quad \text{and} \quad f = 9k \qquad (4.137)$$

$$\left. \begin{aligned} y_{.1} &= y_{11} + y_{21} + \ldots + y_{91} \\ y_{.2} &= y_{12} + y_{22} + \ldots + y_{92} \\ &\cdots \\ y_{.k} &= y_{1k} + y_{2k} + \ldots + y_{9K} \end{aligned} \right\} \qquad (4.138)$$

$$S_\beta = \frac{1}{r_0 r}(M_1 y_{.1} + M_2 y_{.2} + \ldots + M_k y_{.k})^2 \quad \text{and} \quad f = 1 \qquad (4.139)$$

where r_0 is the number of runs under A_1 and therefore,

$$r_0 = 9 \qquad (4.140)$$

$$r = M_1^2 + M_2^2 + \ldots + M_k^2 \qquad (4.141)$$

$$S_{\text{row}} = \frac{1}{k}\left(y_1^2 + y_2^2 + \ldots + y_9^2\right) - \frac{\left(y_1 + y_2 + \ldots + y_9\right)^2}{r_0 k} \quad \text{and} \quad f = 8$$

$$(4.142)$$

where k is the number of data points in each run.

$$S_e = S_T - S_\beta - S_{\text{row}} \quad \text{and} \quad f = 9k - 9 \tag{4.143}$$

$$V_e = \frac{S_e}{9k - 9} \tag{4.144}$$

$$\eta = 10 \log \frac{\frac{1}{r_0 r}\left(S_\beta - V_e\right)}{V_e} \tag{4.145}$$

Table 4.16 shows the results of B_1. From Table 4.14, it is seen that there are 6 experiments under B_1: No. 1, 2, 3, 10, 11, and 12.

Table 4.16   Results of B_1

Experiment No.	M_1	M_2	...	M_k	Total
1	y_{11}	y_{12}	...	y_{1k}	y_1
2	y_{21}	y_{22}	...	y_{2k}	y_2
...	...	...	...	...	...
12	$y_{12.1}$	$y_{12.2}$	...	$y_{12.k}$	y_{12}
Total	$y_{.1}$	$y_{.2}$	...	$y_{.k}$	

$$S_T = y_{11}^2 + y_{12}^2 + \ldots + y_{12.k}^2 \quad \text{and} \quad f = 6k \tag{4.146}$$

$$\left. \begin{array}{l} y_{.1} = y_{11} + y_{21} + y_{31} + y_{10.1} + y_{11.1} + y_{12.1} \\[2mm] y_{.2} = y_{12} + y_{22} + y_{32} + y_{10.2} + y_{11.2} + y_{12.2} \\[2mm] \ldots \\[2mm] y_{.k} = y_{1k} + y_{2k} + y_{3k} + y_{10.k} + y_{11.k} + y_{12.k} \end{array} \right\} \tag{4.147}$$

$$S_\beta = \frac{1}{r_0 r}(M_1 y_{.1} + M_2 y_{.2} + \ldots + M_k y_{.k})^2 \qquad \text{and} \qquad f = 1 \qquad (4.148)$$

where r_0 is the number of runs under B_1, and therefore,

$$r_0 = 6 \qquad (4.149)$$

$$r = M_1^2 + M_2^2 + \ldots + M_k^2 \qquad (4.150)$$

$$S_{\text{row}} = \frac{1}{k}\left(y_1^2 + y_2^2 + \ldots + y_{12}^2\right) - \frac{(y_1 + y_2 + \ldots + y_{12})^2}{r_0 k} \qquad \text{and} \qquad f = 5$$
$$(4.151)$$

where k is the number of data points in each run.

$$S_e = S_T - S_\beta - S_{\text{row}} \qquad \text{and} \qquad f = 6k - 6 \qquad (4.153)$$

$$V_e = \frac{S_e}{6k - 6} \qquad (4.154)$$

$$\eta = 10 \log \frac{\frac{1}{r_0 r}(S_\beta - V_e)}{V_e} \qquad (4.155)$$

Example

Continuing with the conditions presented in the previous example, the results of A_1 are shown in Table 4.17.

In the case of the **zero-point proportional equation**, the SN ratio is calculated as follows:

$$S_T = 5.1^2 + 7.3^2 + \ldots + 17.5^2 = 3305.06 \qquad \text{and} \qquad f = 27 \qquad (4.156)$$

$$S_\beta = \frac{1}{r_0 r}(M_1 y_{.1} + M_2 y_{.2} + M_3 y_{.3})^2$$

$$= \frac{1}{9 \times 29}(2 \times 60.5 + 3 \times 86.3 + 4 \times 129.2)^2 \qquad (4.157)$$

$$= 3080.7314 \qquad \text{and} \qquad f = 1$$

Table 4.17   Results of A_1

No.	A B C D E F G H 1 2 3 4 5 6 7 8	$M_1 = 2$	$M_2 = 3$	$M_3 = 4$	Total
1	1	5.1	7.3	18.9	31.3
2	1	6.7	9.0	11.8	27.5
3	1	5.3	8.1	14.8	28.2
4	1	9.2	12.0	17.9	39.1
5	1	6.3	8.9	12.8	28.0
6	1	7.4	10.1	13.9	31.4
7	1	3.4	4.9	5.9	14.2
8	1	8.0	12.3	15.7	36.0
9	1	9.1	13.7	17.5	40.3
Total		60.5	86.3	129.2	276.0

$$r = 2^2 + 3^2 + 4^2 = 29 \tag{4.158}$$

$$S_{\text{row}} = \frac{1}{k} + \left(y_1^2 + y_2^2 + \ldots + y_9^2\right) - \frac{(y_1 + y_2 + \ldots + y_9)^2}{r_0 k}$$

$$= \frac{1}{3}\left(31.3^2 + 27.5^2 + \ldots + 40.3^2\right) - \frac{276^2}{27} \tag{4.159}$$

$$= \frac{8951.68}{3} - 2821.3333$$

$$= 162.5600 \quad \text{and} \quad f = 8$$

$$S_e = S_T - S_\beta - S_{\text{row}}$$

$$= 3305.06 - 3080.7314 - 162.5600 \tag{4.160}$$

$$= 61.7686 \quad \text{and} \quad f = 18$$

$$V_e = \frac{S_e}{18} = \frac{61.7686}{18} = 3.4317 \tag{4.161}$$

$$\eta = 10 \log \frac{\frac{1}{r_0 r}(S_\beta - V_e)}{V_e}$$

$$= 10 \log \frac{\frac{1}{9 \times 29}(3080.7314 - 3.4317)}{3.4317} \tag{4.162}$$

$$= 10 \log 3.4357$$

$$= 5.36 (\text{db})$$

4.7 CUSTOM-WRITTEN SN RATIOS

So far, we have seen various types of SN ratios. But there are still many special cases that do not fit any of them. Therefore, sometimes we may need to custom-write the equations to calculate a specific SN ratio.

4.7.1 Chemical Reaction I

In this section, an example of a chemical reaction is used to explain the considerations involved in custom-writing an SN-ratio equation.

The function of a chemical reaction is to change the combining condition of molecules or atoms. In this section, one of the simplest of chemical reactions, in which substances **a** and **b** react to produce substance **c** is discussed. Let the initial amounts of **a** and **b** on the equivalent basis be denoted by a and b, respectively. Also, let the amount of substance **c** produced after time t be Y. The following equation shows the relationship based on theory of the chemical reaction.

$$\frac{dY}{dt} = \beta(a - Y)(b - Y) \tag{4.163}$$

Initially, $t = 0$ and $Y = 0$. The above equation is solved to give

$$\frac{1}{b - a} \ln \frac{a(b - Y)}{b(a - Y)} = \beta t \tag{4.164}$$

For the experiment, many control factors are assigned to an orthogonal array. There are k levels of time, which are set as t_1, t_2, ..., t_k, and the amount of reacted product, Y, is observed at each level of time. Time, t, is called the signal factor, denoted by M. Since $y = \beta t$, by letting the observations at time M_1, M_2, ..., M_k be Y_1, Y_2, ..., Y_k, we can rewrite Eq. (4.164) as

$$y = \frac{1}{b-a} \ln \frac{a(b-Y)}{b(a-Y)} \tag{4.165}$$

The ideal function is expressed by the following equation:

$$y = \beta M \tag{4.166}$$

In a chemical reaction, considering a noise factor N_1 and N_2 requires two experiments at N_1 and N_2, which is costly. By observing more levels of the signal factor, the noise factor may not need to be considered. Thus, it is advantageous to convert the data collected for Y into data for y. This can be done by using Eq. (4.165) as shown in Fig. 4.7.

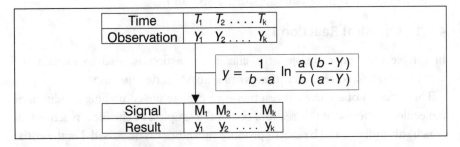

Figure 4.7 Data transformation

From the results in Fig. 4.7, the SN ratio and sensitivity are calculated as follows:

$$S_T = y_1^2 + y_2^2 + \ldots + y_k^2 \quad \text{and} \quad f = k \tag{4.167}$$

$$S_\beta = \frac{1}{r}(M_1 y_1 + M_2 y_2 + \ldots + M_k y_k)^2 \quad \text{and} \quad f = 1 \tag{4.168}$$

$$r = M_1^2 + M_2^2 + \ldots + M_k^2 \tag{4.169}$$

$$S_e = S_T - S_\beta \quad \text{and} \quad f = k - 1 \tag{4.170}$$

$$V_e = \frac{S_e}{k - 1} \tag{1.171}$$

$$\eta = 10 \log \frac{\frac{1}{r}(S_\beta - V_e)}{V_e} \tag{1.172}$$

$$S = 10 \log \frac{1}{r}(S_\beta - V_e) \tag{4.173}$$

It is seen that this example uses the regular SN ratio equation. The only difference is to convert observation Y into y using Eq. (4.165).

4.7.2 Chemical Reaction II

A chemical reaction is a process involving the connection, as well as the separation, of molecular or atomic units. In many cases, it is impossible to measure the behavior of individual molecules or atoms. Instead, only the behavior of a whole group can be measured. For example, when substance **a** and substance **b** chemically react to produce substance **c**, the quantity of substance **c** is measured to get the reaction rate. The reaction rate indicates the percentage of substance **c** produced from the amounts of **a** and **b**. When related to the reaction that takes place between gasoline and air (oxygen) in an internal combustion engine, let a represent the amount of gasoline and b represent the amount of oxygen. Since gasoline is the more expensive of the two, the tendency would be lean towards an excess amount of air instead of the exact amount of each as determined by a chemical-reaction equation. The excess amount is referred to as **excess rate**. When Quality Engineering techniques for design optimization are used, **excess rate** would be a selected control factor. For the purpose of data analysis, the reaction amount of the gasoline, one of the two major constituents in the reaction, would be observed.

A chemical reaction occurs gradually in one case and explosively in another case, only a matter of difference in reaction speed. In this example, the following equation—derived from chemical-reaction theory—is used to show the relationship between the yield (in fraction) and the length of time from the start:

$$p = 1 - e^{-\beta T} \tag{4.174}$$

In Quality Engineering, Eq. (4.174) may be converted into Eq. (4.175) so that the ideal function between input and output has a proportional relationship.

$$y = \beta T \tag{4.175}$$

where y is the result after transforming yield, p, through the following equation:

$$y = \ln \frac{1}{1-p} \tag{4.176}$$

For the chemical reaction that takes place in gasoline combustion, $(1 - p)$ indicates the amount of **unreacted gasoline**. The initial amount is considered as a unit quantity. Letting T_1, T_2, ..., T_k and p_1, p_2, ..., p_k be time and reacted fraction, respectively, we get

$$y_i = \ln \frac{1}{1-p_i} \tag{4.177}$$

where $(i = 1, 2, \ldots, k)$

Eq. (4.177) is substituted into Eq. (4.175) to show the ideal function with a proportional relationship. This approach can be used when there are no side reactions.

4.7.3 Dynamic Operating Window

In the previous section, substances **a** and **b** react to produce substance **c**. When side reactions occur, substances such as **d** are produced.

$$\mathbf{a} + \mathbf{b} \rightarrow \mathbf{c} + \mathbf{d}$$

As shown in Fig. 4.9, let the reacted fraction of **a** be denoted by q, and the produced yield (fraction) of the objective substance, **c**, be denoted by p. Both p and q are observed. $(1 - q)$ is the unreacted fraction of substance, **a**, and $(q - p)$ is the fraction of the side-reacted product, **d**. Table 4.18 shows the observations of p and q at time levels of T_1, T_2, ..., T_k.

Table 4.18   Cases where side reactions exist

T_1	T_2	...	T_k
p_1	p_2	...	p_k
q_1	q_2	...	q_k

When there are no side reactions, p is equal to q. The existence of some variables (noise factors) makes p smaller than q. Let M_1 be the situation showing the reaction rate of substance **a** and let M_2 be the situation showing the rate of side reactions. Also, let the reaction speeds at M_1 and M_2 be β_1 and β_2, respectively. Since we want to maximize the difference between β_1 and β_2, the values of y are calculated as follows:

$$y_{1i} = \ln \frac{1}{1 - q_i} \tag{4.178}$$

and

$$y_{2i} = \ln \frac{1}{1 - (q_i - p_i)} \tag{4.179}$$

where $i = 1, 2, \ldots, k$

The results after conversion are shown in Table 4.19.

Table 4.19   Results after conversion

	T_1	T_2	...	T_k	L
M_1	y_{11}	y_{12}	...	y_{1k}	L_1
M_2	y_{21}	y_{22}	...	y_{2k}	L_2

When side reactions occur, the ideal situation is to minimize these reactions and maximize the total reactions; in other words, maximize the slope of situation M_1 and minimize the slope of situation M_2. This is the same as maximizing the dynamic operating window, the gap between the two slopes, as described in Fig. 4.9. The SN ratio for this dynamic operating window is calculated as shown below.

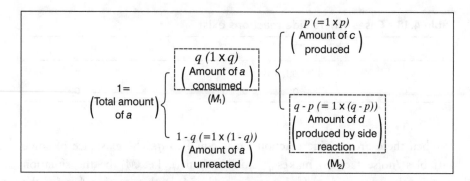

Figure 4.8 Chemical reaction with side reactions

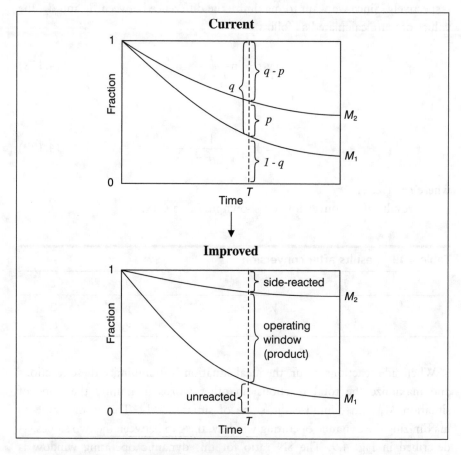

Figure 4.9 Dynamic operating window

In order to maximize the difference between cases M_1 and M_2, the SN ratio is calculated as follows:

$$\left.\begin{array}{l} L_1 = T_1 y_{11} + T_2 y_{12} + \ldots + T_k y_{1k} \\ L_2 = T_1 y_{21} + T_2 y_{22} + \ldots + T_k y_{2k} \end{array}\right\} \tag{4.180}$$

$$S_T = y_{11}^2 + y_{12}^2 + \ldots + y_{2k}^2 \quad \text{and} \quad f = 2k \tag{4.181}$$

$$S_\beta = \frac{(L_1 + L_2)^2}{2r} \quad \text{and} \quad f = 1 \tag{4.182}$$

$$S_{M \times \beta} = \frac{(L_1 - L_2)^2}{2r} \quad \text{and} \quad f = 1 \tag{4.183}$$

$$r = T_1^2 + T_2^2 + \ldots + T_k^2 \tag{4.184}$$

$$S_e = S_T - (S_\beta + S_{M \times \beta}) \quad \text{and} \quad f = 2k - 2 \tag{4.185}$$

$$V_e = \frac{S_e}{2k - 2} \tag{4.186}$$

$$\eta = 10 \log \frac{\frac{1}{2r}(S_{M \times \beta} - V_e)}{V_e} \tag{4.187}$$

$$S = 10 \log \frac{1}{2r}(S_\beta - V_e) \tag{4.188}$$

In this case, the SN ratio, η, is very important, because we do not want substance **a** to react differently from what we expect. Should this happen, substance **a** would be converted, due to side reactions or over-reactions, to substances other than the objective product. For this case, we must custom-write Eq. (4.187) as the SN ratio.

The above SN ratio is determined from p and q, which were observed some time during one reaction, or for one run in an orthogonal array, such as L_{18}. The rate of the objective substance produced is p, the rate of substance **a** consumed is q; therefore, the former is smaller than the latter. In other words, M_1 shows the total reaction speed, and M_2, the side-reaction speed. Using the data that were transformed by Eq. (4.178) and (4.179), we would like to adjust the reaction speed of M_1 at a certain level. Also, we would like to minimize the reaction speed of M_2. Time, T, is also a signal. Only one experiment can generate the results for cases M_1 and M_2. In other words, we need to perform a single experiment to generate the data needed for optimizing this reaction.

Comparing the above two chemical reaction examples, the reader will notice a difference: the first example is strictly data conversion of original observations into the outputs that follow the basic function. After the conversion, calculation of the SN ratio is similar to the basic formula.

In the second example, there is not only a conversion of data for the same purpose as just described, but there also is consideration of the SN ratio. In addition, there is interpretation as to what should be considered as the noise, or the harmful portion, to be used as the denominator of the equation.

Example

In a chemical reaction, raw materials **a** and **b** react to produce an objective product, **c**, and side-reacted product, **d**.

$$\mathbf{a} + \mathbf{b} \rightarrow \mathbf{c} + \mathbf{d}$$

Table 4.20 shows the results of an experimental condition.

Table 4.20 Results and converted data

	Time (hr)	1	2	3	4	5
	Objective product (p)	36.88	62.30	84.13	91.93	92.78
Yield (%)	Side-reacted product ($q - p$)	0.00	0.40	2.21	5.59	7.02
	Total reacted product (q)	36.88	62.70	86.34	97.52	99.80
M_1	$\ln \frac{1}{1-q}$	0.46	0.99	1.99	3.70	6.21
M_2	$\ln \frac{1}{1+p-q}$	0.00	0.00	0.02	0.06	0.07

In Table 4.20, $p =$ is amount of **c**, $q - p$ amount of **d**, and q is amount of **c+d**. Yields in percent were converted into fractions, then converted into two situations, M_1 and M_2.

The SN ratio and sensitivity are calculated using the equations in this section.

$$L_1 = T_1 y_{11} + T_2 y_{12} + \ldots + T_5 y_{15}$$

$$= 1 \times 0.46 + 2 \times 0.99 + \ldots + 5 \times 6.21 \qquad (4.189)$$

$$= 54.26$$

$$L_2 = T_1 y_{21} + T_2 y_{22} + \ldots + T_5 y_{25}$$

$$= 1 \times 0.00 + 2 \times 0.00 + \ldots + 5 \times 0.07 \qquad (4.190)$$

$$= 0.65$$

$$S_T = y_{11}^2 + y_{22}^2 + \ldots + y_{25}^2$$

$$= 0.46^2 + 0.99^2 + \ldots + 0.07^2 \qquad (4.191)$$

$$= 57.4148 \quad \text{and} \quad f = 10$$

$$r = T_1^2 + T_2^2 + \ldots + T_5^2$$

$$= 1^2 + 2^2 + \ldots + 5^2 = 55 \qquad (4.192)$$

$$S_\beta = \frac{(L_1 + L_2)^2}{2r}$$

$$\qquad (4.193)$$

$$= \frac{(54.26 + 0.65)^2}{2 \times 55} = 27.4101 \quad \text{and} \quad f = 1$$

$$S_{M \times \beta} = \frac{(L_1 - L_2)^2}{2r}$$

$$\qquad (4.194)$$

$$= \frac{(54.26 - 0.65)^2}{2 \times 55} = 26.1276 \quad \text{and} \quad f = 1$$

$$S_e = S_T - \left(S_\beta + S_{M \times \beta}\right)$$

$$= 57.4148 - (27.4101 + 26.1276) \tag{4.195}$$

$$= 3.8771 \quad \text{and} \quad f = 8$$

$$V_e = \frac{S_e}{8} = \frac{3.8771}{8} \tag{4.196}$$

$$= 0.48464$$

$$\eta = 10 \log \frac{\frac{1}{2 \times 55}(26.1276 - 0.48464)}{0.48464} = -3.18(\text{db}) \tag{4.197}$$

$$S = 10 \log \frac{1}{2 \times 55}(27.4101 - 0.48464) = 6.11(\text{db}) \tag{4.198}$$

This example shows the calculation of the SN ratio of one experimental condition for a dynamic operating window. In order to maximize the whole reaction rate and minimize the side reaction rate, Parameter Design is conducted in the same way as for other cases. A reminder of how to optimize Parameter Design is given below. Here is a summary of the similarities and differences in various cases for optimization.

4.7.4   Optimization of Performance

1. Nondynamic, Nominal-is-Best Parameter Design (see Chapter 5)

   ▶ Maximize SN ratio for maximum robustness.
   ▶ Use a control factor that has a minimum effect on the SN ratio, but a maximum effect on the average (m) or sensitivity (S_m) to adjust the average to the target.

2. Dynamic Parameter Design

   ▶ Maximize SN ratio for maximum robustness.
   ▶ Use a control factor that has a minimum effect on the SN ratio, but a maximum effect on the slope (β) or sensitivity (S_β), to adjust the slope to the desired value. Such an adjustment

determines how sensitive the output should be when the input changes.

3. Nondynamic Operating Window Parameter Design (see Chapter 5)
   ▶ Maximize SN ratio for robustness.
   ▶ Use a control factor that has a minimum effect on SN ratio, but a maximum effect on the average, to adjust the operating window to a desired position. In the case of a paper feeder, the average refers to the average interval between misfeed and multifeed conditions.

4. Dynamic Operating Window Parameter Design
   ▶ Maximize SN ratio for robustness.
   ▶ Use a control factor that has a minimum effect on SN ratio, but a maximum effect on sensitivity $(\beta \text{ or } S_\beta)$. This adjustment controls the balance between the total reacted fraction and the side-reacted fraction.

4.8   CASE WHEN TRUE VALUES OF SIGNAL FACTOR ARE UNKNOWN

Since SN ratio is the ratio of signal and noise, it is necessary to calculate the numerator and denominator, and then calculate the ratio. In the case of dynamic characteristics, the numerator is the linearity of the output caused by the input signal. Without knowing the true values of the signal-factor levels, there is no way to calculate linearity. However, there are some ways to set up the levels of the signal factor in an experiment so that the linearity can be calculated without knowing the true values of the signal.

Since the true values of the signal factor are unknown, there is no way to use either the zero-point proportional equation or the reference-point proportional equation. Accordingly, the linear equation is used.

4.8.1   Case When Level Interval of Signal Factor is Known

If the signal-factor level interval is known, the linear effect can be calculated. In a chemical analysis, for example, we try to set the levels of the content of a certain ingredient.

Suppose there is a sample containing a certain ingredient, such as the alcohol content in soy bean sauce, but its true value is unknown. In order to set up levels as signal, the following samples are prepared: M_1: unknown sample containing $x\%$ alcohol, $M_2 : M_1$ plus 2% alcohol, $M_3 : M_1$ plus 4% alcohol, and $M_4 : M_1$ plus 6% alcohol. Thus, the signal-factor levels M_1, M_2, M_3, and M_4 have an equal level interval. Chebyshev's table of the orthogonal polynomial equation can be used to calculate the linearity and thus, SN ratios.

The SN ratio of this case is calculated as follows:

$$S_T = y_{11}^2 + y_{12}^2 + \ldots + y_{34}^2 - S_m \quad \text{and} \quad f = 11 \tag{4.199}$$

$$S_m = \frac{(y_{11} + y_{12} + \ldots + y_{34})^2}{12} \tag{4.200}$$

and the following definitions apply:

Level interval: $h = 2$
Number of levels: $k = 4$
Number of repetitions: $r_0 = 3$

From Table 3.7,

$$W_1 = -3 \quad W_2 = -1 \quad W_3 = 1 \quad W_4 = 3$$

$$A_1 = y_1 \quad A_2 = y_2 \quad A_3 = y_3 \quad A_4 = y_4$$

$$\lambda^2 S = 20$$

$$S_\beta = \frac{(W_1 A_1 + W_2 A_2 + W_3 A_3 + W_4 A_4)^2}{r_0 \lambda^2 S} \tag{4.201}$$

$$= \frac{(-3y_1 - y_2 + y_3 + 3y_4)}{3 \times 20} \quad \text{and} \quad f = 1$$

$$S_e = S_T - S_\beta \quad \text{and} \quad f = 10 \tag{4.202}$$

$$V_e = \frac{S_e}{10} \tag{4.203}$$

$$\eta = 10 \ \log \ \frac{\frac{1}{r_0\lambda^2 S b^2}(S_\beta - V_e)}{V_e} \tag{4.204}$$

Table 4.21   Case with equal level interval

Sample	$M_1 = x$	$M_2 = x + 2\%$	$M_3 = x + 4\%$	$M_4 = x + 6\%$
Reading	y_{11}	y_{12}	y_{13}	y_{14}
	y_{21}	y_{22}	y_{23}	y_{24}
	y_{31}	y_{32}	y_{33}	y_{34}
Total	y_1	y_2	y_3	y_4

Example

There are two analysis methods to quantify the alcohol content in soy bean sauce using a gas chromatograph (see Reference 7).

Control factor: Holding time (minutes)
$A_1 = 10$
$A_2 = 20$

Signal factor: Alcohol content (%)
$M_1 = x\%$ (unknown)
$M_2 = x + 0.3$
$M_3 = x + 0.6$
$M_4 = x + 0.9$

Noise factor: Operator, R_1, R_2

In this situation, the true values of the signal factor are unknown. As a result, neither the zero-point proportional equation nor the reference-point proportional equation can be used. Therefore, in the calculation, the linear equation described in Section 3.4 is used.

Table 4.21 shows the results of the experiment.

The SN ratio of A_1 is calculated as follows:

Table 4.22 Results of the experiment

		M_1	M_2	M_3	M_4	Total
A_1	R_1	0.46	0.96	1.48	1.79	
	R_2	0.48	0.92	1.36	1.56	
	Total	0.94	1.88	2.84	3.35	9.01
A_2	R_1	1.12	1.93	2.58	3.06	
	R_2	1.08	1.94	2.60	3.10	
	Total	2.10	3.87	5.18	6.16	17.41

$$S_m = \frac{(0.46 + 0.48 + \ldots + 1.56)^2}{8} = 10.1475 \quad \text{and} \quad f = 1 \quad (4.205)$$

$$S_T = 0.46^2 + 0.48^2 + \ldots + 1.56^2 - S_m$$
$$= 1.7402 \quad \text{and} \quad f = 7 \quad (4.206)$$

$$\overline{M} = \frac{[x + (x + 0.3) + (x + 0.6) + (x + 0.9)]}{4}$$
$$= x + 0.45 \quad (4.207)$$

From Eq. (3.42),

$$r_0 r = r_0 = \left[(M_1 - \overline{M})^2 + (M_2 - \overline{M})^2 + (M_3 - \overline{M})^2 + (M_4 - \overline{M})^2 \right]$$
$$= 2 \left[(-0.45)^2 + (-0.15)^2 + 0.15^2 + 0.45^2 \right] = 0.9 \quad (4.208)$$

From Eq. (3.45),

$$S_\beta = \frac{1}{0.9}[(-0.45) \times 0.94 + (-0.15) \times 1.88 + 0.15 \times 2.84 + 0.45 \times 3.35]^2$$

$$= 1.6769 \quad \text{and} \quad f = 1 \tag{4.209}$$

$$S_e = S_T - S_\beta$$
$$\tag{4.210}$$
$$= 1.7402 - 1.6769 = 0.0633 \quad \text{and} \quad f = 6$$

$$V_e = \frac{S_e}{6} = \frac{0.0633}{6}$$
$$\tag{4.211}$$
$$= 0.01055$$

$$\eta = 10 \log \left[\frac{\left(\frac{1}{0.9}\right)(1.6769 - 0.01055)}{0.01055} \right]$$
$$\tag{4.212}$$
$$= 10 \log 175.4976 = 22.44 \ (\text{db})$$

The SN ratio of A_2 is calculated similarly.

$$\eta(A_1) = 22.4(\text{db}) \tag{4.213}$$

$$\eta(A_2) = 26.7(\text{db}) \tag{4.214}$$

Therefore, A_2 is better than A_1 by 4.3 db.

Example

There are two samples, A and B, whose true contents are unknown but denoted by a and b.

In order to calculate linearity, the two samples are mixed to set the following four levels:

$M_1 : A : B = 0.8 : 0.2$
$M_2 : A : B = 0.6 : 0.4$
$M_3 : A : B = 0.4 : 0.6$
$M_4 : A : B = 0.2 : 0.8$

The four levels are rewritten as

$$\left.\begin{array}{l} M_1 = 0.8\,a + 0.2\,b = (1 - 0.2)\,a + 0.2\,b = a + 0.2\,(b - a) \\[2mm] M_2 = 0.6\,a + 0.4\,b = (1 - 0.4)\,a + 0.4\,b = a + 0.4\,(b - a) \\[2mm] M_3 = 0.4\,a + 0.6\,b = (1 - 0.6)\,a + 0.6\,b = a + 0.6\,(b - a) \\[2mm] M_4 = 0.2\,a + 0.8\,b = (1 - 0.8)\,a + 0.8\,b = a + 0.8\,(b - a) \end{array}\right\} \tag{4.215}$$

Although a and $(b - a)$ are unknown, we can set an equal level interval (0.2) for the signal factor M.

S_β can be calculated by the following equations:

$$\overline{M} = \frac{M_1 + M_2 + M_3 + M_3}{4}$$

$$= \frac{4a + (0.2 + 0.4 + 0.6 + 0.8)(b - a)}{4} \tag{4.216}$$

$$= a + 0.5(b - a)$$

$$M_1 - \overline{M} = a + 0.2(b - a) - [a + 0.5(b - a)]$$

$$= -0.3\,(b - a) \tag{4.217}$$

$$M_2 - \overline{M} = -0.1\,(b - a) \tag{4.218}$$

$$M_3 - \overline{M} = 0.1\,(b - a) \tag{4.219}$$

$$M_4 - \overline{M} = 0.3\,(b - a) \tag{4.220}$$

$$
\begin{aligned}
S_\beta &= \frac{\left[(M_1 - \overline{M})y_1 + (M_2 - \overline{M})y_2 + (M_3 - \overline{M})y_3 + (M_4 - \overline{M})y_4\right]^2}{(M_1 - \overline{M})^2 + (M_2 - \overline{M})^2 + (M_3 - \overline{M})^2 + (M_4 - \overline{M})^2} \\[2mm]
&= \frac{\left[(-0.3)(b-a)y_1 + (-0.1)(b-a)y_2 + 0.1(b-a)y_3 + 0.3(b-a)y_4\right]^2}{\left[(-0.3)^2 + (-0.1)^2 + 0.1^2 + 0.3^2\right](b-a)^2} \\[2mm]
&= \frac{(-0.3y_1 - 0.1y_2 + 0.1y_3 + 3y_4)^2}{0.2}
\end{aligned}
$$

$$\tag{4.221}$$

Thus, S_β can be calculated without knowing the true values of samples A and B. The calculations of S_T, S_e, and V_e are made similarly to those shown in other cases.

Figure 4.10 shows the levels have equal intervals. A linear equation is used as in the previous example.

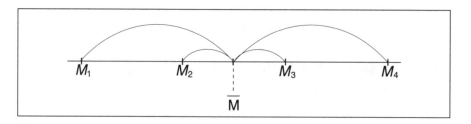

Figure 4.10   Case with equal level interval

4.8.2   Case When Level Ratio is Known

In some cases, the signal-factor level ratio can be set at a certain level, although the absolute values of the levels are unknown. In chemical analysis, for example, a sample of unknown concentration is diluted with a certain ratio, such as 1/2 of the original concentration, then to 1/4, 1/8, etc. For the case presented here, assume the following:

$M_1 = 1/8$
$M_2 = 1/4$
$M_3 = 1/2$
$M_4 = 1$

The sensitivity, S, is calculated as

$$S_\beta = \frac{1}{r_0 r}\left(\frac{1}{8}y_1 + \frac{1}{4}y_2 + \frac{1}{2}y_3 + y_4\right)^2 \tag{4.222}$$

where

$$r = \left[\left(\frac{1}{8}\right)^2 + \left(\frac{1}{4}\right)^2 + \left(\frac{1}{2}\right)^2 + 1^2\right] \tag{4.223}$$

The SN ratio is given by

$$\eta' = 10 \log \frac{\frac{1}{r_0 r}(S_\beta - V_e)}{V_e} \tag{4.224}$$

This ratio is calculated based on $M_4 = 1$, which means that the antilog value is not the original unit. However, it is all right to use since SN ratios are compared *relatively*. If it is necessary to use the original unit, η' may be converted as follows:

$$\eta = \frac{\eta'}{M_s} \tag{4.225}$$

where M_s is the unit of the base level.

Since the absolute value of levels are unknown, it is not realistic to apply the **reference-point proportional equation**. But the following two equations are possible to use in the cases specified:

1. **Zero-point proportional equation:** This is the case when the signal is zero, the output is zero; the input and output relationship is

$$y = \beta M \tag{4.226}$$

2. **Linear equation:** This is the case when there is no specific restriction between the input and the output:

$$y = a + \beta M \qquad (4.227)$$

Example

In the analysis of potassium bromide, four analysis methods are compared (see Reference 6). Each represents one of four levels of control factor A: A_1 Titration using silver nitrate, A_2 Specific-gravity measurement, A_3 Fluorescent x-ray measurement, and A_4 Atomic absorption.

An unknown solution ($x\%$) is diluted to 1/2 and 1/4 of the original concentration. The three values ($x\%$, $x/2\%$, $x/4\%$) define the three levels of the signal factor, M, as follows:

$M_1 = x\%$
$M_2 = 1/2$ of $x\%$
$M_3 = 1/4 \ x\%$

Three repetitions R_1, R_2, and R_3 are considered to be the noise factor.

Table 4.23 shows the results of the analysis, which are graphed, in Fig. 4.11.

The SN ratio of A_1 is calculated as follows:

$$S_T = 635^2 + 640^2 + \ldots + 160^2 = 1,606,127 \qquad \text{and} \qquad f = 9 \qquad (4.228)$$

$$r_0 r = r_0 \left(M_1^2 + M_2^2 + M_3^2 \right) = 3 \left[1^2 + \left(\frac{1}{2} \right)^2 + \left(\frac{1}{4} \right)^2 \right] = 3.9375 \qquad (4.229)$$

$$S_\beta = \frac{1}{r_0 r} \left(M_1 y_1 + M_2 y_2 + M_3 y_3 \right)^2$$

$$= \frac{1}{3.9375} \left(1910 \times 1 + 961 \times \frac{1}{2} + 496 \times \frac{1}{4} \right)^2 \qquad (4.230)$$

$$= 1,605,767.683 \qquad \text{and} \qquad f = 8$$

Table 4.23   Potassium bromide analysis

		$M_1 = x$	$M_2 = x/2$	$M_3 = x/4$
A_1	R_1	635	315	160
	R_2	640	326	176
	R_3	635	320	160
	Total	1910	961	496
A_2	R_1	2098	1038	530
	R_2	2091	1028	532
	R_3	2100	1078	530
	Total	6289	3144	1592
A_3	R_1	92	51	21
	R_2	100	54	23
	R_3	99	51	22
	Total	291	156	66
A_4	R_1	57	26	13
	R_2	58	25	12
	R_3	60	27	12
	Total	175	78	37

$$S_e = S_T - S_\beta$$

$$= 1,606,127 - 1,605,767.683 \tag{4.231}$$

$$= 359.31746 \quad \text{and} \quad f = 8$$

$$V_e = \frac{S_e}{8} = \frac{359.31746}{8} = 44.9146825 \tag{4.232}$$

$$\eta = 10 \log \frac{\frac{1}{r_0 r}(S_\beta - V_e)}{V_e}$$

$$= 10 \log \left[\frac{\left(\frac{1}{3.9375}\right)(1,605,767.683 - 44.9147)}{44.9147} \right] \tag{4.233}$$

$$= 10 \log 9079.49 = 39.58 \, (\text{db})$$

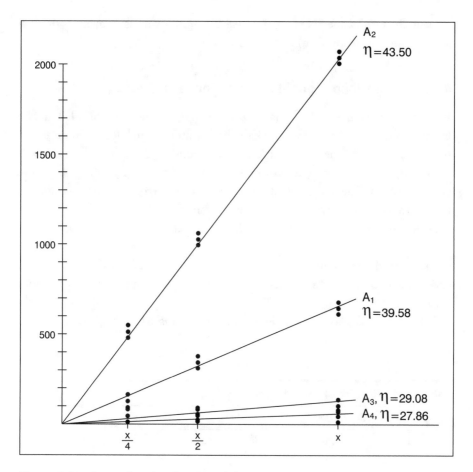

Figure 4.11   Case when level ratio is known

SN ratios of A_2, A_3, and A_4 are calculated similarly.

$$\left.\begin{aligned}
\eta(A_1) &= 39.58 \,(\text{db}) \\
\eta(A_2) &= 43.50 \,(\text{db}) \\
\eta(A_3) &= 29.08 \,(\text{db}) \\
\eta(A_4) &= 27.86 \,(\text{db})
\end{aligned}\right\} \qquad (4.234)$$

From the results, the SN ratio of A_2 (specific-gravity measurement) is the best and A_4 (atomic absorption) is the worst.

4.8.3 Case When Signal-Factor Variance is Used

When the true values of the signal factor are unknown, we cannot calculate the linear effect. There is no way to include the deviation from linearity in the error. But, if it is assumed that the input/output relationship is linear, the variation of the signal, S_M, is calculated and subtracted from the total variation to obtain the error variation. The variances of the signal and the error are used to calculate the SN ratio. However, this is not a very accurate method.

Depending on the assumptions that are made about the input/output relationship, the following two equations may be used: zero-point proportional equation, and linear equation. The calculation of SN ratios is similar for both, except the equations of S_M, the general mean, S_m, and the degrees of freedom are different.

Table 4.24 is the layout of an experiment to compare the SN ratio of A_1. The results for A_2 are not shown.

Table 4.24 Results of experiment

	M_1	M_2	...	M_k
A_1	y_{11}	y_{12}	...	y_{1k}
	y_{21}	y_{22}	...	y_{2k}
	...	...	...	...
	$y_{r_0 1}$	$y_{r_0 2}$	...	$y_{r_0 k}$
Total	y_1	y_2	...	y_k

In the case where the zero-point proportional equation is used, the total variation is calculated by

$$S_T = y_{11}^2 + y_{12}^2 + \ldots + y_{r_0 k}^2 \qquad \text{and} \qquad f = kr_0 \qquad (4.235)$$

Since the true values of the signal factor are unknown, there is no way to calculate its linear effect. Instead, the whole variation of the signal factor is considered as the signal-factor effect.

$$S_M = \frac{y_1^2 + y_2^2 + \ldots + y_k^2}{r_0} \quad \text{and} \quad f = k \quad (4.236)$$

The error variance, S_e, is calculated as

$$S_e = S_T - S_M \quad \text{and} \quad f = kr_0 - k \quad (4.237)$$

The variance of the signal, V_M, and the error, V_e, are

$$V_M = \frac{S_M}{k} \quad (4.238)$$

$$V_e = \frac{S_e}{kr_0 - k} \quad (4.239)$$

The SN ratio is determined by

$$\eta = 10 \log \frac{\frac{1}{r_0}(V_M - V_e)}{V_e} \quad (4.240)$$

Example

A portable hardness tester, denoted by A_1, is a simple piece of measuring equipment. It is convenient for measuring nonflat surfaces. However, the penetrator for this tester is V-shaped, and this probably results in less precise measurements than measurements made with the Telebrinell hardness tester, A_2, which has a U-shaped penetrator. The quality of the two testers can be compared using their respective SN ratios as a quality characteristic (see Reference 7).

The factors in this study are as follows:

Control factors: A_1 = Portable hardness tester (V-shaped penetrator)

                   A_2 = Telebrinell hardness tester (U-shaped penetrator)

Signal factor (material tested): M_1, M_2, M_3

Noise factor (persons doing the measuring): R_1, R_2

Since there is only one control factor, all combinations of the three types of factors can be investigated. For each combination, three measurements are made. The layout and results are shown in Table 4.25.

Table 4.25 Hardness tester experiment

		M_1			M_2			M_3		
A_1	R_1	165	175	205	125	135	133	168	182	190
	R_2	130	158	170	125	148	163	190	212	192
A_2	R_1	170	183	192	152	170	160	225	221	221
	R_2	178	193	181	159	170	170	208	208	221

For data simplification, a working mean, 170, is subtracted from each observation as shown in Table 4.26.

Table 4.26 Simplified data

		M_1			M_2			M_3		
A_1	R_1	-5	5	35	-45	-35	-37	-2	12	20
	R_2	-40	-12	0	-45	-22	-7	20	42	22
A_2	R_1	0	13	22	-18	0	-10	55	51	51
	R_2	8	23	11	-11	0	0	38	38	51

Level totals of the data in Table 4.26 are shown in Table 4.27.

Table 4.27 Level totals

		M_1	M_2	M_3	Total
A_1	R_1	35	-117	30	-52
	R_2	-52	-74	84	-42
	Total	-17	-191	114	-94
A_2	R_1	35	-28	157	164
	R_2	42	-11	127	158
	Total	77	-39	284	322

The SN ratio of A_1 is calculated from Tables 4.26 and 4.27 as follows:

$$S_T = (-5)^2 + 5^2 + \ldots + 22^2 - \frac{(-94)^2}{18}$$

(4.241)

$$= 13392 - \frac{(-94)^2}{18} = 12901 \quad \text{and} \quad f = 17$$

$$S_M = \frac{y_1^2 + y_2^2 + y_3^2}{6} - \frac{(y_1 + y_2 + y_3)^2}{18}$$

$$= \frac{(-17)^2 + (-191)^2 + 114^2}{6} - \frac{(-94)^2}{18}$$

(4.242)

$$= 7803 \quad \text{and} \quad f = 2$$

$$S_e = S_T - S_M = 12901 - 7803$$

$$= 5098 \quad \text{and} \quad f = 15$$

(4.243)

$$V_M = \frac{S_M}{2} = \frac{7803}{2}$$

$$= 3902$$

(4.244)

$$V_e = \frac{S_e}{15} = \frac{5098}{15}$$

$$= 339.9 \tag{4.245}$$

The SN ratio of A_1 is

$$\eta(A_1) = 10 \log \frac{\frac{1}{r_0}(V_M - V_e)}{V_e}$$

$$= 10 \log \frac{\frac{1}{6}(3902 - 339.9)}{339.9} = 10 \log 1.75 \tag{4.246}$$

$$= 2.43 \text{ (db)}$$

The SN ratio of A_2 is

$$\eta(A_2) = 10 \log \frac{\frac{1}{6}(4462 - 62.9)}{62.9} = 10 \log 11.6 \tag{4.247}$$

$$= 10.67 \text{ (db)}$$

The Telebrinell hardness tester, A_2 is better than the portable hardness tester, A_1 by

$$10.67 - 2.43 = 8.24 \text{(db)} \tag{4.247}$$

5

Nondynamic SN Ratios

5.1 INTRODUCTION

In the previous two chapters, the determination of SN ratios for various cases was discussed. Those cases belong to so-called dynamic-type SN ratios. In this chapter, the cases requiring nondynamic-type SN ratios will be discussed.

Briefly speaking, dynamic SN ratios are used to improve the robustness of product functions within a certain output range, whereas nondynamic SN ratios are used to do the same for only a specific or a fixed output target, instead of the whole range.

For example, a study was conducted to produce carbon resistors of 100 ohms. Parameter Design determined the optimum control factor combination to reduce variability around the mean, and adjust the average to a target of 100 ohms. This is a nondynamic approach. Suppose sometime later, the company planned to produce 200-ohm resistors. For this new product, a separate Parameter Design would have to be conducted to determine the optimum condition for the carbon resistors of 200 ohms.

In the dynamic approach, a range of the outputs, such as from 50 to 20,000 ohms, is considered before product development, so that the range covers the outputs of the future products. Parameter Design is conducted to improve the robustness of this product group using a dynamic SN ratio. It also includes the study of how to adjust the output (mean) to any level in the range. By planning this way, a redundant study can be avoided whenever a new product is planned. Thus, it is easy to understand that the dynamic approach is far more powerful and efficient than the nondynamic approach.

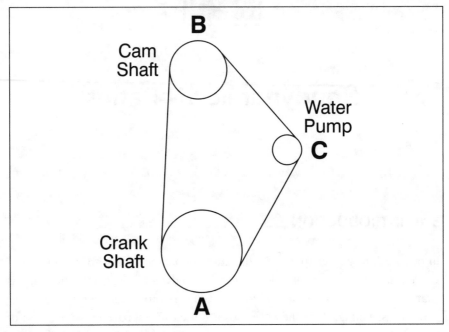

Figure 5.1 Timing belt

It is important to emphasize that in product development, we must always consider using a dynamic approach first. A nondynamic approach is used only as the last alternatives.

Why, then, is the nondynamic approach discussed in this chapter? The reason is that the nondynamic approach should be used when the dynamic SN ratio cannot be used. In other words, the nondynamic approach should be used only when there is no way to measure the input and the output of the function. Inability of measurement is caused by a poor technological level, either in a company or in an industry. For example, the torque of a timing belt in a car cannot be measured. Or, there is no measuring method to quantify a certain quality item available in the industry.

Another reason, which happens frequently, stems from the existing paradigm of engineers. For example, consider an automobile timing belt that links three pulleys together: crank shaft, cam shaft, and the water pump.

The belt manufacturer experienced warranty claims due to audible noise during vehicle operation, and therefore started a series of problem-solving projects. Although carefully considering the control and noise factors, the engineers always measured audible noise as the output response, a smaller-is-better type of nondynamic quality characteristic. Since the measurement approach was always the same, the project results were also always the same: every new design ended up with audible noise, and shorter belt life.

The problem with measuring audible noise as the output response is that such an approach does not focus on the design intent of the product, but rather on a symptom of poor product function. From the paradigm of Quality Engineering, the intended function of the belt is to transfer energy from the crank shaft to the cam shaft and the water pump:

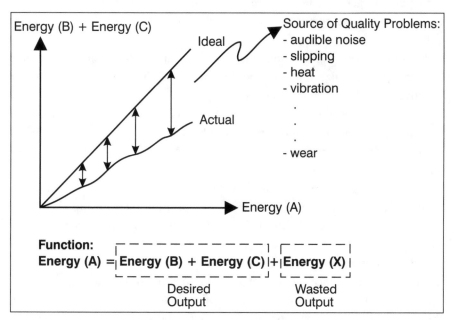

Figure 5.2 Decomposition of energy for timing belt

When the actual performance of the belt deviates from the ideal function, the waste energy creates various problems, including audible noise. By only focusing on minimizing one symptom (audible noise), the performance of the new design may still have the same amount of waste energy. This waste energy does not show up much in the form of audible noise; therefore, it now creates more slipping, heat, vibration, and ultimately more wear, and hence the belt life becomes shorter.

Redirecting waste energy from one symptom to other symptoms is a very common pitfall in problem solving. Often, engineers find themselves chasing back and forth between different problems and still not achieving much progress. The dynamic approach focuses on optimizing the intended function, so that the actual performance gets close to the ideal function, in other words, actively minimizes waste-energy losses that are the source of quality problems.

Every engineered system exists for an intent, and for each intent, there exists an input/output function. This is the most fundamental issue of the system's performance. If the function is optimized, so that the actual performance is very close to the ideal function, most downstream smaller-is-better and larger-is-better requirements will be met. However, attempts to only achieve downstream requirements do not guarantee that the function will be improved.

Therefore, even though nondynamic approaches exist, using a dynamic approach to optimize function should always be the top consideration for effective and efficient engineering efforts.

There are three issues in dynamic SN ratios: reduce variability, improve sensitivity, and improve linearity. It is obvious that reducing variability is essential to quality improvement. As was discussed earlier, improving sensitivity has the same value as reducing variability.

The last issue, improving linearity makes the output of a system easily adjustable because the input and the output relationship is linear (proportional) after the SN ratio has been improved. An output means a target value of a certain product, such as its dimension or output voltage. When the output in a certain range can be easily adjusted, then we can avoid redundancy since we do not have to go through product development for any new product whose output is within that range. Thus, we can save the time and cost of development. That is the power of using dynamic SN ratios.

In nondynamic SN ratios, there are two issues: reduce variability and adjust the average to the target. Once variability is reduced and the average is adjusted to the target, there will be no more issues of moving or adjusting the target. It is seen that nondynamic approach is useful for **a specific product** with a fixed output, in contrast to dynamic approach where the output can be easily adjusted within a range.

There are four types of nondynamic output response applications: nominal-is-best, smaller-is-better, larger-is-better, and nondynamic operating window.

5.2   NOMINAL-IS-BEST APPLICATION

A nominal-is-best application is the type where there is a finite target point to achieve. There are typically upper and lower specification limits on both sides of the target. Examples are the plating thickness of a component, the length of a part, or the output current of a resistor at a given input voltage.

There is a direct relationship between nominal-is-best and dynamic characteristics applications: the target in nominal-is-best is simply a point on the dynamic output response. From the engineering perspective, every application has a dynamic input/output function, and from the customer's standpoint, every application has a target point to achieve. In the case of a resistor, the dynamic function describes the relationship between the input voltage and the output current. As the customer uses the resistor, a target output current is specified for a given input voltage. In the case of injection-molding technology, the intent is to transfer dimensions, and therefore the dynamic function is the relationship between the mold dimensions as the input and the product dimensions as the output. For the final product, there could be a critical dimension on the molded component with a specific target, or, in fact, every dimension could have a specified target. The most thorough and effective optimization approach, especially for technology development, is the dynamic function approach. In the molding example, once the dynamic function is optimized, all dimensions will be accurate and on target. However, there are times when a problem needs to be solved quickly and the situation does not allow for the use of a dynamic approach, since it usually requires more upfront effort. In such a case, it might be feasible only to conduct the experiment using the nominal-is-best approach. Therefore, one should recognize that although the nominal-is-best approach can be effective, it is not the most complete approach.

The objectives of the nominal-is-best approach are to minimize variability around the average and to center the average to the target. Therefore, two types of information are needed to achieve the objectives: which factors affect the variability, and which affect the average. In the two-step optimization for a nominal-is-best application, the first step is to maximize the SN ratio and thereby minimize variability around the average; then, the second step is to adjust the average to the target.

The nominal-is-best SN analysis provides information regarding the factors that affect variability. Conceptually, the nominal-is-best SN is described as

$$SN = \frac{\text{Desired output}}{\text{Undesired output}}$$

$$= \frac{\text{Effect of the average}}{\text{Variability around the average}}$$

The nominal-is-best approach, is applied to two types of cases, as follows:
Case 1: Nonnegative data. This is the case when all data have positive values.
Case 2: Positive and negative data. This is the case when some data are positive and some are negative.

5.2.1 Case 1: Non-Negative Data

In most nominal-is-best applications, the data are non-negative. This is especially true if the output response is energy related, where zero input to the system should produce zero output; thus, there are no negative data.

The calculations for a nominal-is-best SN ratio are as follows:

There are n pieces of data:

$$y_1, y_2, \ldots, y_n$$

The total variation, S_T, is

$$S_T = y_1^2 + y_2^2 + \ldots + y_n^2 \quad \text{and } f = n \tag{5.1}$$

The average variation, S_m, is

$$S_m = \frac{(y_1 + y_2 + \ldots + y_n)^2}{n} \quad \text{and } f = 1 \tag{5.2}$$

Table 5.1   Control and noise factors

Noise Factor	Level 1	Level 2	
N: Part location in plating tank	Off-center	Center	
Control Factors	Level 1	Level 2	Level 3
A: Gold concentration	0.70 – 0.75	1.10 – 1.15	
B: Current density	2.0	1.5	1.0
C: Temperature	95	105	115
D: Barrel speed	10	15	20
E: Anode size	1/4	1/2	1/1
F: Load Size	1/4	1/3	1/2
G: pH	4.20	4.30	4.40
H: Nickel concentration	600	650	700

The error variation, S_e, is

$$S_e = S_T - S_m \quad \text{and} \quad f = n - 1 \tag{5.3}$$

The variance, V_e, is the error variation divided by its degrees of freedom

$$V_e = \frac{S_e}{n - 1} \tag{5.4}$$

The SN ratio, denoted by η, is given by

$$\eta = 10 \log \frac{\frac{1}{n}(S_m - V_e)}{V_e} \tag{5.5}$$

Example

In a gold plating process (see Reference 9), the measured output response is

$$y = \text{Plating thickness } (\mu m)$$

The purpose of gold plating is to provide protection against corrosion and to provide conductance; the minimum specification for these purposes is 50 μm. Since gold is expensive, the cost objective is to minimize the amount of

Table 5.2   Layout and results

L_{18}	A	B	C	D	E	F	G	H	N_1		N_2		η	$\bar{y}$
1	1	1	1	1	1	1	1	1	83	88	90	91	27.9	88.00
2	1	1	2	2	2	2	2	2	73	73	83	81	23.4	77.50
3	1	1	3	3	3	3	3	3	57	58	65	69	20.7	62.25
4	1	2	1	1	2	2	3	3	55	59	61	67	21.6	60.50
5	1	2	2	2	3	3	1	1	73	75	76	79	29.6	75.75
6	1	2	3	3	1	1	2	2	58	60	68	72	19.8	64.50
7	1	3	1	2	1	3	2	3	44	49	55	58	18.3	51.50
8	1	3	2	3	2	1	3	1	50	54	57	64	19.6	56.25
9	1	3	3	1	3	2	1	2	64	65	66	68	31.7	65.75
10	2	1	1	3	3	2	2	1	74	79	86	94	19.6	82.25
11	2	1	2	1	1	3	3	2	75	78	90	94	19.2	84.50
12	2	1	3	2	2	1	1	3	70	76	52	88	19.7	79.75
13	2	2	1	2	3	1	3	2	71	80	87	95	18.2	83.25
14	2	2	2	3	1	2	1	3	48	56	59	65	18.1	57.00
15	2	2	3	1	2	3	2	1	66	67	79	86	17.7	74.50
16	2	3	1	3	2	3	1	2	45	53	58	64	16.7	55.00
17	2	3	2	1	3	1	2	3	60	67	66	73	21.9	66.50
18	2	3	3	2	1	2	3	1	57	65	79	83	15.3	71.00

gold plated to the parts. Therefore, the final objective of the project is to minimize plating thickness variation around the average, and then adjust the average as close to 50 μm as possible.

The control and noise factors of the experiment are shown in Table 5.1.

The experimental layout is shown in Table 5.2.

On each plated part, two thickness measurements were obtained at each part location (noise, n). The signal-to-noise ratio calculations for trial number 1 are

$$S_T = 83^2 + 88^2 + 90^2 + 91^2 = 3014 \quad \text{and} \quad f = 4 \tag{5.6}$$

$$S_m = \frac{(83 + 88 + 90 + 91)^2}{4} = \frac{352^2}{4} = 30976 \quad \text{and} \quad f = 1 \tag{5.7}$$

Table 5.3   Response table (SN ratio)

Level	Factor							
	A	B	C	D	E	F	G	H
1	23.6	21.7	20.4	23.3	19.7	21.2	23.9	21.6
2	18.5	20.8	21.9	20.7	19.8	21.6	20.1	21.4
3		20.6	20.8	19.1	23.6	20.3	19.1	20.1
Δ	5.1	1.1	1.5	4.2	3.9	1.3	4.8	1.5

$$S_e = 83^2 + 88^2 + 90^2 + 91^2 - 30976 = 38 \quad \text{and} \quad f = 3 \qquad (5.8)$$

$$V_e = \frac{S_e}{n-1} = \frac{38}{3} = 12.67 \qquad (5.9)$$

$$\eta = 10 \log \frac{\frac{1}{n}(S_m - V_e)}{V_e}$$

$$= 10 \log \frac{\frac{1}{4}(30976 - 12.67)}{12.67} \qquad (5.10)$$

$$= 10 \log 610.96 = 27.86 \,(\text{db})$$

The response tables for SN and mean are shown in Tables 5.3 and 5.4, respectively.

For example, the averages of A_1 and B_1 in Table 5.3 are calculated as follows:

$$\overline{A}_1 = \frac{1}{9}(27.9 + 23.4 + \ldots + 31.7) = 23.6 \qquad (5.11)$$

$$\overline{B}_1 = \frac{1}{6}(27.9 + 23.4 + 20.7 + 19.6 + 19.2 + 19.7) = 21.7 \qquad (5.12)$$

Based on results in the response tables, the two-step optimization can be performed as follows:

1. Reduce variability around the average (maximize SN ratio):

Table 5.4   Response table (mean)

Level	Factor							
	A	B	C	D	E	F	G	H
1	66.9	79.2	70.3	73.3	69.4	73.0	70.2	74.8
2	72.8	69.3	69.6	73.1	67.3	69.2	69.6	71.8
3		61.0	69.6	63.0	72.8	67.3	69.6	62.9
Δ	5.9	18.2	0.7	10.3	5.5	5.7	0.6	11.9

From Table 5.3, it is seen that factors A, D, E, and G have larger effects than the others. Therefore, levels A_1, D_1, E_3, and G_1, are selected to give the highest SN ratio.

2. Adjust the mean to target:

    Factors B and H both have strong effects on the average and weak effects on the SN ratio, and factor B (current density) is easier to adjust than factor H (nickel concentration); therefore, factor B is the most ideal average adjustment factor, and then H_1 (lowest nickel concentration, 600) is selected to reduce the cost of nickel.

In addition, C_1 (lowest temperature) is selected to reduce the cost of the operating process, and F_3 (maximum load size) is selected to maximize the quantity processed.

To predict the SN ratio for any combination of factors, the stronger SN effects — A, D, E, G — are used. For the optimum combination $A_1 D_1 E_3 G_1$, the SN ratio is

$$\hat{\eta}_{opt} = \overline{T} + (\overline{A}_1 - \overline{T}) + (\overline{D}_1 - \overline{T}) + (\overline{E}_3 - \overline{T}) + (\overline{G}_1 - \overline{T})$$

$$= 21.0 + (23.6 - 21.0) + (23.3 - 21.0) + (23.6 - 21.0) + (23.9 - 21.0)$$

$$= 31.4 \text{ (db)} \tag{5.13}$$

Suppose the initial combination was $A_2 B_2 C_2 D_2 E_2 F_2 G_2 H_2$, the prediction then becomes

$$\hat{\eta}_{opt} = \overline{T} + (\overline{A}_2 - \overline{T}) + (\overline{D}_2 - \overline{T}) + (\overline{E}_2 - \overline{T}) + (\overline{G}_2 - \overline{T})$$

$$= 21.0 + (18.5 - 21.0) + (20.7 - 21.0) + (19.8 - 21.0) + (20.1 - 21.0)$$

$$= 16.1 \text{ (db)} \tag{5.14}$$

The predicted gain therefore is

$$\text{Gain} = 31.4 - 16.1 = 15.3 \text{ (db)} \tag{5.15}$$

After the confirmation runs are conducted for both the optimum and the initial combinations, the SN ratios should be calculated for both combinations. The actual gain hence can be calculated, and the closer it is to the predicted gain, the more reproducible is the experimental conclusion.

Once the SN ratio is confirmed (variability reduction confirmed), simply observe the average of the optimum confirmation run, then adjust it to the target, using factor B, if necessary.

5.2.2   Case 2: Positive and Negative Data

Occasionally in a nominal-is-best application, the output data can take on positive and negative values due to the method of measurement. This usually is the case when the output response is the plus/minus deviation from a nominal target. For example, a set of data for tubing length is 12.55, 13.19, 16.68, etc. If the target of 14.00 is subtracted from each data point, then the data become: -1.45, -0.81, 2.68, etc.

But in such a case, instead of using the deviations from the target (which include positive/negative data), the raw data, which are all positive, can be used to calculate the SN ratios as described in the previous case.

In the case of temperature, the data may be positive and negative: i.e., above and below zero. For this particular case, the Kelvin scale can be used to avoid positive and negative data. Sometimes when positive and negative data coexist, a different approach should be made; examples are the warping upward and downward of a material, or deformation on the rightside and the leftside, etc.

If the SN ratio equation previously described in this section were used for data with negative values, it would lead to wrong conclusions. Therefore, a different approach must be taken.

The two-step optimization for nominal-is-best Case 1 applies just the same here, except the signal-to-noise ratio is given as conceptually

$$SN = \frac{1}{\text{Variability around the average}} \qquad (5.16)$$

This SN ratio is different from nominal-is-best Case 1 in that the numerator does not include the effect of the average. In other words, the variability around the mean is not associated to the average. Thus, it only evaluates the amount of undesired output and has no representation of the desired output (numerator). If the average value varies greatly in an application, the conclusion drawn using this SN ratio may be quite different from that using the SN ratio for nominal-is-best Case 1.

Since the SN ratio for Case 1 evaluates variability around the average against the average itself, it is recommended over this, Case 2, SN ratio. From another perspective, the target value should not be subtracted from the raw data when calculating the SN ratio. The adjustment of the average to the target is taken care of in the second step of the two-step optimization.

The calculations for the SN ratio here are:

For n data: $y_1, y_2, y_3, ..., y_n$

Here, the total variation around the average is equal to the error variation. Therefore, variation, S_T, is

$$S_T = y_1^2 + y_2^2 + ... + y_n^2 - S_m = S_e \quad \text{and} \quad f = n - 1 \qquad (5.17)$$

and variance, V_e, is

$$V_e = \frac{S_e}{n - 1} \qquad (5.18)$$

SN ratio, η, is

$$\eta = -10 \ \log V_e \qquad (5.19)$$

For data points 1.25, -1.48, -2.70, 0.19, the SN ratio for the nominal-is-best Case 2 is

$$S_m = \frac{(1.25 - 1.48 - 2.70 + 0.19)^2}{4} = 1.8769 \qquad (5.20)$$

$$S_T = 1.25^2 + (-1.48)^2 + (-2.70)^2 + 0.19^2 - 1.8769$$
$$= 9.2021 \quad \text{and} \quad f = 3 \qquad (5.21)$$

$$V_e = \frac{S_e}{n-1} = \frac{9.2021}{3} = 3.0674 \qquad (5.22)$$

$$\eta = -10 \ \log \ 3.0674$$
$$= -4.87 \,(\text{db}) \qquad (5.23)$$

5.3   SMALLER-IS-BETTER APPLICATION

The smaller-is-better output response is the type when the desire is to minimize the result and so the ideal target is zero. Examples include the wear on a component, the amount of engine audible noise, the amount of air pollution, the amount of heat loss, etc. Notice that all these examples represent things we don't want, and not the intended system functions. Minimizing wrongs is typically done for short-term problem solving, but fixing a symptom or two does not necessarily mean that the system function is improved. When there are problems with a system, it is an indication that the system's input energy is not entirely performing its intended function and a portion of the output energy is producing undesirable effects. Quite often in solving manufacturing problems, suppressing one symptom results in redirecting the harmful output energy, to cause other problems. The best approach is to use the dynamic application to optimize the system function, so that the input energy will be utilized as much as possible to perform the intended task. The harmful output energy thereby will be minimized, and problems will be prevented. Therefore, the smaller-is-better approach is one of the last alternatives used in Quality Engineering.

The calculations for a smaller-is-better SN ratio are as follows:
For n data, $y_1, y_2, \ldots, \ldots, y_n,$ the SN ratio is given by

$$\eta = -10 \ \log \frac{1}{n} \left(y_1^2 + y_2^2 + \ldots + y_n^2 \right) \qquad (5.24)$$

Example

For data points 0.13, 0.18, 0.14, the smaller-is-better SN ratio is

$$\eta = -10 \ \log\left[\frac{1}{3}\left(0.13^2 + 0.18^2 + 0.14^2\right)\right]$$

$$= 16.4 \ (\text{db})$$

(5.25)

5.4   LARGER-IS-BETTER APPLICATION

The larger-is-better output response is the type when the desire is to maximize the result and so the ideal target is infinity. Examples include the strength of a material, fuel efficiency, etc. Percentage yield seems to be a larger-is-better application, but it does not belong in this category in Quality Engineering, since the ideal value is 100%, not infinity. If we want to apply SN ratios to percent yield, the yield may be subtracted from 100 and then treated as a smaller-is-better case. Similar to small-is-better, a larger-is-better response is also usually a downstream measure of quality. In development, addressing the function of the system and using the dynamic type of output response is the most effective approach. In the case of material strength, for example, a force/displacement function can be considered to evaluate the strength property. The traditional approach of measuring a breakage strength is really testing for failure, not testing how well the intended function is performed. In the paradigm of Quality Engineering, once the further upstream function is optimized, all or most of the downstream requirements can also be achieved.

In practical experience, when engineers cannot reproduce predicted results, the reason is mostly due to the poor selection of the measured output response. Many engineers have in the past utilized larger-is-better and smaller-is-better approaches, but achieved only mediocre results. Therefore, although the SN ratio exists, the larger-is-better approach is also a last alternative.

The calculations of a larger-is-better SN ratio are as follows:

For n data, $y_1, y_2, \ldots, y_n$, the SN ratio is given by

$$\eta = -10 \ \log \ \frac{1}{n} \left(\frac{1}{y_1^2} + \frac{1}{y_2^2} + \ldots + \frac{1}{y_n^2}\right)$$

(5.26)

Example

For date points 32.5, 45.0, 35.0, 50.0, the larger-is-better SN ratio is

$$\eta = -10 \ \log \ \frac{1}{4} \left(\frac{1}{32.5^2} + \frac{1}{45.0^2} + \frac{1}{35.0^2} + \frac{1}{50.0^2} \right) \qquad (5.27)$$
$$= 31.77(\text{db})$$

5.5 NONDYNAMIC OPERATING WINDOW

Quite often in the past, experiments were performed using attribute-type (0/1) data. The problem with 0/1 data is that in nature, the data are discrete and therefore tend to be nonadditive. In the case of having two categories of data, Good and Bad, the data collected represent the count of good pieces or bad pieces. The confusion here is that all the good pieces are perceived as equally good, and all the bad pieces, equally bad. With respect to product function, however, not all good pieces perform equally well, or all bad pieces equally poorly. Due to the ambiguity of data, experiments using this approach rarely achieve reproducible results.

The operating window approach was an alternative when 0/1 data were first considered. The strategy is to measure the threshold values at the transient stages where 0 becomes 1 and 1 becomes 0, and hence use the continuous data in the analysis.

Example

The typical method for testing paper jams in a photocopying machine's paper feeding device is to sample 5000 feedings, record the number of failed trials, and use this as the measured data for the analysis. This approach addresses the customer's complaint; however, it poses difficulties in the engineering analysis. First of all, there are actually two types of failure modes: misfeed, where no paper is fed; and multifeed, where more than one sheet of paper is fed. Counting the total number of failures does not distinguish between the two failure modes. Furthermore, the 0/1 data analysis treats all 0's equally and all 1's equally. This

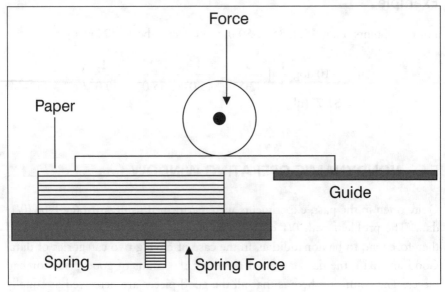

Figure 5.3 Paper feeder

type of data will provide only vague informations and most likely, the project conclusion will not be reproducible; therefore, improvement will be very limited, if any.

The paper feeder is a spring-loaded mechanism in which the spring force pushes the stack of paper up against the feed roller, as shown in Fig. 5.3.

The paper feeder misfeeds when there is too little spring force, and multifeeds when the spring force is too large. Consider the following measures:

x = minimal spring force to feed one sheet of paper
z = maximal spring force before two sheets are fed

If the spring force is below x, misfeeding occurs, and if the spring force is above z, multifeeding occurs. The objectives of the project then becomes to minimize x to decrease number of misfeeds, and to maximize z to decrease number of multifeeds.

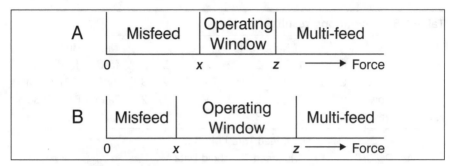

Figure 5.4 Operating window

The range, $z-x$, is called the operating window, and the objective of Parameter Design is to maximize $z-x$. Instead of counting the number of jams (defects), x and z are threshold values, where 0 becomes 1 and 1 becomes 0. Measuring these continuous data will help achieve reproducible experimental results.

The calculations of the operating window signal-to-noise ratio are
For n data, $x_1, x_2, \ldots, \ldots, x_n$ and $z_1, z_2, \ldots, z_n$. Then, the SN ratio is

$$
\eta = \left[-10 \log \frac{1}{n} \left(x_1^2 + x_2^2 + \ldots + x_n^2 \right) \right] \\
+ \left[-10 \log \frac{1}{n} \left(\frac{1}{z_1^2} + \frac{1}{z_2^2} + \ldots + \frac{1}{z_2^2} \right) \right]
\tag{5.28}
$$

Figure 5.4 shows two situations of an operating window. The operating window of situation B is wider and has a greater SN ratio than the window for situation A.

Example

In a paper-feeder design for a copy machine (see Reference 10), eight control factors (— such as feed-roll configuration and retard-pad force —) and four noise factors (— such as paper weight and paper orientation —) were assigned to L_{18} and L_9 arrays, respectively, as shown in Table 5.5.

Table 5.5   Layout and results

No.	Control Factory Array ABCDEFGH	N O P Q	1 1 1 1	1 2 2 2	Noise-Factor Array L_9 1 3 3 3	2 1 2 3	2 2 3 1	2 3 1 2	3 1 3 2	3 2 1 3	3 3 2 1	Mis- feed S/N Ratio η_x	Multi- feed S/N Ratio η_z	SN Ratio Sum η

No.	ABCDEFGH	Misfeed Threshold Data Multifeed Threshold Data								η_x	η_z	η
1	1 1 1 1 1 1 1 1	0.4 0.2 0.6 0.75 0.8 0.4 0.8 0.3 0.1								5.29		6.31
		0.8 1.0 3.0 0.55 3.0 1.2 3.0 3.0 3.0									1.02	
2	1 1 2 2 2 2 2 2									13.63	7.84	21.47
3	1 1 3 3 3 3 3 3									15.39	9.54	24.93
4	1 2 1 1 2 2 3 3									-0.38	-4.55	-4.93
5	1 2 2 2 3 3 1 1									11.98	4.51	16.50
6	1 2 3 3 1 1 2 2									15.74	1.14	17.21
7	1 3 1 2 1 3 2 3									3.78	0.37	4.15
8	1 3 2 3 2 1 3 1									4.73	3.09	7.82
9	1 3 3 1 3 2 1 2									19.53	13.54	6.00
10	2 1 1 3 3 2 2 1									-0.04	2.06	2.02
11	2 1 2 1 1 3 3 2									-2.21	6.86	4.65
12	2 1 3 2 2 1 1 3									10.10	8.98	19.08
13	2 2 1 2 3 1 3 2									-3.46	-11.40	-14.85
14	2 2 2 3 1 2 1 3									3.29	-14.02	-10.73
15	2 2 3 1 2 3 2 1									1.92	-4.80	-2.88
16	2 3 1 3 2 3 1 2									-2.49	-10.50	-12.98
17	2 3 2 1 3 1 2 3									13.31	7.3	20.61
18	2 3 3 2 1 2 3 1									2.22	6.57	8.79

In the table, only the results of experiment no. 1 are shown. The upper row shows the threshold values of misfeed, and the lower row, the threshold values of multifeed. From the results of misfeed, the SN ratio, η is calculated as follows:

Table 5.6 Response table

Factor	Level 1	Level 2	Level 3
A	11.0511	1.5233	
B	13.0767	0.0533	5.7317
C	-3.3800	10.0533	12.1883
D	4.9600	9.1900	4.7117
E	5.0633	4.5967	9.2017
F	9.3633	3.7700	5.7283
G	4.0300	10.4300	4.4017

$$\eta_x = -10 \log \frac{1}{9} \left(0.4^2 + 0.2^2 + \ldots + 0.1^2 \right)$$
$$= 5.29 \text{(db)}$$
(5.29)

The SN ratio of multifeed, η_z, is calculated similarly

$$\eta_z = -10 \log \frac{1}{9} \left(\frac{1}{0.8^2} + \frac{1}{1.0^2} \ldots + \frac{1}{3.0^2} \right)$$
$$= 1.02 \text{(db)}$$
(5.30)

The SN ratio of the operating window is then calculated by

$$\eta = \eta_x + \eta_z = 5.29 + 1.02 = 6.31 \text{ (db)}$$
(5.31)

Table 5.6 shows the response table. From the table, the optimum conditions are selected, followed by the gain calculation. The gain is then compared with one from the confirmatory experiment.

Note (5.1a):

In the case of nominal-is-best, the decomposition of the total variation is summarized in Table 5.7.

The SN ratio for a nominal-is-best case is an estimate:

Table 5.7   ANOVA table for nominal-is-best case

Source	Degrees of Freedom	Variation	Variance	Expectation of Variance, E (V)
m	1	S_m	V_m	$nm^2 + \sigma^2$
e	$n - 1$	S_e	V_e	σ^2

$$\eta \rightarrow 10 \log \frac{m^2}{\sigma^2} \tag{5.32}$$

where m is the population average.

From $E(V)$ in Table 5.1*,

$$\eta = 10 \log \frac{\frac{1}{n}(S_m - V_e)}{V_e} \tag{5.33}$$

Note (5.1b):

When there are n pieces of data,

$$y_1, y_2, \ldots, y_n$$

and the variation from a target, S_T, is

$$S_T = \sum (y_i - t)^2 \tag{5.34}$$

where t is a target.

Equation (5.34) can be written as

$$\begin{aligned}
S_T &= \sum (y_i - t)^2 \\
&= \sum (y_i - \bar{y} + \bar{y} - t)^2 \\
&= \sum (y_i - \bar{y})^2 + 2 \sum (y_i - \bar{y})(\bar{y} - t) + \sum (\bar{y} - t)^2 \\
&= \sum (y_i - \bar{y}) + \eta(\bar{y} - t)^2 \tag{5.35}
\end{aligned}$$

S_T divided by the number of data points is called **mean squared deviation,** and is denoted by MSD.

$$MSD = \frac{1}{n} \sum (y_1 - \bar{y})^2 + (\bar{y} - t)^2 \qquad (5.36)$$

In the case of smaller-is-better, the target is zero. Therefore, Eq. (5.5*) is

$$MSD = \frac{1}{n} \sum (y_i - \bar{y})^2 + (\bar{y})^2 \qquad (5.37)$$

This is the estimation of

$$MSD \rightarrow \sigma^2 + m^2 \qquad (5.38)$$

where

m = population average.
σ^2 = population variance.

Minimizing MSD means minimizing both the variance and the mean. The SN ratio can be written as

$$\eta = -10 \log \frac{1}{n} \left(y_1^2 + y_2^2 + \ldots + y_n^2 \right)$$
$$= -10 \log (MSD) \qquad (5.39)$$

Note (5.1c):

The SN ratio for larger-is-better case is

$$\eta = -10 \log \left(\frac{1}{n} \sum \frac{1}{y_i^2} \right) \qquad (5.40)$$

The estimation of

$$\frac{1}{n} \sum \frac{1}{y_i^2}$$

can be rewritten as

$$E\left(\frac{1}{n}\sum\frac{1}{y_i^2}\right)$$

$$= E\left[\frac{1}{n}\sum\frac{1}{(m+y_i-m)^2}\right]$$

$$= E\left[\frac{1}{n}\sum\frac{1}{m^2\left(1+\frac{y_i-m}{m}\right)^2}\right]$$

$$= \frac{1}{m^2}E\left[\frac{1}{n}\sum\left(1+\frac{y_i-m}{m}\right)^{-2}\right] \qquad (5.41)$$

Since

$$(1+x)^n = 1 + nx + \frac{n(n-1)}{2!}x^2 + \ldots \qquad (5.42)$$

Equation (5.41) becomes

$$E\left(\frac{1}{n}\sum\frac{1}{y_i^2}\right) = \frac{1}{m^2}$$

$$\times E\left\{\frac{1}{n}\sum\left[1-2\frac{y_i-m}{m}+\frac{-2\times(-2-1)}{2!}\times\left(\frac{y_i-m}{m}\right)^2+\ldots\right]\right\} \qquad (5.43)$$

In the above equation,

$$E\left[\frac{1}{n}\sum(1)\right] = 1 \qquad (5.44)$$

$$E\left[\frac{1}{n}\sum\left(\frac{y_i-m}{m}\right)\right] = 0 \qquad (5.45)$$

$$E\left\{\frac{1}{n}\sum\left[\frac{-2\times(-2-1)}{2!}\left(\frac{y_i-m}{m}\right)\right]\right\} = \frac{3\sigma^2}{m^2} \qquad (5.46)$$

Therefore,

$$E\left(\frac{1}{n}\sum\frac{1}{y_i^2}\right) = \frac{1}{m^2}\left(1 + \frac{3\sigma^2}{m^2}\right) \tag{5.47}$$

When the mean increases and the variance decreases, the magnitude of Eq. (5.47) decreases, and therefore the SN ratio increases.

Classified Attributes

6.1 DIFFERENCE BETWEEN CONTINUOUS VARIABLES AND CLASSIFIED ATTRIBUTES

There are different types of classified attributes, but they have one point in common: classified attribute data consist of 0 and 1, or digital data. For example, the number of defects can be expressed by 0 for a good product and 1 for a bad product, or vice versa. This examplifies the case when results are classified into two categories. In the case when results are classified into three or more categories, such as good, normal, and bad, the number of data points in each category can also be expressed by 0 and 1.

Classified attributes are very widely used for data collection and analysis, but they are *not* good quality characteristics from a Quality Engineering viewpoint. That's because they waste information, are inefficient, and can lead to interactions.

6.1.1 Wasted Information

To understand this problem, consider the following example, a product's dimensions are measured by a go and no-go gauge and then are classified into two categories: good and bad. The design specifies a tolerance of 10 ± 0.1 mm for the product. One product has a dimension of 10.5 mm and another, 9.8 mm. These two products are considered as being equally bad products. But the important information regarding the variability—the first one is too large and the second, too small—disappears by this kind of classification. For another example, consider the case when one student scores 60 on an examination and another student, 90. If they are classified by pass/fail, then these two grades are treated as being equal. But no one thinks that scores of 60 and 90 are equal. Go and no-go gauges are very widely used in industries, or at least were until recent years. It is one of the reasons why the quality of the products produced by these industries could not (and cannot) be improved.

6.1.2   Inefficiency

A quality characteristic called **fraction defective** seemingly belongs to continuous variables, but substantially, it is 0/1 data. This is because products are classified into good and bad classes, and then the number of bad products are divided by the total number of products to get a fraction. **Reliability data** is another example where the number of failed tests are divided by the total number of tests.

When the sample size is small in a study using the fraction defective method, we do not believe the figure. When reliability tests are conducted only a few times, no one believes the conclusion. The number of products used to determine the fraction of defective products or the number of tests needed to establish reliability of data have to be very large, and that makes the studies inefficient.

6.1.3   Interactions

The third reason—and the one causing the greatest problem—for not using classified attributes such as good or bad, pass or failed in research is that such quality characteristics tend to generate many interactions.

Interaction is synonymous with inconsistency, nonadditivity or nonreproducibility. To explain the reason why classified attributes may lead to interactions, let's use the following example. In an experiment, two factors A and B with two levels each were evaluated using good and bad as the quality characteristics, and the following results were collected:

This type of experiment is called a **"one-factor-at-a-time experiment"** because only one factor or condition is varied from one experiment to another. By comparing experiments 1 and 2, we know A_2 is better than A_1. From experiments 1 and 3, we see that B_2 is better than B_1. From these three experiments, we may infer that condition $A_2 B_2$ would be the best. However, if a confirmatory experiment were conducted for $A_2 B_2$, it could show that $A_2 B_2$ is

Experiment	Condition	Result
1	A_1B_1	Bad
2	A_2B_1	Good
1	A_1B_1	Bad
3	A_1B_2	Good

the worst instead of the best condition. In such a case, we say that an interaction exists between factors A and B. When there is no interaction between A and B, A_2 must always be better than A_1, no matter how the condition of B changes, and B_2 must be better than B_1, irrespective of the condition of A. Figure 6.1 shows the cases with and without interactions.

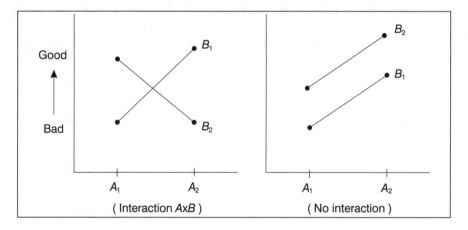

Figure 6.1 Interaction

The reason for the occurrence of such an unexpected interaction lies in using the wrong quality characteristic for the study: good and bad. To understand why, let's use an example of a welding experiment. The conditions of A and B are:

A = current
A_1 = low current
A_2 = high current

B = welding time
  B_1 = short
  B_2 = long

It is obvious that combination $A_1 B_1$ involved low current and short welding time. Because the input energy was very low, no weld occurred, giving a bad result. Combination $A_2 B_2$ involves high current and long welding time, causing a weld that is burnt through, which is bad also. But from the above-noted three experiments, we would expect condition $A_2 B_2$ — which was not included in the original experiment—to yield the best result, not the worst. Thus, the effects of both A and B are not consistent. The effect of changing A from A_1 to A_2 cannot be added to the effect of changing B from B_1 to B_2 and give the expected result. This is termed **poor additivity.** The estimation of the best condition was not reproduced in the confirmatory experiment; this is called **nonreproducibility.**

A one-factor-at-a-time experiment is efficient and easy to conduct. But, when there are many interactions, the best condition indicated by this type of experiment may not, in reality, be the best, and thus, we are betrayed by the results of our own experiment because we used good/bad type of quality characteristics.

When interactions exist, the best condition has to be found from all combinations of all factors. This type of experiment is called a **factorial** or a **full factorial experiment.**

There are only two factors in the above experiment; therefore, to consider all combinations means we need to add just one more experiment, i.e., conduct 4 runs instead of 3. However, when there are 13 factors with three level each, the total number of combinations is 1,594,323. A need to evaluate as many as 13 factors at three levels is common in experimentation. How can we spend tens of years finishing one robust design effort using a full factorial experiment?

When conclusions are not reproducible, small-scale laboratory experimentation cannot be applied to the larger scale of manufacturing; the conclusions also will not be applicable when the products are used by customers. For example, two kinds of materials, A_1 and A_2, are compared in the laboratory with a result that A_1 is better than A_2. But in manufacturing or in the market, A_2 turns out to be better than A_1. If that is the case, the time and money spent in the laboratory was wasted, because the conclusions generated were flawed.

6.2   WHAT ARE THE STRATEGIES TO AVOID
INTERACTIONS?

In Quality Engineering, it is stressed that selection of quality characteristics is the key to avoiding interactions.

Solution 1: Avoid using 0/1 data.

The following are examples of 0/1 data: number of pass/failed tests, number of good/bad products, failure rate, and reliability data. Instead of using these quality characteristics, try to measure continuous variables or convert 0/1 data into continuous variables. For example, stop using go and no-go gauges and measure actual dimensions. Instead of just counting the number of holes that are defective, measure the size of the holes as well. Instead of tasting a food and judging it as being tasty or not tasty, measure items such as sugar content, salt content, and physical properties and then assess their effect on taste.

It must be stressed that the recommendation to avoid the above types of data does not imply such data are not important. They are important for management or marketing people, since it is important to satisfy customers and these data are necessary for monitoring the results of quality-improvement activities. However, we must avoid using these types of data in research, for the purpose of avoiding **interactions.**

Solution 2: Increase the number of classes from two to three or more.

This solution is recommended only for the case in which there is no way of measuring continuous variables.

By increasing the number of classes to three or more, some of the erroneous conclusions likely to be made when only two classes are used can be avoided. For example, the number of defects in a welding process may be classified into

Class 1:   not welded
Class 2:   normal or good
Class 3:   burnt through

In the reliability test of the paper-feeding system in a copy machine, the number of problems can be altered by using the following three classes:

Class 1: misfeed (no paper was fed in)
Class 2: normal
Class 3: multifeed (more than one sheet of paper was fed in)

In both examples, Class 1 is the result of too little energy being put into the system, whereas Class 3 is the case of too much energy being put in. In the two-class scheme, these sorts of distinctions are lost because such opposite and extreme conditions are lumped together in one category; this essentially hides the actual conditions. That is the reason why interactions exist. Although this solution is better than using a two-class categorization, it is a strategy of last resort when choosing quality characteristics. Unfortunately, in many cases, continuous variables cannot be obtained due to a lack in measurement technology.

Solution 3: Use robust quality characteristics.

Nondynamic-type SN ratios are called robust quality characteristics. The chance of having interactions when using them is much less than when classified attributes or ordinary continuous variables are used.

Solution 4: Use functional quality characteristics.

Functional quality is expressed by dynamic-type SN ratios. By using this type of quality characteristics, the existence of interactions can be minimized. This will be explained in later chapters.

6.3 CASE WITH TWO CLASSES, ONE TYPE OF MISTAKE

When attribute data are classified into two classes, 0 and 1 are used for classification. With such digital-type data, there are two cases: one type of mistake and two types of mistakes. When using a vending machine, for example, we put coins into the machine and expect to get a product, such as a cola, from the machine. If no product is delivered, there is a mistake. Another type of mistake is that a product comes out of the machine when no coins are put in. Normally, vending machines are designed in such a way that the second type of mistake rarely occurs. In the reliability study of vending machines, only the first type of mistake is studied.

As mentioned in the previous section, the problem of using digital-type data is lack of additivity in factorial effects. For example, a product has a reliability of 99.4%. The company producing it has decided to upgrade the three component parts A, B, and C in the product. Table 6.1 shows the results of conducting a stress test.

Table 6.1   Results of reliability

Component	Current	New
A	90%	99%
B	95%	98%
C	80%	95%

It is obvious that the improvement of all three component parts cannot be arithmetically added together. The improvement of each component is

$$
\begin{array}{rl}
A: & 9\% \\
B: & 3\% \\
C: & 15\% \\
\hline
\text{Total}: & 27\%
\end{array}
$$

If the total improvement were added to the reliability figure before the improvements, the reliability would exceed 100%.

In order to expect a better additivity, a digital-type SN ratio may be used.

Table 6.2 shows the results of testing a vending machine. In the table, y_i is either 0 or 1. Let 1 refer to the case when a product comes out of the machine, and 0 be the other case.

Letting the rate of getting a product be p,

$$
p = \frac{y_1 + y_2 + \ldots + y_n}{n} \tag{6.1}
$$

Table 6.2 Results of 0 and 1

Test No.	1	2	3	...	n
Results	y_1	y_2	y_3	...	y_n

To calculate the SN ratio, data are decomposed as follows. Total variation is given by

$$S_T = y_1^2 + y_2^2 + \ldots + y_n^2 = np \qquad (6.2)$$

The effect of the signal is calculated as the variation of p. Since Eq. (6.1) is a linear equation, its variation, denoted by S_p, is given by

$$S_p = \frac{L^2}{D} \qquad (6.3)$$

where D is the number of units of Eq. (6.1).

$$D = \left(\frac{1}{n}\right)^2 + \left(\frac{1}{n}\right)^2 + \ldots + \left(\frac{1}{n}\right)^2 = \left(\frac{1}{n}\right)^2 \times n = \frac{1}{n} \qquad (6.4)$$

Putting Eq. (6.1) and (6.4) into Eq. (6.3), we get

$$S_p = \frac{p^2}{1/n} = np^2 = S_m \qquad (6.5)$$

The error variation, S_e, is calculated by subtracting S_p from S_T:

$$S_e = S_T - S_p$$
$$= np - np^2 = np\,(1 - p) \qquad (6.6)$$

The SN ratio of digital data is calculated as the ratio of the variation of the signal to the variation of error in decibel (db) units:

$$\eta = 10 \log \frac{S_p}{S_e} = 10 \log \frac{np^2}{np(1-p)}$$

$$= 10 \log \frac{p}{1-p} = -10 \log \left(\frac{1}{p} - 1\right)$$

(6.7)

This is the same equation used in the **omega transformation**.

Table 6.3   SN ratios (db)

Component	Current	New	Gain
A	9.54	19.91	10.37
B	12.79	16.90	4.11
C	6.03	12.79	6.76

The results of Table 6.1 are used to explain the application. The gains of using new components are calculated as shown in Table 6.3.

For example, the gain by component A is calculated as

$$\left.\begin{array}{ll} \text{Current:} & -10 \log(1/0.90 - 1) = 9.54 \text{(db)} \\ \text{New:} & -10 \log(1/0.99 - 1) = 19.91 \text{(db)} \\ \text{Gain} = & 19.91 - 9.54 = 10.37 \text{(db)} \end{array}\right\}$$

(6.9)

The total gain of upgrading all component parts would be

$$\text{Total gain} = 10.37 + 4.11 + 6.76 = 21.24 \text{(db)}$$

(6.10)

Since the reliability of the current product is 0.994, its SN ratio is

$$-10\log\left(\frac{1}{0.994} - 1\right) = 22.19(\text{db}) \tag{6.11}$$

The SN ratio after upgrading is calculated by

$$22.19 + 21.24 = 43.43(\text{db}) \tag{6.12}$$

This is equivalent to a reliability of

$$-10\log\left(\frac{1}{p} - 1\right) = 43.43 \tag{6.13}$$

$$p = 0.999954 \tag{6.14}$$

6.4 CASE WITH TWO CLASSES, TWO TYPES OF MISTAKES

This is the case when the input signal is either 0 or 1, while the output can be either 0 or 1. One type of mistake is that when the input is 0, the output is 1. Another type is that when the input is 1, the output is 0. In communication, for example, a transmitter may send out a **mark** signal, but the receiver may receive it as a **space,** or vice versa. For another example, a smoke detector may give an alarm when there is no smoke, or the detector may not give an alarm when a fire breaks out.

Examples

The SN ratio with two types of mistakes has important applications in the chemical industry. For example, the separation of copper ore into product and slag (waste), the results of which are shown in Table 6.4.

There are two types of mistakes:

Impurities are not separated well and go into the product.
Copper is not separated well and goes into the slag.

Table 6.4   Results of copper smelting

		Output	
		Product	Slag
Input	Copper	-	Mistake 2
	Impurities	Mistake 1	-

The objective in a separation process is to minimize both types of mistakes, not just to reduce one of the two. By using the SN ratio of this type, it is possible to evaluate the overall mistake. The following are some examples of applications for this SN ratio:

▶ Purification
▶ Filtration
▶ Air separation
▶ Alarm systems
▶ Safety devices
▶ Defect screening

Table 6.5 is the input/output table for the case with two types of mistakes.

In the table, input 0 was tested n_0 times and input 1 was tested n_1 times. The number mistakes of the former test was n_{01} and of the latter test was n_{10}. The numbers in Table 6.5 are converted into ratios as shown in Table 6.6.

Table 6.5   Input/output table for two types of mistakes

		Output		Total
		0	1	
Input	0	n_{00}	n_{01}	n_0
	1	n_{10}	n_{11}	n_1
Total		r_0	r_1	n

Table 6.6 Input/output table in fraction

		Output		Total
		0	1	
Input	0	$1 - p$	p	1
	1	q	$1 - q$	1

In order to optimize the process in similar such cases, there are two problems:

Problem 1: Two types of mistakes, p and q, vary depending on the threshold value.

Problem 2: When the research is conducted through experimentation, the rates of two mistakes are not equal most of the time.

To explain the first problem, let's use the example of a copper smelting process. When the temperature of the process is raised, copper melts better and more copper goes into the product. Thus, mistake p decreases. On the other hand, the impurities also melt better and more impurities go into the product, thus mistake q increases. When the temperature is lowered, p increases and q decreases. Temperature in this case is not a **control factor**, but an **adjusting factor**.

How, then can we set the threshold value for temperature? The answer depends on the economic viewpoint. In other words, the temperature that minimizes the total loss—which is the loss of copper going into slag plus the loss of impurities going into the product—is the right threshold value.

For the second problem, suppose there is a control factor in the process, such as a raw-material mixing ratio with two levels, A_1 and A_2. Two experiments were conducted with the following results:

A_1: $p = 0.01$
  $q = 0.07$

$$p + q = 0.08$$

$$A_2: \quad p = 0.04$$
$$q = 0.03$$
$$p + q = 0.07$$

If the totals of the two mistakes are compared, it seems that A_2 is better. As described in the previous sections, the assumption of additivity of 0/1 data will lead to flawed conclusions. Therefore, we should not treat such data by either adding p and q or taking their average for comparison. However, it is difficult to tell which condition has a better separating function. In order to compare them on the same basis, the two rates of mistakes of each condition must be adjusted by using an adjusting factor such as temperature so that p and q of A_1 become equal, and then do the same for A_2. In the above example, q is larger than p at level A_1. This implies that the mistake of copper being mixed with slag is smaller than the mistake of impurities being mixed with product. In order to adjust p to be equal to q, temperature was lowered. Assume the adjustment resulted in $p = q = 0.027$. At level A_2, where p is larger than q, the mistake of copper being mixed with slag is larger than the mistake of impurities being mixed with product. Temperature was raised and adjusted until p and q were equal. Assume the result was $p = q = 0.035$. Now, we know that condition A_1 has a better separating function than A_2.

Such an approach is theoretically possible, but just thinking about conducting many tedious and expensive experiments just for the purpose of adjusting p equal to q, it becomes obvious that such a hardware approach is not at all practical. In order to avoid such impractical experimentation, we would like to compare A_1 and A_2 through a data transformation, the **omega transformation**. Experience has shown that omega transformation gives a better additivity. After transforming p and q into the omega scale, then we can either add or subtract them.

Imagine p and q becomes equal after adjustment. This rate of mistake is called the **standard rate of mistake**, denoted by p_0. Then the input/output relationship is as shown in Table 6.7.

Table 6.7   Input/output table after standardization

		Output		Total
		0	1	
Input	0	$1 - p_0$	p_0	1
	1	p_0	$1 - p_0$	1
Total		1	1	2

Comparison of A_1 and A_2 can be made if we obtain the results shown in Table 6.7, where $p = q = p_0$.

6.4.2   Determination of the Standard Rate of Mistakes

From Table 6.6, the SN ratio of input 0 and the one from input 1 are individually calculated:

$$\eta_0 = -10 \log \left(\frac{1}{p} - 1 \right) \tag{6.15}$$

$$\eta_1 = -10 \log \left(\frac{1}{q} - 1 \right) \tag{6.16}$$

As mentioned in the previous section, we can expect arithmetical additivity from the omega transformation. Therefore, if k db is added to η_0, η_1 is affected by k db, or η_1 is reduced by k db. The addition and subtraction are made arithmetically. In order to make p and q equal, k is determined from the following equation:

$$-10 \log \left(\frac{1}{p_0} - 1 \right) = -10 \log \left(\frac{1}{p} - 1 \right) + k = -10 \log \left(\frac{1}{q} - 1 \right) - k \tag{6.17}$$

$$k = \frac{1}{2} \left[10 \log \left(\frac{1}{p} - 1 \right) - 10 \log \left(\frac{1}{q} - 1 \right) \right]$$

$$= 10 \log \sqrt{ \frac{\left(\frac{1}{p} - 1 \right)}{\left(\frac{1}{q} - 1 \right)} } \tag{6.18}$$

Putting Eq. (6.18) into either side of Eq. (6.17), we get

$$-10\log\left(\frac{1}{p_0}-1\right) = -10\log\left(\frac{1}{p}-1\right) + 10\log\sqrt{\frac{\left(\frac{1}{p}-1\right)}{\left(\frac{1}{q}-1\right)}} \tag{6.19}$$

$$= -10\log\sqrt{\left(\frac{1}{p}-1\right)\left(\frac{1}{q}-1\right)}$$

$$\frac{1}{p_0}-1 = \sqrt{\left(\frac{1}{p}-1\right)\left(\frac{1}{q}-1\right)} \tag{6.20}$$

$$p_0 = \frac{1}{1+\sqrt{\left(\frac{1}{p}-1\right)\left(\frac{1}{q}-1\right)}} \tag{6.21}$$

This is the equation for calculating the standard rate of mistake.

6.4.3   Standard SN Ratio

Standard SN ratio is the SN ratio when the two types of mistakes are equal. It is the index for evaluating the proficiency of separation, refining, filtration, purification, or various kinds of detecting devices. To derive the standard SN ratio, Table 6.5 is used again.

Table 6.8   Input/output table for two types of mistakes

		Output		Total
		0	1	
Input	0	n_{00}	n_{01}	n_0
	1	n_{10}	n_{11}	n_1
Total		r_0	r_1	n

The table shows there are n pieces of data (y's), which consist of either 0 or 1. This is true also for other symbols, such as n_{00}, n_{01}, ..., r_0 and r_1.

From Table 6.8, the total variation, S_T, is

$$S_T = y_1^2 + y_2^2 + \ldots + y_n^2 - S_m \tag{6.22}$$

where

$$S_m = \frac{(y_1 + y_2 + \ldots + y_n)^2}{n} = \frac{r_1^2}{n} \tag{6.23}$$

S_T is therefore

$$S_T = r_1 - \frac{r_1^2}{n} = r, \left(1 - \frac{r_1}{n}\right) = \frac{r_1 r_0}{n} \tag{6.24}$$

The linear equation showing the effect of the input signals 0 and 1 is given by

$$L = \frac{n_{11}}{n_1} - \frac{n_{01}}{n_0} \tag{6.25}$$

Its number of units, D, is

$$D = \left(\frac{1}{n_1}\right)^2 \times n_1 + \left(\frac{-1}{n_0}\right)^2 \times n_0 \tag{6.26}$$

Therefore, the variation of L is

$$S_L = \frac{L^2}{D} = \frac{\left(\frac{n_{11}}{n_1} - \frac{n_{01}}{n_0}\right)^2}{\left(\frac{1}{n_1}\right)^2 \times n_1 + \left(\frac{-1}{n_0}\right)^2 \times n_0} \tag{6.27}$$

$$= \frac{(n_0 n_{11} - n_1 n_{01})^2}{n_0^2 n_1 + n_1^2 n_0} = \frac{(n_{00} n_{11} - n_{10} n_{01})^2}{n_0 n_1 n}$$

The SN ratio is the ratio of signal variation to error variation. Let the pure (or net) variation of the linear equation and the error be S_L' and S_e', respectively. The SN ratio is then written as

$$\eta = 10\log\frac{\text{Variation of signal}}{\text{Variation of error}} = 10\log\frac{S'_L}{S'_e}$$

$$\approx 10\log\frac{S_L/S_T}{S_e/S_T} = 10\log\frac{\rho_L}{\rho_e} \qquad (6.28)$$

$$= 10\log\frac{\rho_L}{(1-\rho_L)} = -10\log\left(\frac{1}{\rho_L}-1\right)$$

where ρ_L and ρ_e are the degrees of contribution of the signal and the error, respectively. The degree of contribution, ρ, indicates how much the variability caused by L or e contributes to the total variation. It is measured in terms of ratio or percentage. Strictly speaking, pure variations must be used for calculation. However, the magnitude of error variance, V_e, is much smaller than that of the signal. Therefore, V_e is not subtracted from S_L, which is used as S'_L.

The degree of contribution of L, or ρ_L, is

$$\rho_L \approx \frac{S_L}{S_T} = \frac{\dfrac{(n_{00}n_{11}-n_{01}n_{10})^2}{n_0 n_1 n}}{\dfrac{r_0 r_1}{n}} \qquad (6.29)$$

$$= \frac{(n_{00}n_{11}-n_{01}n_{10})^2}{n_0 n_1 r_0 r_1}$$

If the standard rate of mistake, ρ_0, is used to express Eq. (6.29), then

$$\left. \begin{array}{l} n_{00} = n_{11} = 1 - p_0 \\[1mm] n_{01} = n_{10} = p_0 \\[1mm] r_0 = r_1 = n_0 = n_1 = 1 \end{array} \right\} \qquad (6.30)$$

Therefore, ρ_L is rewritten as

$$\rho_L = \frac{[(1-p_0)(1-p_0)-p_0 \times p_0]^2}{1 \times 1 \times 1 \times 1} \qquad (6.31)$$

$$= (1-2p_0)^2$$

and

$$\eta = -10 \log \left(\frac{1}{\rho_L} - 1 \right) = -10 \log \left[\frac{1}{(1 - 2p_0)^2} - 1 \right] \qquad (6.32)$$

To summarize the procedure of calculating the standard SN ratio,

1. Calculate the standard rate of mistake, p_0:

$$p_0 = \frac{1}{1 + \sqrt{\left(\frac{1}{p} - 1\right)\left(\frac{1}{q} - 1\right)}} \qquad (6.33)$$

2. Calculate the degree of contribution, ρ_L:

$$\rho_L = (1 - 2p_0)^2 \qquad (6.34)$$

3. Calculate the standard SN ratio, η:

$$\eta = -10 \log \left(\frac{1}{\rho_L} - 1 \right) \qquad (6.35)$$

In Section 6.4.1, a numerical example of a copper refining process was discussed. Comparison of the averages calculated from the raw data showed that A_2 is better than A_1. However, using the standard SN ratio will result in a reversed conclusion.

As presented, the two types of mistakes of A_1 were

$$p = 0.01$$

$$q = 0.07$$

Using Eq. (6.33), the standard rate of mistake, p_0, is calculated as

$$p_0 = \frac{1}{1 + \sqrt{\left(\frac{1}{0.01} - 1\right)\left(\frac{1}{0.07} - 1\right)}} \qquad (6.36)$$

$$= 0.02683$$

From Eq. (6.34), the degree of contribution, ρ, is calculated as

$$\rho = (1 - 2p_0)^2$$

$$= (1 - 2 \times 0.02683)^2 \tag{6.37}$$

$$= 0.89556$$

Putting ρ into Eq. (6.35), the SN ratio for A_1 is calculated:

$$\eta = -10 \log \left(\frac{1}{0.89556} - 1 \right) \tag{6.38}$$

$$= 9.33(\text{db})$$

The SN ratio of A_2 is similarly calculated. Here,

$$p = 0.04$$

$$q = 0.03$$

Therefore,

$$p_0 = \frac{1}{1 + \sqrt{\left(\frac{1}{0.04} - 1 \right) \left(\frac{1}{0.03} - 1 \right)}} \tag{6.39}$$

$$= 0.03465$$

$$q = (1 - 2 \times 0.03465)^2 \tag{6.40}$$

$$= 0.86620$$

$$\eta = -10 \log \left(\frac{1}{0.86620} - 1 \right) \tag{6.41}$$

$$= 8.11(\text{db})$$

The conclusion is that the separating capability of A_1 is better than A_2.

6.4.4   Comparison of Screening Machines

There are two types of automatic defective screening machines, A_1 and A_2. The machines were tested under stress conditions to separate go and no-go parts. Table 6.9 shows the results.

Without using the standard SN ratio approach, it seems that the total rate of mistakes for A_1 is smaller than for A_2.

$$\text{Total of mistakes for } A_1 = \frac{30 + 20}{5000} = 0.0100 \qquad (6.42)$$

$$\text{Total of mistakes for } A_2 = \frac{48 + 7}{5000} = 0.0110 \qquad (6.43)$$

Table 6.9   Input/output table of a screening experiment

	A_1				A_2		
	Go	No-go	Total		Go	No-go	Total
Good	2970	30	3000	Good	2952	48	3000
Bad	20	1980	2000	Bad	7	1993	2000
Total	2990	2010	5000	Total	2959	2041	5000

To use the standard SN ratio, we must calculate the rates of mistakes, p and q, for A_1 and A_2. These are shown in Table 6.10.

First, the SN ratio of A_1 is calculated. It happens in this case that $p = q$, Therefore,

$$p = q = p_0 = 0.0100 \qquad (6.44)$$

$$p_0 = (1 - 2p_0)^2 = (1 - 2 \times 0.0100)^2 = 0.9604 \qquad (6.45)$$

$$\eta = -10 \log\left(\frac{1}{0.9604} - 1\right) = 13.85(\text{db}) \qquad (6.46)$$

Table 6.10 Input/output table

	A_1				A_2		
	Go	No-go	Total		Go	No-go	Total
Good	0.9900	0.0100	1.0000	Good	0.9840	0.0160	1.0000
Bad	0.0100	0.9900	1.0000	Bad	0.0035	0.9965	1.0000
Total	1.0000	1.0000	2.0000	Total	0.9875	1.0125	2.0000

Next, the SN ratio of A_2 is calculated.

$$p_0 = \frac{1}{1 + \sqrt{\left(\frac{1}{\bar{p}} - 1\right)\left(\frac{1}{\bar{q}} - 1\right)}}$$

$$= \frac{1}{1 + \sqrt{\left(\frac{1}{0.0160} - 1\right)\left(\frac{1}{0.0035} - 1\right)}} \qquad (6.47)$$

$$= \frac{1}{1 + \sqrt{61.5 \times 284.7}} = 0.007501$$

$$\rho_0 = (1 - 2 \times 0.007501)^2 = 0.9702 \qquad (6.48)$$

$$\eta = -10\log\left(\frac{1}{0.9702} - 1\right) = 15.13(\text{db}) \qquad (6.49)$$

It is seen that A_2 is better than A_1 by

$$15.13 - 13.85 = 1.28(\text{db}) \qquad (6.50)$$

6.5   AIR-SEPARATION PROCESS

In this section, a separation process for tobacco leaves is illustrated. Tobacco leaves that are chopped to make cigarettes include leaf portion and stem portion. These may be separated into product and waste through an air-separation process (Table 6.11).

Table 6.11   Input/output table for tobacco leaf and stem separation process

Input		Output		
		Product	Waste	Total
Input	Leaf	n_{00}	n_{01}	n_0
	Stem	n_{10}	n_{11}	n_1

Table 6.12 shows the control factors and their levels in the process.

Table 6.12   Factors and levels for tobacco leaf/stem separation

Factors	Level 1	Level 2
A: Material flow (kg/min)	5	8
B: Main damper opening (scale)	3.5	4.5
C: Concurrent damper opening	3/4	1
D: Rpm of 1st blower	650	750
E: Rpm of 2nd blower	300	400
F: Opening of shutter A	closed	open
G: Combination of shutters	30/15	15/25

These factors were assigned to an L_{16} array. Results of the experiment and the calculated SN ratios are shown in Table 6.13.

The SN ratio for experiment no. 1 is calculated as an example. The values for the input/output are shown in Table 6.14.

As described in the previous section, the SN ratio for experimental run no. 1 is calculated as follows:

$$p = \frac{n_{01}}{n_0} = \frac{103}{14556} = 0.007076 \tag{6.51}$$

Table 6.13   Layout and results for tobacco leaf/stem separation

	A	B	E	C	F	G	D		Results				
No.	1	2	4	8	10	12	15	n_{00}	n_{01}	n_{10}	n_{11}	η	p_0
1	1	1	1	1	1	1	1	14453	103	47	71	4.993	0.064
2	1	1	1	2	2	2	2	14335	204	55	186	4.361	0.072
3	1	1	2	1	1	2	2	14395	121	55	118	5.453	0.059
4	1	1	2	2	2	1	1	14206	609	24	242	5.251	0.061
5	1	2	1	1	2	1	2	14420	179	50	39	1.799	0.112
6	1	2	1	2	1	2	1	14299	50	71	14	1.494	0.118
7	1	2	2	1	2	2	1	13976	256	74	43	-0.211	0.151
8	1	2	2	2	1	1	2	14507	48	41	13	2.951	0.093
9	2	1	1	1	1	1	2	21165	983	49	140	1.740	0.113
10	2	1	1	2	2	2	1	22137	1202	58	132	0.634	0.134
11	2	1	2	1	1	2	1	22040	870	76	94	-0.250	0.152
12	2	1	2	2	2	1	2	21340	1357	50	118	0.270	0.141
13	2	2	1	1	2	1	1	22832	1106	57	83	-0.380	0.154
14	2	2	1	2	1	2	2	21829	1118	121	75	-3.550	0.223
15	2	2	2	1	2	2	2	22481	987	90	72	-2.036	0.190
16	2	2	2	2	1	1	1	22412	793	82	78	-0.734	0.163

Table 6.14   Input/output values for tobacco leaf/stem separation

		Output		Total
		Product (0)	Waste (1)	
Input	Leaf (0)	$n_{00} = 14453$	$n_{01} = 103$	$n_0 = 14556$
	Stem (1)	$n_{10} = 47$	$n_{11} = 71$	$n_1 = 118$
Total		$r_0 = 14500$	$r_1 = 174$	$n = 14674$

$$q = \frac{n_{10}}{n_1} = \frac{47}{118} = 0.398305 \qquad (6.52)$$

$$p_0 = \cfrac{1}{1 + \sqrt{\left(\frac{1}{0.007076} - 1\right)\left(\frac{1}{0.398305} - 1\right)}} \tag{6.53}$$

$$= \frac{1}{1 + \sqrt{140.32 \times 1.510}} = 0.064283$$

$$p_0 = (1 - 2 \times 0.064283)^2 = 0.759397 \tag{6.54}$$

$$\eta = -10 \log\left(\frac{1}{0.759397} - 1\right) = 4.993 \text{(db)} \tag{6.55}$$

The SN ratios for other experiments are shown in Table 6.13. Table 6.15 is the response table.

Table 6.15 Response table for SN ratios

	Level 1	Level 2	Difference
A	3.26	-0.54	3.80
B	2.81	-0.08	2.89
E	1.39	1.34	0.05
C	1.39	1.34	0.05
F	1.51	1.21	0.30
G	1.99	0.74	1.25
D	1.35	1.37	0.02

From the response table, factors A, B, and G, are significant. The best condition is $A_1 B_1 G_1$, which is estimated by

$$\overline{T} = \frac{4.993 + 4.361 + \ldots - 0.734}{16} = 1.36 \tag{6.56}$$

$$\begin{aligned} \hat{\eta}_{A_1 B_1 G_1} &= \overline{T} + (\overline{A_1} - \overline{T}) + (\overline{B_1} - \overline{T}) + (\overline{G_1} - \overline{T}) \\ &= \overline{A_1} + \overline{B_1} + \overline{G_1} - 2\overline{T} \\ &= 3.26 + 2.81 + 1.99 - 2 \times 1.36 \\ &= 5.33 \text{(db)} \end{aligned} \tag{6.57}$$

6.6   CASE WITH TWO CLASSES WHERE TRUE VALUES OF SIGNAL FACTORS ARE UNKNOWN

This is the case when the results of measurement are either 0 or 1, such as go/no-go or pass/fail criteria, but unlike in Sections 6.4, here there is no signal factor.

Consider the case of sensory tests in which the true values of the samples to be tested are unknown and there are two inspectors, A_1 and A_2. Each inspector tests k pieces of samples, namely, $M_1, M_2, \ldots, M_k$. Each sample is tested r_0 times, with the results shown in Table 6.16.

Table 6.16   Sensory test results

Sample	M_1	Sub-total	M_2	Sub-total	...	M_k	Sub-total	Total
Repetition	$R_1 R_2 \ldots R_{r_0}$		$R_1 R_2 \ldots R_{r_0}$		...	$R_1 R_2 \ldots R_{r_0}$		
A_1	0 1 ... 1	y_{11}	1 1 ... 0	y_{12}	...	1 0 ... 1	y_{1k}	y_1
A_2	1 1 ... 0	y_{21}	0 1 ... 1	y_{22}	...	0 0 ... 0	y_{2k}	y_2

The SN ratio of A_1 is calculated as follows:
The correction factor is

$$S_m = \frac{(\text{Total})^2}{kr_0} = \frac{y_1^2}{kr_0} \tag{6.58}$$

The total variation is

$$S_T = 0^2 + 1^2 + \ldots + 1^2 - S_m$$

$$= y_1 - \frac{y_1^2}{kr_0} \quad \text{and} \quad f = kr_0 - 1 \tag{6.59}$$

The variation of the signal factor is

$$S_M = \frac{y_{11}^2 + y_{12}^2 + \ldots + y_{1k}^2}{r_0} - S_m \quad \text{and} \quad f = k - 1 \tag{6.60}$$

Note that there are two similar and therefore confusing symbols: S_m and S_M. S_m is the magnitude of the mean of kr_0 pieces of data in square terms. S_M is the variation of k pieces of samples around the mean.

The error variation is

$$S_e = S_T - S_M \quad \text{and} \quad f = k(r_0 - 1) \tag{6.61}$$

The variance of the signal factor is

$$V_M = \frac{S_M}{k-1} \tag{6.62}$$

The error variance is

$$V_e = \frac{S_e}{k(r_0 - 1)} \tag{6.63}$$

The SN ratio is

$$\eta = 10 \log \frac{\frac{1}{r_0}(V_M - V_e)}{V_e} \tag{6.64}$$

The SN ratio of A_2 is similarly calculated.

Example

Two inspectors, A_1 and A_2, inspected the feeling of four fabric samples, M_1, M_2, M_3, and M_4 by hand. Five repeated inspections were made, and the results were graded good and bad, as shown in Table 6.17. In the table, 1 and 0 represent good and bad, respectively.

The SN ratio of A_1 is calculated as follows:

$$S_m = \frac{8^2}{20} = 3.20 \tag{6.65}$$

$$S_T = 8 - \frac{8^2}{20} = 4.80 \quad \text{and} \quad f = 19 \tag{6.66}$$

Table 6.17   Fabric inspection

		M_1	M_2	M_3	M_4	Total
	R_1	1	1	0	0	
	R_2	1	0	0	0	
A_1	R_3	1	0	0	0	
	R_4	0	1	1	0	
	R_5	1	1	0	0	
	Total	4	3	1	0	8
	R_1	1	1	1	0	
	R_2	1	1	0	0	
A_2	R_3	0	0	1	1	
	R_4	0	1	0	0	
	R_5	1	1	1	0	
	Total	3	4	3	1	11

$$S_M = \frac{4^2 + 3^2 + 1^2 + 0^2}{5} - S_m \tag{6.67}$$

$$= 2.00 \quad \text{and} \quad f = 3$$

$$S_e = 4.80 - 2.00 = 2.80 \quad \text{and} \quad f = 16 \tag{6.68}$$

$$V_e = \frac{2.80}{16} = 0.175 \tag{6.69}$$

$$\eta(A_1) = 10 \log \frac{\frac{1}{5}\left(\frac{2.00}{(4-1)} - 0.175\right)}{0.175} \tag{6.70}$$

$$= 10 \log 0.562 = -2.50 (\text{db})$$

Similarly, the SN ratio of A_2 is calculated:

$$\eta(A_2) = -12.73 (\text{db}) \tag{6.71}$$

$A_1 z$ is better than A_2 by

$$\eta(A_1) - \eta(A_2) = -2.50 - (-12.73) = 10.23(\text{db}) \qquad (6.72)$$

6.7   CASE WITH THREE OR MORE CLASSES WHERE TRUE VALUES OF SIGNAL FACTORS ARE KNOWN

6.7.1   Equations for Calculation

In the case of sensory tests or pattern recognition, there are usually three or more samples or signal-factor levels. For example, there are k brands of beer to be recognized by two panel members. The test results are shown in Table 6.18.

In the table, sample M_1 was tested m_1 times; M_2 was tested m_2 times, etc. If sample M_1 was tested and judged as M_1', then y_{11} is expressed as 1, otherwise it is expressed as 0. If M_1' was judged as M_2', then y_{12} is expressed as 1, and so on.

The SN ratio is calculated by the following steps:

$$\left. \begin{array}{l} \text{weight of } M_1' \text{ is } \omega_1 = \dfrac{T^2}{y_1(T-y_1)} \\[3mm] \text{likewise, weight of } M_2' \text{ is } \omega_2 = \dfrac{T^2}{y_2(T-y_2)} \\[2mm] \cdots \\[1mm] \text{and weight of } M_k' \text{ is } \omega_k = \dfrac{T^2}{y_k(T-y_k)} \end{array} \right\} \qquad (6.73)$$

$$S_T = \left(y_1 - \frac{y_1^2}{T} \right) \times \omega_1 + \left(y_2 - \frac{y_2^2}{T} \right) \omega_2 + \ldots + \left(y_k - \frac{y_k^2}{T} \right) \times \omega_k \qquad (6.74)$$

$$= k \times T \qquad \text{and} \qquad f_T = (k-1)(T-1)$$

Table 6.18   Brand-name-recognition test

			Output			Total
		M'_1	M'_2	...	M'_k	
A_1						
	M_1	y_{11}	y_{12}	...	y_{1k}	m_1
Input	M_2	y_{21}	y_{22}	...	y_{2k}	m_2
	...	...	...	...	...	...
	M_k	y_{k1}	y_{k2}	...	y_{kk}	m_k
Total		y_1	y_2	...	y_k	T
A_2						
	M_1	y_{11}	y_{12}	...	y_{1k}	m_1
Input	M_2	y_{21}	y_{22}	...	y_{2k}	m_2
	...	...	...	...	...	...
	M_k	y_{k1}	y_{k2}	...	y_{kk}	m_k
Total		y_1	y_2	...	y_k	T

$$S_M = \left(\frac{y_{11}^2}{m_1} + \frac{y_{21}^2}{m_2} + \ldots + \frac{y_{k1}^2}{m_k} - \frac{y_1^2}{T}\right) \times \omega_1$$

$$+ \left(\frac{y_{12}^2}{m_1} + \frac{y_{22}^2}{m_2} + \ldots + \frac{y_{k2}^2}{m_k} - \frac{y_2^2}{T}\right) \times \omega_2 + \ldots \tag{6.75}$$

$$+ \left(\frac{y_{1k}^2}{m_1} + \frac{y_{2k}^2}{m_2} + \ldots + \frac{y_{kk}^2}{m_k} - \frac{y_k^2}{T}\right)$$

$$\times \omega_k \quad \text{and} \quad f_M = (k-1)(k-1)$$

$$S_e = S_T - S_M \quad \text{and} \quad f_e = (k-1)(T-k) \tag{6.76}$$

$$\frac{1}{\bar{r}} = \frac{1}{k}\left(\frac{1}{m_1} + \frac{1}{m_2} + \ldots + \frac{1}{m_k}\right) \tag{6.77}$$

where $\bar{r}$ is the harmonic mean of $m_1, m_2, \ldots m_k$.

$$V_M = \frac{S_M}{f_m} = \frac{S_M}{(k-1)(k-1)} \tag{6.78}$$

$$V_e = \frac{S_e}{f_e} = \frac{S_e}{(k-1)(T-k)} \tag{6.79}$$

$$\eta = 10 \log \frac{\frac{1}{\bar{r}}(V_M - V_e)}{V_e} \tag{6.80}$$

6.7.2 Beer-Taste Recognition

Experimentation was conducted on test groups to document their ability to differentiate the taste of beer provided by several suppliers. The test groups were defined by cigarette-smoking habits: eight smoking and five nonsmoking people were selected. Three different beers were tested, twice each.

In this case, the control factor is cigarette smoking ("yes" versus "no"); the signal factor is beer brand, and the noise factor is repetition. The panels were informed of the brands of beer being tested. The results are shown in Table 6.19.

The SN ratio of A_1 is calculated as follows:

$$\omega_1 = \frac{48^2}{18 \times (48 - 18)} = 4.267$$

$$\omega_2 = \frac{48^2}{15 \times 33} = 4.655 \tag{6.81}$$

$$\omega_3 = \frac{48^2}{15 \times 33} = 4.655$$

$$S_T = \left(18 - \frac{18^2}{48}\right)\omega_1 + \left(15 - \frac{15^2}{48}\right)\omega_2 + \left(15 - \frac{15^2}{48}\right)\omega_3 \tag{6.82}$$

$$= 48 + 48 + 48 = 144 \quad \text{and} \quad f = 94$$

Table 6.19 Beer-taste recognition

		Out					Out				Out			
	R_1	M'_1	M'_2	M'_3	T	R_2	M'_1	M'_2	M'_3	T	M'_1	M'_2	M'_3	T
A_1														
	M_1	4	4	1	9	M_1	5	4	1	10	M_1	9	8	2	19
In	M_2	4	3	2	9	M_2	2	4	1	7	M_2	6	7	3	16
	M_3	2	0	4	6	M_3	1	0	6	7	M_3	3	0	10	13
	T	10	7	7	24	T	8	8	8	24	T	18	15	15	48
A_2														
	M_1	4	0	0	4	M_1	2	1	0	3	M_1	6	1	0	7
In	M_2	1	3	0	4	M_2	1	5	0	6	M_2	2	8	0	10
	M_3	0	0	7	7	M_3	2	1	3	6	M_3	2	1	10	13
	T	5	3	7	15	T	5	7	3	15	T	10	10	10	30

$$S_M = \left(\frac{9^2}{19} + \frac{6^2}{16} + \frac{3^2}{13} - \frac{18^2}{48}\right)\omega_1 + \left(\frac{8^2}{19} + \frac{7^2}{16} + \frac{0^2}{13} - \frac{15^2}{48}\right)\omega_2$$

$$+ \left(\frac{2^2}{19} + \frac{3^2}{16} + \frac{10^2}{13} - \frac{15^2}{48}\right)\omega_3 \tag{6.83}$$

$$= 0.453 \times 4.267 + 1.743 \times 4.655 + 3.779 \times 4.655$$

$$= 27.64 \quad \text{and} \quad f = 4$$

$$S_e = S_T - S_M = 144 - 27.64 = 116.36 \quad \text{and} \quad f = 90 \tag{6.84}$$

$$\frac{1}{\bar{r}} = \frac{1}{3}\left(\frac{1}{19} + \frac{1}{16} + \frac{1}{13}\right) = 0.0640 \tag{6.85}$$

$$\eta = 10\log\frac{\frac{1}{\bar{r}}(V_M - V_e)}{V_e} = 10\log\frac{0.0640(6.91 - 1.29)}{1.29} \tag{6.86}$$

$$= 10\log 0.279 = -5.54 (\text{db})$$

SN ratio of A_2 is calculated as follows:

$$\left.\begin{array}{c} \omega_1 = \dfrac{30^2}{10 \times 20} = 4.5 \\[3mm] \omega_2 = \dfrac{30^2}{10 \times 20} = 4.5 \\[3mm] \omega_3 = \dfrac{30^2}{10 \times 20} = 4.5 \end{array}\right\} \tag{6.87}$$

$$S_T = 30 + 30 + 30 = 90 \quad \text{and} \quad f = 58 \tag{6.88}$$

$$S_M = \left(\frac{6^2}{7} + \frac{2^2}{10} + \frac{2^2}{13} - \frac{10^2}{30}\right)\omega_1 + \left(\frac{1^2}{7} + \frac{8^2}{10} + \frac{1^2}{13} - \frac{10^2}{30}\right)\omega_2$$

$$+ \left(\frac{0^2}{7} + \frac{0^2}{10} + \frac{10^2}{13} - \frac{10^2}{30}\right)\omega_3 \tag{6.89}$$

$$= 2.518 \times 4.5 + 3.287 \times 4.5 + 4.359 \times 4.5$$

$$= 45.74 \quad \text{and} \quad f = 4$$

$$S_e = 90.00 - 45.74 = 44.26 \quad \text{and} \quad f = 54 \tag{6.90}$$

$$\frac{1}{\bar{r}} = \frac{1}{3}\left(\frac{1}{7} + \frac{1}{10} + \frac{1}{13}\right) = 0.1066 \tag{6.91}$$

$$\eta = 10\log\frac{\frac{1}{\bar{r}}(V_M - V_e)}{V_e} = 10\log\frac{0.1066(11.44 - 0.0820)}{0.820} \tag{6.92}$$

$$= 10\log(1.38) = 1.40(\text{db})$$

From the results, the SN ratio of A_2 is better than A_1 by

$$1.40 - (-5.54) = 6.94(\text{db}) \tag{6.93}$$

6.8 CASE WITH THREE OR MORE CLASSES WHERE TRUE VALUES OF SIGNAL FACTORS ARE UNKNOWN

This is when there are three or more classes, but the order between classes has a technical meaning, such as when classes are categorized into good, normal, and bad, etc. **Accumulation analysis** is used for the analysis.

For example, two qualitative analysis methods, A_1 and A_2, are compared using k pieces of standard samples, $M_1, M_2, \ldots M_k$. The number of repetitions is three. In this case, A is a control factor, M is the signal factor, and repetition is a noise factor. The results of A_1 are shown in Table 6.20.

Table 6.20   Results of A_1*

Signal Factor	Results			Noncumulative Frequency			Cumulative Frequency		
	R_1	R_2	R_3	G	N	B	I	II	III
M_1	G	N	N	1	2	0	1	3	3
M_2	G	N	G	2	1	0	2	3	3
...	...	...	...	...	...	...	...	...	...
M_k	B	B	B	0	0	3	0	0	3
Total				T_G	T_N	T_B	T_I	T_{II}	T_{III}

**Note:* G=good; N=normal; B=bad; R=repetition;

The results of testing sample M_1 are: two normal and one good. For M_2, there are two good and one normal. These results are expressed under the columns G, N, and B of noncumulative frequency. For the columns of cumulative frequency,

$$I = G$$
$$II = G + N$$
$$III = G + N + B$$

In accumulation analysis, the results of cumulative frequency are used, (instead of using noncumulative frequency, as was done in the previous section). For the details of accumulation analysis, see Reference (1).

Since the results under column III are all equal, there is no necessity to analyze them, so only the results under columns I and II are analyzed. That is, only two classes are analyzed instead of three. The weights of case I and class II are calculated as

$$
\left.\begin{array}{l}
\omega_1 = \dfrac{T_{III}^2}{T_I(T_{III}-T_I)} \\[4mm]
\omega_2 = \dfrac{T_{III}^2}{T_{II}(T_{III}-T_{II})}
\end{array}\right\} \tag{6.94}
$$

The correction factor, S_m, is given by

$$
S_m = \frac{T_I^2}{T_{III}} \times \omega_1 + \frac{T_{II}^2}{T_{III}} \times \omega_2 \tag{6.95}
$$

The total variation, S_T, is

$$
S_T = \left(T_I - \frac{T_I^2}{T_{III}}\right) \times \omega_1 + \left(T_{II} - \frac{T_{II}^2}{T_{III}}\right) \times \omega_2
$$

$$
= (\textit{Number of classes analyzed} - 1) \times (\textit{Number of total Results})
$$

$$
= 2 \times T_{III} \quad \text{and} \quad f_T = 2 \times (T_{III} - 1) \tag{6.96}
$$

The variation of the signal, S_M, is

$$
S_M = \frac{1}{3}\left(1^2 + 2^2 + \ldots + 0^2\right) \times \omega_1
$$

$$
+ \frac{1}{3}\left(3^2 + 3^2 + \ldots + 0^2\right) \times \omega_2 \tag{6.97}
$$

$$
-S_m \quad \text{and} \quad f_M = 2 \times (k - 1)
$$

The error variation, S_e, is

$$S_e = S_T - S_M \quad \text{and} \quad f_e = f_T - f_M \tag{6.98}$$

The variance of the signal, V_M is

$$V_M = \frac{S_M}{f_M} \tag{6.99}$$

The error variance, V_e, is

$$V_e = \frac{S_e}{f_e} \tag{6.100}$$

The SN ratio is given by

$$\eta = 10 \log \frac{\frac{1}{r_0}(V_M - V_e)}{V_e} \tag{6.101}$$

where r_0 is the number of repetitions. In this case, $r_0 = 3$.

Example

In the example of qualitative analysis in this section, 5 standard samples were used to compare analysis methods A_1 and A_2. From each sample, four observations were made, meaning there were four repetitions. The results of A_1 are shown in Table 6.21.

Table 6.21   Results of experiment

Signal Factor	Results				Noncumulative Frequency			Cumulative Frequency		
	R_1	R_2	R_3	R_3	G	N	B	I	II	III
M_1	G	N	G	G	3	1	0	3	4	4
M_2	N	G	G	N	2	2	0	2	4	4
M_3	B	N	N	N	1	3	0	1	4	4
M_4	B	N	N	N	0	3	1	0	3	4
M_5	B	B	B	B	0	0	4	0	0	4
Total					6	9	6	6	15	20

The SN ratio of A_1 is calculated from these results, as follows:

$$\left.\begin{array}{l} \omega_1 = \dfrac{20^2}{6(20-6)} \; 4.7619 \\[4mm] \omega_2 = \dfrac{20^2}{15(20-15)} = 5.3333 \end{array}\right\} \tag{6.102}$$

$$S_m = \frac{6^2}{20} \times 4.7619 + \frac{15^2}{20} \times 5.3333 \tag{6.103}$$

$$= 68.5710$$

$$S_T = \left(6 - \frac{6^2}{20}\right) \times 4.7619 + \left(15 - \frac{15^2}{20}\right) \times 5.3333$$

$$= 20.0000 + 20.0000 = 40.0000 \quad \text{and} \quad f_T = 2 \times (20-1) = 38 \tag{6.104}$$

$$S_M = \frac{1}{4}\left(3^2 + 2^2 + 1^2 + 0^2 + 0^2\right) \times 4.7619$$

$$+ \frac{1}{4}\left(4^2 + 4^2 + 4^2 + 3^2 + 0^2\right) \times 5.3333 - 68.5710 \tag{6.105}$$

$$= 24.0951 \quad \text{and} \quad f_T = 2 \times (5-1) = 8$$

$$S_e = 40.0000 - 24.0951 = 15.9049 \quad \text{and} \quad f_T = 30 \tag{6.106}$$

$$V_M = \frac{24.0951}{8} = 3.0119 \tag{6.107}$$

$$V_e = \frac{15.9049}{30} = 0.53016 \tag{6.108}$$

$$\eta = 10 \log \frac{\frac{1}{4}(3.0119 - 0.53016)}{0.53016} \tag{6.109}$$

$$= 10 \log 1.1703 = 0.68 (\text{db})$$

6.9   CASE WITH THREE OR MORE CLASSES WITHOUT A SIGNAL FACTOR (CLASSES HAVE AN ORDER)

This is the case when there are only control and noise factors, but no signal factors, and results are classified into three or more classes with technical meaning, such as ranked data. In a welding experiment, for example, results are classified into five classes: class 1 is the best, and 5 is the worst, as shown in Table 6.22.

Table 6.22   Appearance of welded products

Grade	1	2	3	4	5
Results	Best	Better	Good	Worse	Worst
No. of data points	y_1	y_2	y_3	y_4	y_5
Distance	0	1	2	3	4

In the table, grade 1 is the best, so it can be considered as the ideal situation: The larger the grade number, the greater the distance from the ideal situation. Therefore, we can set a distance for each class shown in the table, and treat the results as a smaller-is-better characteristic. The SN ratio for a smaller-is-better case is given by

$$\sigma^2 = \frac{1}{y_1 + y_2 + y_3 + y_4 + y_5}$$
$$\times \left(0^2 \times y_1 + 1^2 \times y_2 + 2^2 \times y_3 + 3^2 \times y_4 + 4^2 \times y_5\right) \tag{6.110}$$

$$\eta = -10\log\sigma^2 \tag{6.111}$$

Example

Two kinds of welding rods, A_1 and A_2, were compared in an experiment, and the appearance was classified into five classes, as shown in Table 6.23.

Table 6.23 Welding experiment

	Best	Better	Good	Worse	Worst	Total
A_1	2	1	8	0	3	14
A_2	2	2	5	5	0	14
Distance	0	1	2	3	4	

The SN ratio of A_1 is

$$\eta_{A_1} = -10 \log \frac{1}{14} \left(0^2 \times 2 + 1^2 \times 1 + 2^2 \times 8 + 3^2 \times 0 + 4^2 \times 3 \right)$$

(6.112)

$$= -10 \log 5.78 = -7.62 \text{ (db)}$$

SN ratio of A_2 is

$$\eta_{A_2} = -10 \log \frac{1}{14} \left(0^2 \times 2 + 1^2 \times 2 + 2^2 \times 5 + 3^2 \times 5 + 4^2 \times 0 \right)$$

$$= 10 \log 4.79 = -6.80 \text{ (db)}$$

(6.113)

Therefore, A_2 is better than A_1 by

$$\text{gain} = -680 - (-7.62)$$

(6.114)

$$= 0.82 \text{ (db)}$$

7

SN Ratio With Complex Numbers

7.1 THE IDEAL FUNCTION OF ELECTRIC CIRCUITS _____

The input and output of alternating electric circuits are commonly defined by using complex numbers. To improve the stability of these circuits, it is recommended that SN ratios be used, as we have been doing for noncomplex numbers.

The ideal function of alternating current circuits with complex numbers, such as RC circuits, RL circuits, or RLC circuits, is the basic function of transforming voltage into current. The approaches we have discussed so far are the ways of analyzing data that consist of either real numbers only or imaginary numbers only. Generally, both types of numbers are equally important. Therefore, it is desirable to have a method by which we can analyze data that includes both real and imaginary numbers.

In the case of a simple RC circuit, its impedance, denoted by Z, is given by

$$Z = R + \frac{1}{j\omega C} \qquad (7.1)$$

where

R = resistance
ω = angular velocity
C = capacitance
j = $\sqrt{-1}$

It is seen from the above equation that the impedance consists of both real numbers and imaginary components. The imaginary portion is called **reactance**.

It is important that both the real and imaginary numbers have consistent values, so that the robustness of the function can be improved.

7.2   SN RATIO FOR COMPLEX NUMBERS

When real and imaginary numbers coexist, the real part and the imagimary part have been separately analyzed. Since all circuit theories are expressed as a complex number, it would be better to analyze the real and imaginary components together. The use of the Hermitian form makes it possible to do so.

In this section, the calculation of the SN ratios with complex numbers is illustrated. For the decomposition of variation that includes imaginary numbers, the so-called Hermitian form is used.

In the case of real numbers, the ideal function of the input, M, and the output, y, is given by

$$y = \beta M \tag{7.2}$$

The total variation of the following data

$$y_1, y_2, \ldots y_n$$

is calculated as

$$S_T = y_1^2 + y_2^2 + \ldots y_n^2 \tag{7.3}$$

This total variation is then decomposed into useful and harmful parts.

In the case of complex numbers, the total variation is defined as

$$S_T = y_1 \bar{y}_1 + y_2 \bar{y}_2 + \ldots + y_n \bar{y}_n \tag{7.4}$$

where $\bar{y}_i$ is the conjugate number of y_i.

S_T is then decomposed into the proportional part, S_β, and the rest. The proportional constant, β, is a complex number. But S_T, S_β, and S_e are all positive real numbers.

For example, a complex number, y, consists of two parts:

$$y = R + jX \tag{7.5}$$

where

R = resistance
X = reactance

Its conjugate number is

$$\bar{y} = R - jX \tag{7.6}$$

The product of y and $\bar{y}$ is

$$y\bar{y} = (R + jX)(R - jX)$$
$$= R^2 + X^2 \tag{7.7}$$

Note that the above value is a nonnegative real number, which corresponds to the magnitude of the total output.

We also discussed before that the proportional constant, β, is given by

$$
\begin{aligned}
S_\beta &= \frac{(M_1 y_1 + M_2 y_2 + \ldots + M_k y_k)^2}{M_1^2 + M_2^2 + \ldots + M_k^2} \\
&= \frac{(M_1 y_1 + M_2 y_2 + \ldots + M_k y_k)^2}{\left(M_1^2 + M_2^2 + \ldots + M_k^2\right)^2} \; (M_1^2 + M_2^2 + \ldots + M_k^2) \\
&= \beta^2 \left(M_1^2 + M_2^2 + \ldots + M_k^2\right)
\end{aligned} \tag{7.8}
$$

In the case of the complex number, there are two coefficients, namely, β and its conjugate number, $\bar{\beta}$:

$$\beta = \frac{\overline{M}_1 y_1 + \overline{M}_2 y_2 + \ldots + \overline{M}_k y_k}{M_1 \overline{M}_1 + M_2 \overline{M}_2 + \ldots + M_k \overline{M}_k} \tag{7.9}$$

$$\bar{\beta} = \frac{M_1 \bar{y}_1 + M_2 \bar{y}_2 + \ldots + M_k \bar{y}_k}{M_1 \overline{M}_1 + M_2 \overline{M}_2 + \ldots + M_k \overline{M}_k} \tag{7.10}$$

The variation of the proportional term, S_β, is calculated by

$$S_\beta = \beta\bar{\beta}(M_1\overline{M}_1 + M_2\overline{M}_2 + \ldots + M_k\overline{M}_k)$$

$$= \frac{(\overline{M}_1 y_1 + \overline{M}_2 y_2 + \ldots + \overline{M}_k y_k)(M_1\bar{y}_1 + M_2\bar{y}_2 + \ldots + M_k\bar{y}_k)}{M_1\overline{M}_1 + M_2\overline{M}_2 + \ldots + M_k\overline{M}_k} \quad (7.11)$$

The error variation is therefore

$$S_e = S_T - S_\beta \quad (7.12)$$

The SN ratio and sensitivity are calculated in the same way as before:

$$\eta = 10\log\frac{\frac{1}{r_0 r}(S_\beta - V_e)}{V_e} \quad (7.13)$$

$$S = 10\log\frac{1}{r_0 r}(S_\beta - V_e) \quad (7.14)$$

where r is the magnitude of the input and is given by

$$r = M_1\overline{M}_1 + M_2\overline{M}_2 + \ldots + M_k\overline{M}_k \quad (7.15)$$

Table 7.1 shows the results of an experiment with a noise factor of 3 levels.

Table 7.1   Results with complex numbers

	M_1	M_2	...	M_k	Linear Equation
N_1	y_{11}	y_{12}	...	y_{1k}	L_1
N_2	y_{21}	y_{22}	...	y_{2k}	L_2
N_3	y_{31}	y_{32}	...	y_{3k}	L_3

The linear equations are calculated by

$$\left.\begin{aligned}
L_1 &= \overline{M}_1 y_{11} + \overline{M}_2 y_{12} + \ldots + \overline{M}_k y_{1k} \\
L_2 &= \overline{M}_1 y_{21} + \overline{M}_2 y_{22} + \ldots + \overline{M}_k y_{2k} \\
L_3 &= \overline{M}_1 y_{31} + \overline{M}_2 y_{32} + \ldots + \overline{M}_k y_{3k}
\end{aligned}\right\} \quad (7.16)$$

Using the above equations, the SN ratio and sensitivity are calculated after the decomposition of data is made.

Total variation, S_T, is

$$S_T = y_{11}\bar{y}_{11} + y_{12}\bar{y}_{12} + \ldots + y_{3k}\bar{y}_{3k} \qquad \text{and} \qquad f = 3k \qquad (7.17)$$

The variation of the proportional constant, S_β, is

$$S_\beta = \frac{(L_1 + L_2 + L_3)(\bar{L}_1 + \bar{L}_2 + \bar{L}_3)}{3r} \qquad \text{and} \qquad f = 1 \qquad (7.18)$$

where

$$r = M_1\bar{M}_1 + M_2\bar{M}_2 + \ldots + M_k\bar{M}_k \qquad (7.19)$$

The variation of sensitivity, $S_{N\times\beta}$, is

$$S_{N\times\beta} = \frac{L_1\bar{L}_1 + L_2\bar{L}_2 + L_3\bar{L}_3}{r} - S_\beta \qquad \text{and} \qquad f = 2 \qquad (7.20)$$

The error variation, S_e, is

$$S_e = S_T - S_\beta - S_{N\times\beta} \qquad \text{and} \qquad f = 3k - 3 \qquad (7.21)$$

The total noise variation, S_N, is

$$S_N = S_e + S_{N\times\beta} \qquad \text{and} \qquad f = 3k - 1 \qquad (7.22)$$

The error variance for correction, V_e, is

$$V_e = \frac{S_e}{3k - 3} \qquad (7.23)$$

The variance of noise including nonlinearity, V_N, is

$$V_N = \frac{S_N}{3k - 1} \qquad (7.24)$$

The SN ratio, η, then is

$$\eta = 10\log\frac{\frac{1}{3r}(S_\beta - V_e)}{V_N} \qquad (7.25)$$

and the sensitivity, S, is

$$S = 10 \log \frac{1}{3r} (S_\beta - V_e) \tag{7.26}$$

7.3 THE HERMITIAN FORM

In matrix A, when the element of the ith column and kth row, denoted by a_{ik}, is equal to the conjugate complex number of a_{ki}, A is called the Hermitian matrix.

The form using the Hermitian matrix, (a_{ik}), is called the Hermitian form and is expressed by

$$\sum_{ik} a_{ik} \bar{x}_i x_k$$

where $\bar{x}$ is the conjugate complex number of x. This value is always a real number. The Hermitian form is the extention of the quadratic form. The theorems in quadratic form are mostly applicable to the Hermitian form.

Table 7.2 Inputs and outputs

	M_1	M_2	...	M_n
Output	y_1	y_2	...	y_n

In the case of real numbers, the error variation, S_e, is given by

$$S_e = S_T - S_\beta \tag{7.27}$$

By definition, S_e can be written as

$$
\begin{aligned}
S_e &= (y_1 - \beta M_1)^2 + (y_2 - \beta M_2)^2 + \ldots + (y_n - \beta M_n)^2 \\
&= \left(y_1^2 + y_2^2 + \ldots + y_n^2 \right) - 2\beta (M_1 y_1 + M_2 y_2 + \ldots + M_n y_n) \\
&\quad + \beta^2 \left(M_1^2 + M_2^2 + \ldots + M_n^2 \right) + \frac{(M_1 y_1 + M_2 y_2 + \ldots + M_n y_n)^2}{M_1^2 + M_2^2 + \ldots + M_n^2} \\
&\quad - \frac{(M_1 y_1 + M_2 y_2 + \ldots + M_n y_n)^2}{M_1^2 + M_2^2 + \ldots + M_n^2}
\end{aligned}
\tag{7.28}
$$

The value of β for minimizing S_e is given by

$$\beta = \frac{M_1 y_1 + M_2 y_2 + \ldots + M_n y_n}{M_1^2 + M_2^2 + \ldots + M_n^2} \tag{7.29}$$

In the case of a complex number, S_e is defined by

$$
\begin{aligned}
S_e &= (y_1 - \beta M_1)\overline{(y_1 - \beta M_1)} + \ldots + (y_n - \beta M_n)\overline{(y_n - \beta M_n)} \\
&= (y_1 \bar{y}_1 + \ldots + y_n \bar{y}_n) - \beta(M_1 \bar{y}_1 + \ldots + M_n \bar{y}_n) \\
&\quad - \bar{\beta}(\overline{M}_1 y_1 + \ldots + \overline{M}_n y_n) + \beta\bar{\beta}(M_1 \overline{M}_1 + \ldots + M_n \overline{M}_n) \\
&\quad + \frac{(\overline{M}_1 y_1 + \ldots + \overline{M}_n y_n)(M_1 \bar{y}_1 + \ldots + M_n \bar{y}_n)}{M_1 \overline{M}_1 + \ldots + M_n \overline{M}_n} \\
&\quad - \frac{(\overline{M}_1 y_1 + \ldots + \overline{M}_n y_n)(M_1 \bar{y}_1 + \ldots + M_n \bar{y}_n)}{M_1 \overline{M}_1 + \ldots + M_n \overline{M}_n} \tag{7.30} \\
&= (y_1 \bar{y}_1 + \ldots + y_n \bar{y}_n) \\
&\quad + \left(\beta\sqrt{M_1 \overline{M}_1 + \ldots + M_n \overline{M}_n} - \frac{M_1 \bar{y}_1 + \ldots + M_n \bar{y}_n}{\sqrt{M_1 \overline{M}_1 + \ldots + M_n \overline{M}_n}}\right) \\
&\quad \times \left(\bar{\beta}\sqrt{M_1 \overline{M}_1 + \ldots + M_n \overline{M}_n} - \frac{\overline{M}_1 y_1 + \ldots + \overline{M}_n y_n}{\sqrt{M_1 \overline{M}_1 + \ldots + M_n \overline{M}_n}}\right) \\
&\quad - \frac{(\overline{M}_1 y_1 + \ldots + \overline{M}_n y_n)(M_1 \bar{y}_1 + \ldots + M_n \bar{y}_n)}{M_1 \overline{M}_1 + \ldots + M_n \overline{M}_n}
\end{aligned}
$$

The values of β and $\bar{\beta}$ for minimizing S_e are

$$\beta = \frac{\overline{M}_1 y_1 + \ldots + \overline{M}_n y_n}{M_1 \overline{M}_1 + \ldots + M_n \overline{M}_n} \tag{7.31}$$

$$\bar{\beta} = \frac{M_1 \bar{y}_1 + \ldots + M_n \bar{y}_n}{M_1 \overline{M}_1 + \ldots + M_n \overline{M}_n} \tag{7.32}$$

The error variation is given by

$$S_e = y_1 \bar{y}_1 + \ldots + y_n \bar{y}_n$$

$$- \frac{(M_1 \bar{y}_1 + \ldots + M_n \bar{y}_n)(\overline{M}_1 y_1 + \ldots + \overline{M}_n y_n)}{(M_1 \overline{M}_1 + \ldots + M_n \overline{M}_n)} \qquad (7.33)$$

Example

A phase advancer is used in a car phone to advance the input signal by a certain degree. Its basic function is to make the input voltage be proportional to the output voltage.

In an experiment (see Reference 8) to improve a phase advancer, control factors such as coil type, phase-advancer combination, condenser type, and resistor type were investigated with the following signal factor:

$$M_1 = 224 + j \times 0 (\text{ mV})$$

$$M_2 = 707 + j \times 0$$

$$M_3 = 2236 + j \times 0$$

In this case, the signal-factor levels are real numbers.

Frequency was considered as an indicative factor and was varied as follows:

$$\omega_1 = 0.9 (\text{ MHz})$$

$$\omega_2 = 1.0 (\text{ MHz})$$

$$\omega_3 = 1.1 (\text{ MHz})$$

Two noise factor conditions were set:

$$N_1 = 10^\circ \text{C}$$

$$N_2 = 60^\circ \text{C}$$

Table 7.3 shows the results of experiment no. 1.

Table 7.3   Results of experiment

Noise	Freq.	M_1	M_2	M_3	L	L
	ω_1	77+j101	248+j322	769+j1017	1912068+j2524290	L_{11}
N_1	ω_2	87+j104	280+j330	870+j1044	2162768+j2590990	L_{21}
	ω_3	97+j106	311+j335	970+j1058	2410525+j2626277	L_{31}
	ω_1	77+j102	247+j322	784+j1025	1944901+j2542402	L_{12}
N_2	ω_2	88+j105	280+j331	889+j1052	2205476+j2609809	L_{22}
	ω_3	98+j107	311+j335	989+j1068	2453233+j2648861	L_{32}

The SN ratio is calculated as follows:
The total variation, S_T, is

$$S_T = y_{111}\bar{y}_{111} + y_{121}\bar{y}_{121} + \ldots + y_{332}\bar{y}_{332}$$

$$= (77 + j101)(77 - j101) + \ldots + (989 + j1068)(989 - j1068) \quad (7.34)$$

$$= 12448150 \quad \text{and} \quad f = 18$$

The variation of the proportional term, S_β, is

$$S_\beta = \frac{(L_{11} + L_{21} + \ldots + L_{32})(\bar{L}_{11} + \bar{L}_{21} + \ldots + \bar{L}_{32})}{6r}$$

$$= \frac{\left(13088971^2 + 15542629^2\right)}{6 \times 5549721} \quad (7.35)$$

$$= 12399857 \quad \text{and} \quad f = 1$$

The magnitude of input, r, is

$$r = M_1\bar{M}_1 + M_2\bar{M}_2 + M_3\bar{M}_3$$

$$= (224 + j0)(224 - j0) + (707 + j0)(707 - j0) + (2236 + j0)(2236 - j0)$$

$$= 5549721 \quad (7.36)$$

The linear equations of the proportional term, L, are

$$
\begin{aligned}
L_{11} &= \overline{M}_1 y_{111} + \overline{M}_2 y_{121} + \overline{M}_3 y_{131} \\
&= (224 - j0)(77 + j101) + (707 - j0) + (248 + j322) \\
&\quad + (2236 - j0)(769 + j1017) \\
&= 1912068 + j2524290 \\
L_{21} &= \overline{M}_1 y_{211} + \overline{M}_2 y_{221} + \overline{M}_3 y_{231} \\
&= 2162768 + j2590990 \\
&\cdots \\
L_{32} &= \overline{M}_1 y_{312} + \overline{M}_2 y_{322} + \overline{M}_3 y_{332} \\
&= 2453233 + j2648861
\end{aligned}
\right\} \tag{7.37}
$$

The variation of the proportional constant due to frequency, $S_{\omega \times \beta}$, is given by

$$
S_{\omega \times \beta} = \frac{(L_{11} + L_{12})(\overline{L}_{11} + \overline{L}_{12}) + (L_{21} + L_{22})(\overline{L}_{21} + \overline{L}_{22}) + (L_{31} + L_{32})(\overline{L}_{31} + \overline{L}_{32})}{2r}
$$

$$
- S_\beta \tag{7.38}
$$

$$
= 47676 \quad \text{and} \quad f = 2
$$

The variation due to temperature, $S_{N(\omega) \times \beta}$, is

$$
S_{N(\omega) \times \beta} = \frac{(L_{11}\overline{L}_{11} + L_{21}\overline{L}_{21} + L_{31}\overline{L}_{31} + L_{12}\overline{L}_{12} + L_{22}\overline{L}_{22} + L_{32}\overline{L}_{32})}{r}
$$

$$
- S_\beta - S_{\omega \times \beta} \tag{7.39}
$$

$$
= 533 \quad \text{and} \quad f = 3
$$

The error variation, S_e, is

$$S_e = S_T - S_\beta - S_{\omega \times \beta} - S_{N(\omega) \times \beta}$$

$$= 12448150 - 12399857 - 47676 - 533 \qquad (7.40)$$

$$= 84 \quad \text{and} \quad f = 12$$

The error variance for correction, V_e, is

$$V_e = \frac{S_e}{12} = 7 \qquad (7.41)$$

The total noise variation, S_N, is

$$S_N = S_e + S_{N(\omega) \times \beta}$$

$$= 84 + 533 = 617 \quad \text{and} \quad f = 15 \qquad (7.42)$$

The total noise variance, V_N, is

$$V_N = \frac{S_N}{15} = \frac{617}{15}$$

$$= 41 \qquad (7.43)$$

The SN ratio, η, is

$$\eta = 10 \log \frac{\dfrac{1}{6r}\left(S_\beta - V_e\right)}{V_N}$$

$$= 10 \log \frac{\dfrac{1}{6 \times 5549721}\left(12399857 - 1\right)}{41} \qquad (7.44)$$

$$= 10 \log 0.0090825$$

$$= -20.42 (\text{db})$$

and the Sensitivity, S, is

$$S = 10 \log \frac{1}{6r} \left(S_\beta - V_e \right)$$

$$= 10 \log 0.37239 = -4.29 (\text{db})$$

(7.45)

7.4 DEVELOPMENT OF A FILTER CIRCUIT

A filter circuit used in a car audio system has been customarily designed to meet the requirements of a new car. This is an example of designing a circuit through the robust technology development approach so that the circuit may be used for a group of cars (see Reference 12).

7.4.1 Explanation of the System

Because car audio systems generate music in a limited space, they require a special device called a filter circuit. Figure 7.1 shows the frequency response

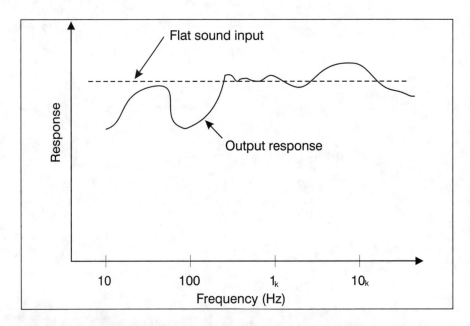

Figure 7.1 Acoustic characteristic in a car

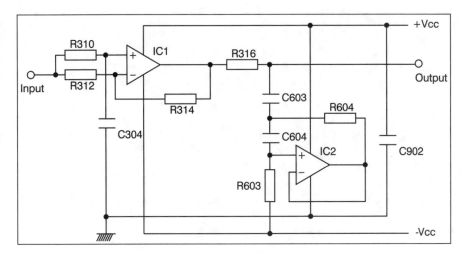

Figure 7.2   Filter circuit

characteristic of a flat sound input measured at the driver's seat. Since the response is not flat, a compensating circuit is needed to power the amplifier. Figure 7.2 is an example of a filter circuit.

Customarily, the frequency-characteristic curve is tuned to the target curve as the first step of design. Then an attempt is made to reduce variability. However, tuning is made by calculation from the constants of individual component parts, followed by assembling the hardware for confirmation. This is tedious and time-consuming. Needless to say, reducing variability is even more difficult.

In Quality Engineering, Parameter Design must be conducted by improving robustness first and tuning next. In this particular case, the target is a curve consisting of the outputs at many different frequencies. To adjust multiple targets, the method of least squares is used.

7.4.2   The Ideal Function

The ideal function of a filter circuit is that output voltage be proportional to input voltage.

$$y = \beta M$$

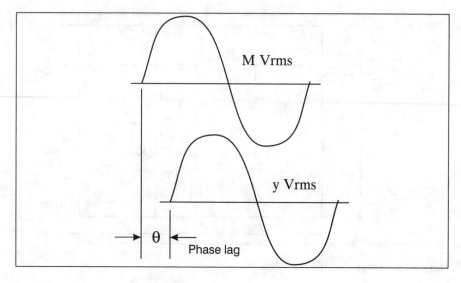

Figure 7.3   Input/output relationship

where

y = output voltage
M = input voltage

In such a circuit, output voltage has a phase lag from input voltage. The lag is denoted by θ, as shown in Fig. 7.3. M is a real number, while y and β are complex numbers. The zero-point proportional equation is used to define the ideal function.

7.4.3   Target Frequency Characteristic

Figure 7.4 is an example of the frequency characteristic to be targeted.

7.4.4   Factors, Levels, and Layout

Table 7.4 shows control factors and their levels. Table 7.5 shows the compounded noise factor. Compounding was made after a preliminary study to find the trend of each noise factor. Tables 7.6 and 7.7 show the signal factor

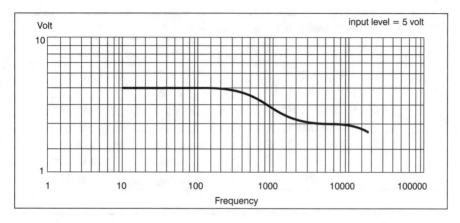

Figure 7.4   Target frequency characteristic

and the indicative factor, respectively, and their levels. The input/output format for data collection is shown in Table 7.8. An L_{18} was used for the layout. Table 7.9 shows the results of one experimental run.

In the L_{18} orthogonal array, there are 18 control-factor combinations. In each combination, there are 4 signal-factor levels, 2 compounded noise factor levels. In addition, there are 18 frequency levels for each of the above combination. The total number of outputs to calculate will be

$$18 \times 4 \times 2 \times 18 = 2592$$

Table 7.4   Control factors and levels

	Factor	Level 1	Level 2	Level 3
A	R310*C304	6.435 x E-4	1.287 x E-3	2.574 x E-3
B	C304	2.200 x E-8	3.900 x E-8	6.800 x E-8
C	C603*C604*R604*R603	8.424 x E-9	1.053 x E-8	1.264 x E-8
D	C603*R604	5.265 x E-5	1.053 x E-4	2.106 x E-4
E	C603*(R604 + R316)	2.182 x E-4	2.727 x E-4	3.272 x E-4
F	C603	1.800 x E-8	2.700 x E-8	4.700 x E-8
G	C604	6.800 x E-10	1.000 x E-9	1.800 x E-9

Table 7.5   Compounded noise factor and levels

		N_1	N_2
	R310*C304	Small	Large
	C304	Small	Large
	C603*C604*R604*R603	Large	Medium
N	C603*R604	Small	Large
	C603*(R603 + R316)	Small	Large
	C604	Small	Medium
	C604	Small	Medium

Table 7.6   Signal factor and levels

		Level 1	Level 2	Level 3	Level 4
M	Input Voltage	5 μV	500 μV	50 mV	5 V

Table 7.7   Indicative factor

		Level 1	...	Level 18
f	Frequency	10 Hz	...	25 kHz

Table 7.8   Input/output format

		M_1	M_2	M_3	M_4	L
	f_1	y_{11}	y_{12}	y_{13}	y_{14}	L_1
	f_2	y_{21}	y_{22}	y_{23}	y_{24}	L_2
N_1	...	....	....	....	....	....
	f_{17}	y_{171}	y_{172}	y_{173}	y_{174}	L_{17}
	f_{18}	y_{181}	y_{182}	y_{183}	y_{184}	L_{18}
	f_1	y_{191}	y_{192}	y_{193}	y_{194}	L_{19}
	f_2	y_{201}	y_{202}	y_{203}	y_{204}	L_{20}
N_2	...	....	....	....	....	....
	f_{17}	y_{351}	y_{352}	y_{353}	y_{354}	L_{35}
	f_{18}	y_{361}	y_{362}	y_{363}	y_{364}	L_{36}

Calculation

The equations to calculate the SN ratio and sensitivity follow:

$$\left.\begin{aligned} L_1 &= M_1 y_{11} + M_2 y_{12} + M_3 y_{13} + M_4 y_{14} \\ &\cdots \\ L_{36} &= M_1 y_{361} + M_2 y_{362} + M_3 y_{363} + M_4 y_{364} \end{aligned}\right\} \qquad (7.46)$$

$$S_T = y_{11}\bar{y}_{11} + y_{12}\bar{y}_{12} + \cdots + y_{363}\bar{y}_{363} + y_{364}\bar{y}_{364} \quad \text{and} \quad f = 144 \quad (7.47)$$

$$r = M_1^2 + M_2^2 + M_3^2 + M_4^2 \qquad (7.48)$$

$$L = L_1 + L_2 + L_3 + \cdots + L_{34} + L_{35} + L_{36} \qquad (7.49)$$

$$S_\beta = \frac{L \times \bar{L}}{18 \times 2 \times r} \quad \text{and} \quad f = 1 \qquad (7.50)$$

$$\left.\begin{aligned} L_{N_1} &= L_1 + L_2 + \cdots + L_{17} + L_{18} \\ L_{N_2} &= L_{19} + L_{20} + \cdots + L_{35} + L_{36} \end{aligned}\right\} \qquad (7.51)$$

$$S_{N\times\beta} = \frac{L_{N_1}\bar{L}_{N_1} + L_{N_2}\bar{L}_{N_2}}{18 \times r} - S_\beta \quad \text{and} \quad f = 1 \qquad (7.52)$$

$$\left.\begin{aligned} L_{f_1} &= L_1 + L_{19} \\ L_{f_{18}} &= L_{18} + L_{36} \end{aligned}\right\} \qquad (7.53)$$

$$S_{f\times\beta} = \frac{L_{f_1}\bar{L}_{f_1} + \cdots + L_{f_{18}}\bar{L}_{f_{18}}}{2 \times r} - S_\beta \quad \text{and} \quad f = 17 \qquad (7.54)$$

$$V_e = \frac{S_T - S_\beta - S_{N\times\beta} - S_{f\times\beta}}{18 \times 2 \times 4 - 1 - 1 - 17} \qquad (7.55)$$

$$V_N = \frac{S_T - S_\beta - S_{f\times\beta}}{18 \times 2 \times 4 - 1 - 17} \qquad (7.56)$$

$$\eta = 10 \times \log \frac{S_\beta - V_e}{18 \times 2 \times r \times V_N} \, (\mathrm{db}) \qquad (7.57)$$

$$S = 10 \times \log \frac{S_\beta - V_e}{18 \times 2 \times r} \, (\mathrm{db}) \qquad (7.58)$$

Table 7.9 shows part of the results of simulation no. 1 of the L_{18} orthogonal array.

Table 7.9 Results (partial) of simulation no. 1

		M_1	M_2	M_3	M_4
N_1	f_1	4.99E(-6) - j3.8E(-7)	4.99E(-4) - j3.8E(-5)	0.0499 - j0.00376	4.99 - j0.376
	f_2	4.96E(-6) - j5.9E(-7)	4.96E(-4) - j5.9E(-5)	0.0496-j0.00594	4.96 - j0.594
	...	....	....	....	....
	f_{17}	-1.2E(-6) + j2.9E(-7)	-1.2E(-4) + j2.93E(-5)	-0.0120 - j0.00293	-1.20 - j0.293
	f_{18}	-1.1E(-6) + j2.93E(-7)	-1.1E(-4) + j2.93E(-5)	-0.0111 - j0.00293	-1.11 - j0.293
N_2	f_1	4.97E(-6) - j5.3E(-7)	4.97E(-4) - j5.3E(-5)	0.0497 - j0.00535	4.97 - j0.535
	f_2	4.93E(-6) - j8.4E(-7)	4.93E(-4) - j8.4E(-5)	0.0493 - j0.00844	4.93 - j0.844
	...	....	....	....	....
	f_{17}	-1.2E(-6) + j3.1E(-7)	-1.2E(-4) + j3.1E(-5)	-0.0124 + j0.0031	-1.24 - j0.310
	f_{18}	-1.2E(-6) + j2.95E(-7)	-1.2E(-4) + j2.95E(-5)	-0.0115 + j0.00295	-1.15 - j0.295

From the data in Table 7.9, calculations were made to give the following results:

$$S_T = 515.6716 \qquad (7.59)$$

$$r = 25.0025 \qquad (7.60)$$

$$L_1 = 24.92857 - j1.87916$$

$$\left.\begin{array}{l} \cdots \\ L_{36} = -5.77217 + j1.476996 \end{array}\right\} \quad (7.61)$$

$$L = 66.96326 - j200.768 \quad (7.62)$$

$$S_\beta = 49.76395 \quad (7.63)$$

$$\left.\begin{array}{l} L_{N_1} = 50.90719 - j100.546 \\ L_{N_2} = 16.05607 - j100.222 \end{array}\right\} \quad (7.64)$$

$$S_{N \times \beta} = 1.349538 \quad (7.65)$$

$$\left.\begin{array}{l} L_{f_1} = 49.78403 - j4.55382 \\ \cdots \\ L_{f_{18}} = -11.3187 + j2.941412 \end{array}\right\} \quad (7.66)$$

$$S_{f \times \beta} = 459.0557 \quad (7.67)$$

$$V_e = 0.044019 \quad (7.68)$$

$$V_N = 0.054381 \quad (7.69)$$

$$\eta = 0.07(\text{db}) \quad (7.70)$$

$$S = -12.58(\text{db}) \quad (7.71)$$

Table 7.10   SN ratio and sensitivity

Experiment No.	1	2	3	4	5	6
η	0.07	0.59	1.70	0.40	2.33	-0.88
S	-12.58	-12.25	-10.98	-11.80	-9.83	-12.96
Experiment No.	7	8	9	10	11	12
η	-0.75	3.57	5.40	2.47	0.83	0.32
S	-12.73	-8.27	-6.42	-9.84	-12.47	-12.17
Experiment No.	13	14	15	16	17	18
η	5.34	-1.58	-0.21	1.04	7.05	0.26
S	-6.45	-13.80	-12.56	-10.93	-4.64	-11.67

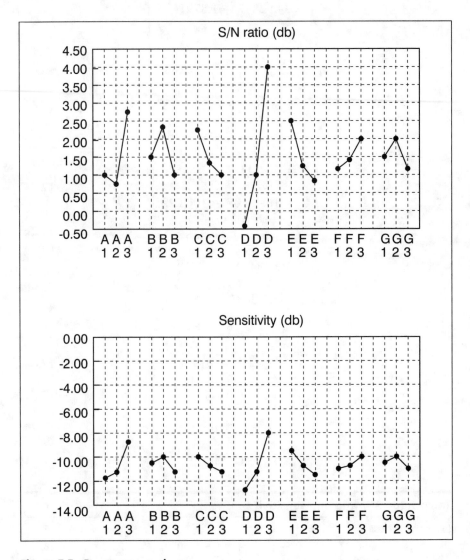

Figure 7.5 Response graph

Table 7.10 shows the SN ratios and sensitivity, and Fig. 7.5 shows their effects. The sensitivity in the table shows the average of the whole frequency spectrum; there is no engineering significance. Instead, the sensitivity of each frequency is important because it will be used for tuning.

Optimum Condition and Estimation

The control-factor combination to maximize the SN ratio is selected as

$$A_3 B_2 C_1 D_3 E_1 F_3 G_2$$

The benchmark condition is

$$A_2 B_3 C_3 D_1 E_3 F_1 G_3$$

From these conditions, the process averages and the gains from estimation and confirmation are calculated, and shown in Table 7.11.

Table 7.11   Confirmation of gain

	Estimation		Confirmation	
	η (db)	S (db)	η (db)	S (db)
Optimum Condition	7.00	-4.69	7.16	-4.58
Worst Condition	-2.22	-14.60	-1.72	-14.09
Gain	9.22	9.91	8.88	9.51

It is seen from the table that the conclusions were well-reproduced. However, the frequency-characteristic curve under the optimum condition significantly deviates from the target, as shown in Fig. 7.6.

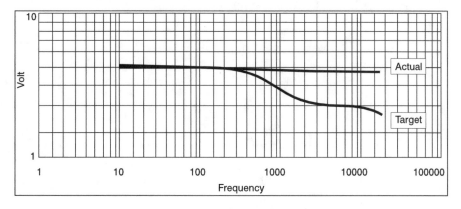

Figure 7.6   Comparison of frequency-characteristic curves

7.4.7 Tuning

The following are the steps to tune the frequency characteristic after maximizing the SN ratio:

Step 1. Calculation of sensitivity for each frequency
Step 2. Selection of control factor(s) for tuning
Step 3. Determination of the empirical equation for frequency
Step 4. Entering the optimum condition levels to the empirical quation
Step 5. Solving simultaneous equations to determine the tuning-factor
       level(s)
Step 6. Confirmation

Step 1. Calculation of sensitivity

From the raw data, the sensitivity of each frequency is calculated from the following format:

	M_1	M_2	M_3	M_4	L
N_1	y_{11}	y_{21}	y_{31}	y_{41}	L_1
N_2	y_{12}	y_{22}	y_{32}	y_{42}	L_2

Calculations are made using the following equations:

$$S_T = y_{11}\bar{y}_{11} + y_{21}\bar{y}_{21} + \ldots + y_{42}\bar{y}_{42} \tag{7.72}$$

$$L_1 = \bar{M}_1 y_{11} + \bar{M}_2 y_{21} + \bar{M}_3 y_{31} + \bar{M}_4 y_{41} \tag{7.73}$$

$$L_2 = \bar{M}_1 y_{12} + \bar{M}_2 y_{22} + \bar{M}_3 y_{32} + \bar{M}_4 y_{42} \tag{7.74}$$

$$r = M_1 \bar{M}_1 + M_2 \bar{M}_2 + M_3 \bar{M}_3 + M_4 \bar{M}_4 \tag{7.75}$$

$$S_\beta = \frac{(L_1 + L_2) \times (\bar{L}_1 + \bar{L}_2)}{2 \times r} \tag{7.76}$$

$$S_{N \times \beta} = \frac{L_1 \bar{L}_1 + L_2 \bar{L}_2}{r} - S_\beta \tag{7.77}$$

$$V_e = \frac{S_T - S_\beta - S_{N \times \beta}}{8 - 1 - 1} \qquad (7.78)$$

$$S = 10 \log \frac{1}{2r}(S_\beta - V_e)(\text{db}) \qquad (7.79)$$

Table 7.12 shows the sensitivity at 4 kHz as an example.

Table 7.12 Calculated sensitivity at 4kHz

No.	1	2	3	4	5	6
Sensitivity	-10.10	-7.39	-3.56	-7.27	-3.57	-9.99
No.	7	8	9	10	11	12
Sensitivity	-13.29	-5.51	-2.05	-2.08	-13.13	-5.50
No.	13	14	15	16	17	18
Sensitivity	-0.27	-11.79	-8.95	-8.93	-0.27	-11.65

Step 2. Selection of control factors for tuning

Figure 7.7 shows the factorial effects on sensitivity. From similar figures at other frequencies (which are not shown here), it was concluded that only factors D and E affect sensitivity. Therefore, D and E were selected to be used for tuning.

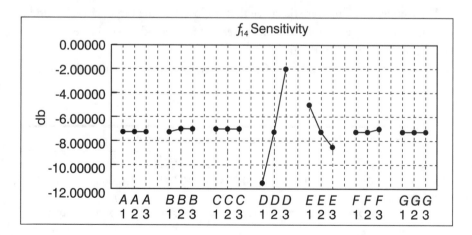

Figure 7.7 Response graph of sensitivity at 4 kHz

Step 3.   Determination of the empirical equation for each frequency

For example, the empirical equation at 4 kHz is determined as follows:

$$S_{4kHz} = -6.96 - 0.0187(\log A + 2.890)$$

$$+ 0.0831(\log B + 7.409)$$

$$- 4063016\left(C - 1.05 \times 10^8\right) \qquad (7.80)$$

$$+ 16.10(\log D + 3.978)$$

$$- 30240(E - 0.000273)$$

Step 4.   Entering the optimum condition levels to the empirical equation

The levels of the optimum condition were put into the empirical equation to get an equation for D and E. For example, the equation at 4 kHz is

$$S_{4Khz} = -6.95 + 16.10(\log D + 3.98) - 30240(E - 0.000273) \qquad (7.81)$$

Since there are 18 frequencies, 18 equations were prepared.

Step 5.   Solving simultaneous equations to determine the tuning-factor levels

The frequency-characteristic curve that is closest to the target curve could be obtained if the sensitivity at each frequency are adjusted closest to the corresponding values in the table.

The target sensitivity at each frequency is converted into the db scale, as shown in Table 7.13.

Table 7.13   Target frequency characteristic (sensitivity)

Frequency	f_1	f_2	f_3	f_4	f_5	f_6
Sensitivity	-0.002	-0.003	-0.008	-0.018	-0.045	-0.110
Frequency	f_7	f_8	f_9	f_{10}	f_{11}	f_{12}
Sensitivity	-0.269	-0.635	-1.390	-2.668	-4.297	-5.791
Frequency	f_{13}	f_{14}	f_{15}	f_{16}	f_{17}	f_{18}
Sensitivity	-6.804	-7.376	-7.736	-8.111	-8.679	-9.474

Each of these 18 values is put to the left side of the corresponding equation shown in Step 4. Thus, there are 18 equations with two unknowns, D and E. The method of least squares is used to determine D and E, which minimizes the differences between both sides of the equations.

The total of the squares of these differences between both sides are calculated. We differentiate this total with respect to D and E, to obtain the following two equations:

$$1962(\log D + 3.98) - 3853740(E - 0.000273) = -68.19 \qquad (7.82)$$

$$-3853740(\log D + 3.98) + 7922619779(E - 0.000273) = 144004 \quad (7.83)$$

Solving these equation gives the following values:

$$D = 0.00011057 \qquad (7.84)$$

$$E = 0.0003012 \qquad (7.85)$$

These are selected as the optimum conditions. The optimum conditions of the factors other than D and E have already been selected based on the SN ratio.

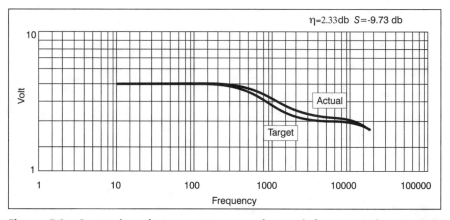

Figure 7.8 Comparison between target and actual frequency-characteristic curves

Step 6. Confirmation

Figure 7.8 shows the comparison between target and actual frequency-characteristic curves.

Because the level of factor D was selected for tuning instead of maximizing the SN ratio, there is an offset in the SN ratio. However, the frequency-characteristic curve is very close to the target, with a significant gain in the SN ratio.

Layout and Analysis of Youden Squares

8.1 PURPOSE OF USING YOUDEN SQUARES _____

Youden squares are a type of layout used in the design of experiments. A Youden square is a fraction of a Latin square, or an incomplete Latin square. The objective of using Youden squares in this section is to efficiently utilize an L_{18} orthogonal array in order to obtain more information from the same number of runs of the array.

Table 8.1 shows a Latin square in two standard formats, (a) and (b). Format (a) is the layout commonly seen in experimental design texts. Format (b) shows the contents using an L_9 orthogonal array, where only the first three columns of the array are shown.

Table 8.2 shows a Youden square; notice that a portion of the layout in Table 8.1 is missing. In the Latin square, factors A, B, and C are orthogonal to each other, and the effect of each factor can be separated. But in Youden squares, factors B and C are not orthogonal. However, the effects of these three factors can be independently determined by solving the equations generated from the relationship shown of this layout. In the table, y's show the responses of the experiment.

Comparing the arrays in Tables 8.2(b) and 8.3, the first two columns of the two arrays correspond to each other, with the exception that there are three repetitions in Table 8.3. In other words, combination $A_1 B_1$ appears once in Table 8.2(b), while the combination appears three times (Nos. 1, 2, and 3) in Table 8.3. Another exception is that column C does not exist in

Table 8.1 Latin square

(a)

	B_1	B_2	B_3
A_1	C_1	C_2	C_3
A_2	C_2	C_3	C_1
A_3	C_3	C_1	C_2

(b)

No.	A 1	B 2	C 3	y
1	1	1	1	y_1
2	1	2	2	y_2
3	1	3	3	y_3
4	2	1	2	y_4
5	2	2	3	y_5
6	2	3	1	y_6
7	3	1	3	y_7
8	3	2	1	y_8
9	3	3	2	y_9

the L_{18} array (see Table 3.10). However, we can obtain the extra information for a 3-level factor without adding extra experimental runs. This is understood from the degrees of freedom in L_{18}. It is known that the number of degrees of freedom means the number of types of information that is available. In the normal assignment of the L_{18}, one 2-level factor and seven 3-level factors are assigned in the array; its total number of degrees of freedom is 15, but the total number of runs in L_{18} is 18, meaning the total number of degrees of freedom is 17. This suggests that 2 more degrees of freedom, or 2 kinds of information are obtainable. The 3-level factor C has 2 degrees of freedom. In this way, one 2-level factor and eight 3-level factors can be assigned to the L_{18} array by using the Youden square, as shown in Table 8.3.

Table 8.2   Youden square

(a)

	B_1	B_2	B_3
A_1	$C_1(y_1)$	$C_2(y_2)$	$C_3(y_3)$
A_2	$C_2(y_4)$	$C_3(y_5)$	$C_1(y_6)$

(b)

	A	B	C	
No.	1	2	3	y
1	1	1	1	y_1
2	1	2	2	y_2
3	1	3	3	y_3
4	2	1	2	y_4
5	2	2	3	y_5
6	2	3	1	y_6

8.2   CALCULATION OF MAIN EFFECTS

In Table 8.3, one 2-level factor (A) and eight 3-level factors $(B, C, ..., I)$ are assigned and results (such as SN ratios) $y'_1, y'_2, ..., y'_{18}$ were obtained. Calculation of the main effects $A, D, E, F, G, H,$ and I are exactly identical to regular calculation. Main effects B and C are calculated after calculating their level averages as follows.

Subtotals $y_1, y_2, ..., y_6$ are calculated as shown in Table 8.3.

$$\left.\begin{array}{l} y_1 = y'_1 + y'_2 + y'_3 \\ y_2 = y'_4 + y'_5 + y'_6 \\ \cdots \\ y_6 = y'_{16} + y'_{17} + y'_{18} \end{array}\right\} \tag{8.1}$$

Table 8.3 Orthogonal array L_{18}

No.	A 1	B 2	C 9	D 3	... ...	I 8	Results	Subtotal
1	1	1	1				y'_1	
2	1	1	1				y'_2	y_1
3	1	1	1				y'_3	
4	1	2	2				y'_4	
5	1	2	2				y'_5	y_2
6	1	2	2				y'_6	
7	1	3	3				y'_7	
8	1	3	3				y'_8	y_3
9	1	3	3				y'_9	
10	2	1	2				y'_{10}	
11	2	1	2				y'_{11}	y_4
12	2	1	2				y'_{12}	
13	2	2	3				y'_{13}	
14	2	2	3				y'_{14}	y_5
15	2	2	3				y'_{15}	
16	2	3	1				y'_{16}	
17	2	3	1				y'_{17}	y_6
18	2	3	1				y'_{18}	

Let the effect of each factor level, A_1, A_2, B_1, B_2, B_3, C_1, C_2, and C_3 be denoted by a_1, a_2, b_1, b_2, b_3, c_1, c_2, and c_3, respectively, as shown in Fig. 8.1.

For example, a_1 is the deviation of A_1 from the grand average, $\overline{T}$. As described previously, a_1 and a_2 can be determined as usual without considering the layout of Youden squares. The effects of factor levels of B and C are calculated as follows:

$$b_1 = \frac{1}{9}(y_1 - y_2 + y_4 - y_6)$$

$$b_2 = \frac{1}{9}(y_2 - y_3 - y_4 + y_5) \qquad (8.2)$$

$$b_3 = \frac{1}{9}(-y_1 + y_3 - y_5 + y_6)$$

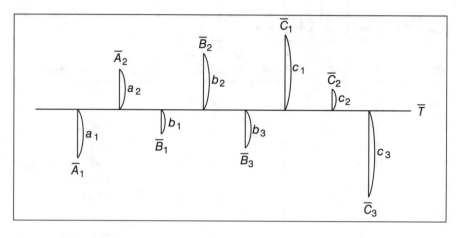

Figure 8.1 Main effects of A, B, and C

$$c_1 = \frac{1}{9}(y_1 - y_3 - y_4 + y_6)$$

$$c_2 = \frac{1}{9}(-y_1 + y_2 + y_4 - y_5) \qquad (8.3)$$

$$c_3 = \frac{1}{9}(-y_2 + y_3 + y_5 - y_6)$$

8.3   NUMERICAL EXAMPLE

In an experiment, a 2-level factor A and eight 3-level factors $B, C, D, E, F, G, H,$ and I were assigned to an L_{18} array by the Youden square layout, as shown in Table 8.4. From the results of 18 runs, subtotals are calculated.

The effect of each factor level of B and C is calculated:

$$b_1 = \frac{1}{9}(y_1 - y_2 + y_4 - y_6)$$

$$= \frac{1}{9}(12.08 - 9.13 + 24.11 - 72.13) \qquad (8.4)$$

$$= -5.01$$

Table 8.4   Results of experiment

No.	A 1	B 2	C 9	D 3	... ...	I 8	η	Subtotal
1	1	1	1				3.82	
2	1	1	1				3.91	12.08(y_1)
3	1	1	1				4.35	
4	1	2	2				3.22	
5	1	2	2				3.08	9.13(y_2)
6	1	2	2				2.83	
7	1	3	3				7.99	
8	1	3	3				8.18	24.17(y_3)
9	1	3	3				8.00	
10	2	1	2				7.71	
11	2	1	2				7.88	24.11(y_4)
12	2	1	2				8.52	
13	2	2	3				-15.81	
14	2	2	3				-13.07	−51.15(y_5)
15	2	2	3				-22.27	
16	2	3	1				24.05	
17	2	3	1				26.53	72.13(y_6)
18	2	3	1				21.55	

$$b_2 = \frac{1}{9}(y_2 - y_3 - y_4 + y_5)$$

$$= \frac{1}{9}(9.13 - 24.17 - 24.11 - 51.15) \tag{8.5}$$

$$= -10.03$$

$$b_3 = \frac{1}{9}(-y_1 + y_3 - y_5 + y_6)$$

$$= \frac{1}{9}(-12.08 + 24.17 + 51.15 + 72.13) \tag{8.6}$$

$$= 15.04$$

$$c_1 = \frac{1}{9}(y_1 - y_3 - y_4 + y_6)$$

$$= \frac{1}{9}(12.08 - 24.17 - 24.11 + 72.13) \tag{8.7}$$

$$= 3.99$$

$$c_2 = \frac{1}{9}(-y_1 + y_2 + y_4 - y_5)$$

$$= \frac{1}{9}(-12.08 + 9.13 + 24.11 + 51.15) \tag{8.8}$$

$$= 8.03$$

$$c_3 = \frac{1}{9}(-y_2 + y_3 + y_5 - y_6)$$

$$= \frac{1}{9}(-9.13 + 24.17 - 51.15 - 72.13) \tag{8.9}$$

$$= -12.02$$

The grand average, $\overline{T}$, is

$$\overline{T} = \frac{1}{18}(12.08 + 9.13 + \ldots + 72.13) = \frac{90.47}{18}$$

$$\tag{8.10}$$

$$= 5.03$$

Therefore, the level averages of B and C are calculated as

$$\overline{B}_1 = \overline{T} + b_1 = 5.03 + (-5.01)$$

$$\tag{8.11}$$

$$= 0.02$$

$$\overline{B}_2 = \overline{T} + b_2 = 5.03 + (-10.03)$$

$$\tag{8.12}$$

$$= -5.00$$

$$\overline{B}_3 = \overline{T} + b_3 = 5.03 + 15.04$$

$$= 20.07 \tag{8.13}$$

$$\overline{C}_1 = \overline{T} + c_1 = 5.03 + 3.99$$

$$= 9.02 \tag{8.14}$$

$$\overline{C}_2 = \overline{T} + c_2 = 5.03 + 8.03$$

$$= 13.06 \tag{8.15}$$

$$\overline{C}_3 = \overline{T} + c_3 = 5.03 + (-12.02)$$

$$= -6.99 \tag{8.16}$$

8.4   DERIVATION

In this section, the derivation of Eq. (8.2) and (8.3) is illustrated.

Table 8.5 is constructed from Table 8.2 (b) using symbols $a_1, a_2, b_1, b_2, b_3, c_1, c_2,$ and c_3, as described in Section 8.2.

Table 8.5   Youden square

	A	B	C	y
No.	1	2		
1	a_1	b_1	c_1	y_1
2	a_1	b_2	c_2	y_2
3	a_1	b_3	c_3	y_3
4	a_2	b_1	c_2	y_4
5	a_2	b_2	c_3	y_5
6	a_2	b_3	c_1	y_6

It is seen from the table that y_1 is the result of $a_1, b_1,$ and c_1; y_2 is the result of $a_1, b_2,$ and c_2, etc. Therefore, the following equations can be written:

$$y_1 = a_1 + b_1 + c_1 \tag{8.17}$$

$$y_2 = a_1 + b_2 + c_2 \tag{8.18}$$

$$y_3 = a_1 + b_3 + c_3 \tag{8.19}$$

$$y_4 = a_2 + b_1 + c_2 \tag{8.20}$$

$$y_5 = a_2 + b_2 + c_3 \tag{8.21}$$

$$y_6 = a_2 + b_3 + c_1 \tag{8.22}$$

In addition, the following three equations exist based on the definition of $a_1, a_2, \ldots, c_3$:

$$a_1 + a_2 = 0 \tag{8.23}$$

$$b_1 + b_2 + b_3 = 0 \tag{8.24}$$

$$c_1 + c_2 + c_3 = 0 \tag{8.25}$$

By solving these equations, b_1, b_2, b_3, c_1, c_2, and c_3 are calculated, as shown in Eq. (8.2) and (8.3).

For example, the effect of C_2 is derived by

$$\text{Eq.}(8.17) - \text{Eq.}(8.18)$$

$$y_1 - y_2 = b_1 - b_2 + c_1 - c_2 \tag{8.26}$$

$$\text{Eq.}(8.20) - \text{Eq.}(8.21)$$

$$y_4 - y_5 = b_1 - b_2 + c_2 - c_3 \tag{8.27}$$

$$\text{Eq.}(8.26) - \text{Eq.}(8.27)$$

$$y_1 - y_2 - (y_4 - y_5) = c_1 - c_2 - (c_2 - c_3) \tag{8.28}$$

$$y_1 - y_2 - y_4 + y_5 = c_1 + c_3 - 2c_2 \tag{8.29}$$

From Eq. (8.25)

$$c_1 + c_2 + c_3 = 0$$

Therefore, Eq. (8.29) can be written as

$$y_1 - y_2 - y_4 + y_5 = c_1 + c_3 + c_2 - 3c_2$$

$$c_2 = \frac{1}{3}(-y_1 + y_2 + y_4 - y_5)$$

This is shown in Eq. (8.3).

9

Incomplete Data

9.1 INTRODUCTION

During Parameter Design experimentation, or simulation using orthogonal arrays, SN ratios are calculated and the optimum conditions are determined. But sometimes the SN ratios of a few runs of an orthogonal array cannot be calculated for various reasons. In the discipline known as design of experiments, the treatments of "missing data" are illustrated and are based on analyses using existing results. However, no distinction is made between different types of incomplete data.

Table 9.1 shows the different types and examples of incomplete data. So-called missing data in design of experiments belong to Type 1 in the table. Examples include misplacement of samples to be measured or of data sheets containing the recorded results. In either of these cases, we don't know if the results of the run were good or bad.

There are other types of incomplete data, such as when the apparatus used in a chemical reaction explodes or when test pieces cannot be produced due to the extreme conditions of a welding experiment. Such types of incomplete data should not be confused with the missing data illustrated in books on the design of experiments.

In this chapter, the treatments for different types of incomplete data are illustrated by using the existing data.

Although it is desirable to collect a complete set of data for analysis, it is not absolutely necessary. In Parameter Design for product or process optimization, it is recommended that control-factor-level intervals must be set wide enough so that a significant quality improvement may be expected. On the other hand, the

Table 9.1 Types of incomplete data

Type		Case
1. All data in one run of an orthogonal array are missing.	1.1	Samples to be measured are missing.
	1.2	Data sheets with the recorded results are misplaced.
	1.3	Some experimental runs were discontinued due to budget, time constraints, or job transfer.
	1.4	The raw materials or test pieces needed to complete the whole runs of experiments were insufficient.
2. The number of data points in one run are different from others.	2.1	The number of signal-factor levels in one run differs from those in the other runs.
	2.2	The number of repetitions in one run are different from other runs.
	2.3	All results in one noise factor level of one run is missing.
3. Part or all results of one run is missing due to extreme conditions.	3.1	The chemical reaction apparatus exploded.
	3.2	No current flowed in an electric circuit.
	3.3	No product was produced.
4. No data are missing, but calculation of the SN ratios results in values of either positive or negative infinity.	4.1	When using the zero-point proportional, reference-point proportional, or linear equation, the error variance (V_e) is greater than the sensitivity (S_β).
	4.2	In the nominal-is-best case, the error variance (V_e) is greater than the sensitivity (S_m).
	4.3	In classified data with 3 classes or more, the error variance (V_e) is greater than the sensitivity (S_m).
	4.4	In the smaller-is-better case, all results are equal to zero.
	4.5	In the larger-is-better case, all results are equal to zero.

levels of conditions must be within a certain range so that undesirable results are not obtained. Such determinations can only be made based on existing knowledge or past experiences.

In the case of new-product development, however, there is no existing knowledge on which to base the determination of the appropriate range of control-factor levels within which a product or a system functions. To avoid generating undesirable results, engineers tend to conduct research within narrow ranges.

It is important to realize that the purpose of product development is not to produce good products, but to generate useful knowledge. If all results from different experimental runs are close to each other, little knowledge can be found. In order to get more knowledge about a new frontier, control-factor-level intervals need to be set wide enough to purposely produce some bad results, such as having explosions or cracked test pieces. Such situations are allowed at the research-and-development stage. In the case of an L_{18} orthogonal array experiment, there may be as many as several runs with incomplete data, but this is still good enough to draw valuable conclusions.

9.2 TREATMENT OF INCOMPLETE DATA

In order to make analysis and optimization possible, the treatments outlined below are suggested.

Cases 1.1, 1.2, 1.3, and 1.4

These are the cases which are referred to as "missing data" in traditional experimental design books. Fisher-Yates' method is commonly used. A method called **sequential approximation** is recommended.

Case 2.1

For example, when the number of signal-factor level of run no. 4 is 3 but all other runs are 5, the SN ratio of run no. 4 is calculated as is and analyzed with the other SN ratios.

Case 2.2

As shown in Table 9.2, this is the case in which the number of repetitions under each signal factor are different.

Table 9.2 Incomplete data

Signal	M_1	M_2	...	M_k
	y_{11}	y_{21}	...	y_{k1}
Repetition	y_{12}	y_{22}	...	y_{k2}
	...		...	
	y_{1r_1}	y_{2r_2}	...	y_{kr_k}
Total	y_1	y_2	...	y_k

In the case of the zero-point proportional equation, the SN ratio is calculated as follows:

$$S_T = y_{11}^2 + y_{12}^2 + \ldots + y_{kr_k}^2 \quad \text{and} \quad f_T = r_1 + r_2 + \ldots + r_k \tag{9.1}$$

$$S_\beta = \frac{(M_1 y_1 + M_2 y_2 + \ldots + M_k y_k)^2}{r_1 M_1^2 + r_2 M_2^2 + \ldots + r_k M_k^2} \quad \text{and} \quad f_\beta = 1 \tag{9.2}$$

$$S_e = S_T - S_\beta \quad \text{and} \quad f_e = f_T - 1 \tag{9.3}$$

$$V_e = \frac{S_e}{f_e} \tag{9.4}$$

$$\eta = 10 \log \frac{\frac{1}{r_1 M_1^2 + r_2 M_2^2 + \ldots + r_k M_k^2}(S_\beta - V_e)}{V_e} \tag{9.5}$$

Table 9.3 is a simple numerical example.

Table 9.3 Numerical example

Signal	$M_1 = 0.1$	$M_2 = 0.3$	$M_3 = 0.5$
	0.098	0.294	0.495
	0.097	0.288	0.493
Result	0.093	0.288	0.489
	0.092	0.296	0.495
		0.297	0.495
		0.287	0.488
Total	0.380	1.750	2.955

$$S_T = 0.098^2 + 0.097^2 + \ldots + 0.488^2$$

$$= 2.002033 \quad \text{and} \quad f_T = 4 + 6 + 6 = 16 \tag{9.6}$$

$$S_\beta = \frac{(0.1 \times 0.380 \times 1.750 \times 0.5 \times 2.955)^2}{4 \times 0.1^2 + 6 \times 0.3^2 + 6 \times 0.5^2}$$

$$= \frac{2.0405^2}{2.08} \tag{9.7}$$

$$= 2.00175012 \quad \text{and} \quad f = 1$$

$$S_e = 2.002033 - 2.00175012$$

$$= 0.00028288 \quad \text{and} \quad f = 16 - 1 = 15 \tag{9.8}$$

$$V_e = \frac{0.00028288}{15}$$

$$= 0.00001886 \tag{9.9}$$

$$\eta = 10 \, \log \frac{\dfrac{1}{2.08}(2.00175012 - 0.00001886)}{0.00001886}$$

$$= 10 \, \log 51027.08 \tag{9.10}$$

$$= 47.08(\text{db})$$

Case 2.3

An example of this case is when there are two compounded noise-factor levels: the positive and negative extreme conditions. If one of these two extreme conditions is totally missing, do not just use the results of another extreme condition to calculate the SN ratio. Instead, treat it the same way as described in Type 1.

Cases 3.1, 3.2, and 3.3

Whether it's an explosion, lack of current, or lack of end product, each such problem indicates that the condition is very bad. Use negative infinity as the SN ratio. It is important to distinguish this case from Type 1, in which it is unknown whether the condition is good or bad.

There are two ways to treat these cases:

▶ Classify the SN ratios, including positive and/or negative infinity, into several categories and analyze the results by accumulation analysis.

▶ Subtract 3 to 5 decibels from the smallest SN ratio in the orthogonal array. Assign that number to the SN Ratio for the missing run(s). Then follow with sequential approximation.

Cases 4.1, 4.2, and 4.3

These cases involve error variance being greater than the sensitivity. Use negative infinity for the SN Ratio and treat these cases in the same way as Case 3.1.

Case 4.4

This is when all results are equal to zero for a smaller-is-better case. Use positive infinity as the SN ratio and

▶ Classify the SN ratio into several categories and conduct accumulation analysis.

▶ Add 3 to 5 decibels to the largest SN ratio in the orthogonal array. Assign that number to the SN ratio of the missing run(s), then followed with sequential approximation.

Case 4.5

This is when all results are equal to zero for a larger-is-better case. Use negative infinity, and treat the problem in the same way as Case 3.1.

9.3 SEQUENTIAL APPROXIMATION

9.3.1 Procedures

To apply sequential approximation, the number of runs with incomplete data could be one or more. The procedure is:
1. Calculate the average from the existing SN ratios. For example, if experiment nos. 3 and 9 are missing in an L_{18} array, calculate the average from the remaining 16 SN ratios. The average is considered as the zero-th approximation.
2. Conduct response analysis and pick up about half of the larger factors.
3. Use these factors to estimate the average of the missing run(s). This average is the first approximation.
4. Conduct the response analysis, and, again, use about half of the larger factors to estimate the second approximated value.
5. Continue approximations until the results converge.

9.3.2 Numerical Example

In the following example, the results of experiment no. 4 are missing, as shown in Table 9.4.

In order to analyze the results, sequential approximation is applied.

Table 9.4 Results with missing data

L_{18}	A	B	C	D	E	F	G	H	N_1		N_2		η
1	1	1	1	1	1	1	1	1	83	88	90	91	27.9
2	1	1	2	2	2	2	2	2	73	73	83	81	23.4
3	1	1	3	3	3	3	3	3	57	58	65	69	20.7
4	1	2	1	1	2	2	3	3					
5	1	2	2	2	3	3	1	1	73	75	76	79	29.6
6	1	2	3	3	1	1	2	2	58	60	68	72	19.8
7	1	3	1	2	1	3	2	3	44	49	55	58	18.3
8	1	3	2	3	2	1	3	1	50	54	57	64	19.6
9	1	3	3	1	3	2	1	2	64	65	66	68	31.7
10	2	1	1	3	3	2	2	1	74	79	86	94	19.6
11	2	1	2	1	1	3	3	2	75	78	90	94	19.2
12	2	1	3	2	2	1	1	3	70	76	52	88	19.7
13	2	2	1	2	3	1	3	2	71	80	57	95	13.5
14	2	2	2	3	1	2	1	3	48	56	59	65	18.1
15	2	2	3	1	2	3	2	1	66	67	79	86	17.7
16	2	3	1	3	2	3	1	2	45	53	58	64	16.7
17	2	3	2	1	3	1	2	3	60	67	66	73	21.9
18	2	3	3	2	1	2	3	1	57	65	79	83	15.3

First, the average of the other 17 SN ratios is calculated:

$$\eta(\text{average}) = \frac{1}{17}(27.9 + 23.4 + \ldots + 15.3)$$

$$= 20.4(\text{db})$$

(9.11)

Next, 20.4 is used as the SN ration of no. 4, and level averages are calculated. These are shown in Table 9.5 and Table 9.6.

A high–low table shows the magnitude of effects in descending order. From Table 9.6, half of the larger effects, A, G, E, and D, are used to estimate the SN ratio of experiment no. 4.

Table 9.5   Response table for 1st iteration

Factor	Level 1	Level 2	Level 3
A	23.4766	17.2901	
B	20.7155	19.8494	20.5853
C	19.3883	21.9716	19.7902
D	23.1385	18.9386	19.0730
E	19.7722	18.5346	22.8434
F	19.3549	21.4177	20.3776
G	22.9170	20.1161	18.1171
H	21.6166	20.7091	18.8244

Table 9.6   High-low table for 1st iteration

	High		Low		
Factor	Level	SN Ratio	Level	SN Ratio	Gap
A	1	23.4766	2	17.2901	6.1865
G	1	22.917	3	18.1171	4.7999
E	3	22.8434	2	18.5346	4.3088
D	1	23.1385	2	18.9386	4.1999
H	1	21.6166	3	18.8244	2.7923
C	2	21.9716	1	19.3883	2.5833
F	2	21.4177	1	19.3549	2.0628
B	1	20.7155	2	19.8494	0.8661

The grand average of 18 SN ratios is calculated:

$$\overline{T} = \frac{1}{18}(27.9 + 23.4 + 20.7 + 20.4 + \ldots + 15.3)$$

$$= 20.38$$

(9.12)

The condition of experiment no. 4 is $A_1 B_1 C_1 D_1 E_2 F_2 G_3 H_3$. Its process average is estimated using A, D, E, and G.

$$\eta = (\text{No. 4}) = \overline{A}_1 + \overline{D}_1 + \overline{E}_2 + \overline{G}_3 - 3\overline{T}$$

$$= 23.47 + 23.13 + 18.53 + 18.12 - 3 \times 20.38 \qquad (9.13)$$

$$= 22.11$$

This is the result of the first iteration. For the second iteration, 22.11 is used as the SN ratio of no. 4, and the same procedure is executed. Iterations should be repeated until the estimated result converges on a certain value.

The results of the iterations were calculated and are given in Table 9.7.

Table 9.7 Result of iterations

Iteration	SN ratio	(%) Difference with previous iteration
1st	22.11	
2nd	22.88	3.37
3rd	23.22	1.47
4th	23.38	0.65

From Chapter 5, the optimum condition is $A_1 D_1 E_3 G_1$. Using 22.11 as SN no. 4, the estimated process average is

$$\eta(\text{optimum}) = \overline{A}_1 + \overline{D}_1 + \overline{E}_3 + \overline{G}_1 - 3\overline{T}$$

$$= 23.66 + 23.42 + 22.84 + 22.92 - 3 \times 20.38 \qquad (9.14)$$

$$= 31.70$$

From Eq. (5.13), the estimate using the original result of experiment no. 4 is

$$\eta(\text{optimum}) = 31.4 \qquad (9.15)$$

These two results are very close.

10

Robust Technology Development

10.1 INTRODUCTION

Robust technology development is a revolutionary approach recently developed and promoted by Dr. Genichi Taguchi. This new approach is used to develop families of products, rather than one product at a time. The direct result of using this approach is the development of robust quality products that are reliable while in use. A by-product of the use of this approach is a dramatic reduction in R&D cycle time.

Can we Reduce R&D Cycle Time to One-Third? This was the theme of the 1992 Quality Engineering Symposium in Nagoya, Japan. Case studies presented offered convincing proof that it is now possible to dramatically reduce product-development cycle time. But this reduction in the product-development cycle time was only a by-product. The main objective of the case studies was to develop products that perform their function and yield high customer satisfaction, even when used under a wide variety of customer-usage patterns and environments.

A revolutionary approach to product development was presented in the case studies that were first introduced by Dr. Genichi Taguchi in 1989. The approach is generally known as technology development when translated from Japanese. However, this sounds rather vague and does not do the method justice. The authors prefer to refer to this approach as **robust technology development**. In order to illustrate its use, several examples of successful applications follow.

10.2   EXAMPLES

10.2.1   Development of Hardness Standards

In 1991, at the American Supplier Institute Taguchi Methods Symposium held in Dearborn, Michigan, a Japanese company called Asahi Industrial Company presented a series of studies on the development of the products used as standards for Rockwell hardness testers. Prior to the completion of these studies, there had been only one source in the world that supplied the hardness standards. In order to develop the standards to a superior quality level, attempts had been made by several large steel companies in Japan. But they did not succeed, despite several years of joint research efforts.

Assisted by the Japanese Bearing Inspection Institute and the National Research Laboratory of Metrology, and using the robust technology development approach, Asahi developed standards whose quality was vastly superior. By previous industry standards, the dispersion of standards was to be within 0.1 HRC (scale of hardness). From the Asahi development, standards are now produced whose variability is as low as 0.02 HRC in terms of standard deviation. The development was completed in only one-and-a-half years.

10.2.2   Development of a Braking System

For more than 20 years, Nissan Motor Company had been struggling to resolve major complaints from customers regarding the squealing of brakes. In efforts to solve the problem, many traditional researching approaches were used, without success in eliminating brake squealing. Recently, Nissan implemented the development of a new nonasbestos brake pad and began to utilize the robust technology development approach. After development, utilizing the new material, the squealing noise level of the redesigned brake was measured. Surprisingly, they discovered that the noise level was so low that even highly sensitive measuring devices could not detect any brake squeal. Furthermore, brake efficiency was improved and brake life increased. The net result of the improved development resulted in a brake system that is smaller and lighter, contributing to improved gas mileage, less pollution, and virtually no detectable squealing noise.

10.2.3 Development of Ammunition

The Aerojet Ordnance Company in Tustin, California, used the robust technology development approach in establishing a broad pyrotechnics database that could be applied to "all future (ammunition) products." The goal was to eliminate the need for Parameter Design for each new product. The company spent three worker-months developing the database, but it was estimated that using traditional approaches, it would have taken 800 worker-months, or one person working 67 years, to establish the broad technology database. Aerojet estimates that this database is conservatively worth over 60 million dollars. The data allows the rapid design of all future products. In this example, R&D cycle time is not merely reduced to one-third ... but to the staggering fraction of 1/266th.

The followings are some important issues related to robust technology development, and how it provides organizations with the potential not only to keep up with competition, but to set the competitive pace for research and product development.

10.3   PARADIGM SHIFT NEEDED: DEVELOPMENT OF QUALITY MUST BEGIN IN R&D

Historically, the quality control function has been performed within the manufacturing organization. Quality engineers, production engineers, and statisticians have played a major role in quality improvement. In contrast, R&D and product-design engineers have been less involved in quality activities. It has been said that the definition of R&D in the U.S. has wrongly excluded the issue of quality.

Thankfully, this paradigm has begun to change. The traditional approach to quality control issues has largely been synonymous with problem solving, or firefighting. It is interesting to note that the U.S. has not been alone in harboring this paradigm. In Japan, it has been called "mole beating" and in China, "cure head for a headache, cure foot for a footache."

Utilizing the robust technology development approach, one does not focus on the symptoms, that is, how the problem manifests itself, or even on the root cause for variation. Instead, the focus is on the study of the generic function of the product. In the case of a brake-system design, the generic function of a brake is, ideally, to convert 100% of the energy to stopping the vehicle, with none of the energy being lost to waste or the brake exhibiting symptoms, such as noisy squealing.

Ford Motor Company has recognized the value of the robust technology development approach and started to implement its use in product design on a large scale. A slogan has been adopted at Ford to promote the use of the new approach: **From root cause analysis to ideal function.** This is the type of major paradigm shift that world-class competitive organizations must adopt in their research and engineering systems in lieu of the old paradigms. Quality must be built into the product in the earliest stages of R&D and product design—and this can be accomplished through the ideal function mindset at the very beginning.

10.4 HOW ROBUST TECHNOLOGY DEVELOPMENT WORKS: THE MAIN CONCEPTS

The followings are the main concepts in robust technology development:

- ▶ Two-step optimization
- ▶ Choice of quality to measure
- ▶ Ideal function
- ▶ SN Ratio

These concepts are explained below.

10.4.1 Two-Step Optimization: Reduce Variability First, Then Place on Target

There are two common paradigms among design engineers: one is trying to hit the target first, and the other is the improvement of quality by using higher quality (more expensive) raw materials or components. Taguchi's approach is a new paradigm - never try to hit the target the first time. The first step in quality engineering is to improve and maximize stability or robustness. Manufacturing will love you for it. Only then do we adjust the average to meet the target, since adjusting the average is easy work in most cases.

In golf for example, the most important thing is to reduce variability in flight distance and direction, not to improve the average. Using a driver, one may hit a ball to a respectable average of 200 yards, with a range of ±50 yards. Using the Parameter Design approach, by changing the levels of control factors such as stance, grip, or swing, etc., variability can be reduced. After that, adjusting the average distance is accomplished simply by the selection of the right club. This Parameter Design approach is now widely recognized as two-step optimization in Taguchi Methods.

In engineering, reducing variability is difficult, but adjusting the average is easy. Many products still remain inferior to others due to differences in variability, not difference in means. Research efficiency will indeed be low if one tries to hit the target by trial and error to accommodate various kinds of noise factors, even with the use of computers and CAD/CAM software.

10.4.2   Choice of Right Output to Measure

Referring back to the Nissan brake example, the traditional mindset has been to improve quality by measuring quality characteristics such as "noise levels." The noise level of the brakes was measured very accurately, but this did nothing to actually solve the problem over the past 20 years. Such a problem-solving mindset has been a major pitfall for engineers; engineering research is highly inefficient if the focus is on the wrong quality characteristics.

Dr. Taguchi defined different levels of quality that need to be considered: downstream, midstream, upstream, and origin. They are described as follows:

Downstream Quality (Customer Quality)

Examples are: noise, vibration, effort in using the product (e.g., closing the car door), or cost (economic/environmental) of using the Product (e.g., gas mileage).

Downstream quality is the type of quality characteristics that is noticed by customers. Such quality characteristics are important to the management of organizations. However, they are of limited value in determining how to improve the quality of the product and one insignificant for engineering research. Not only are they unimportant, it should not be the function of engineers to measure these characteristics as a basis for quality improvement. They serve only to create the wrong focus and are the worst type of quality characteristics to use in quality engineering.

Midstream Quality (Specified Quality)

Examples are: dimension, strength, or specifications.

Midstream quality is important for production engineers, since it is essential to "make the product to print." Today, many engineers have begun to understand that making the product to print does not always mean quality is achieved. These quality characteristics are slightly better to use than downstream quality, but not much.

Upstream Quality (Robust Quality)

Examples are nondynamic SN ratios.

Upstream quality is an index for the stability of product quality. This type of quality—recognized under the name Taguchi Methods—has been widely applied in the past decade. But it is only the second-best type of quality characteristic. The reason is that such quality characteristics can only be used to improve the robustness of particular products, but not a group, or family, of products.

Origin Quality (Functional Quality)

Examples are dynamic SN ratios.

The best and most powerful type, origin quality is the heart of robust technology development. It defines the generic function of a given product. The use of the origin quality characteristic brings the highest possible efficiency to R&D efforts. It also makes the results of small-scale laboratory experiments or simulations from R&D reproducible downstream in manufacturing and in the customer's environment. Numerous examples have proven this to be true.

10.4.3   To Get Quality, Don't Measure Quality!

The above statement was the theme of the 1989 ASI Taguchi Methods Symposium. In other words, to truly improve quality, don't measure symptoms or downstream quality; measure something that relates to the product function itself.

Typically, one of the most controversial issues in Taguchi Methods for statisticians and design-of-experiment experts is the belief that "Taguchi Methods ignores the effects and importance of interactions." On the contrary, Dr. Taguchi's approach urges the use of measurement of functional quality precisely because interactions are the most important issue. The effects of interactions produce results that are inconsistent and not reproducible.

For example, the authors often ask engineers the following question: "Which wine tastes better, white or red?" In most of the cases, the answer is, "It depends." They say that with meat, red is better, and with fish, white is better. There is no consistency about the effect of wine type, so one cannot say which wine is always better.

What laboratory research needs to discover is what kind of factorial effect is consistent or reproducible downstream. When interactions are present, the conclusions from small-scale laboratory experiments cannot be reproduced in manufacturing and the marketplace. This is precisely why many people will not trust laboratory results—they have done so in the past and been burned.

If we can avoid quality characteristics with interactions through our R&D and engineering methodology, research conclusions can be reproduced consistently downstream. In addition, R&D and product-development cycle times are shortened, and the cost of experiments is reduced. Unfortunately, most of our engineering schools have not taught this type of approach. Instead, they have taught that interactions are important to pursue. So our engineers tend to spend countless time and effort pursuing those useless and harmful interactions and trying to manage the downstream effects.

The use of dynamic SN ratios enables us to avoid interactions and, thus, greatly improve engineering efficiency. This will be discussed in some detail later.

10.4.4 Energy Transformation and Definition of Ideal Function

Functional quality is based on the engineering perspective. In the case of car brakes, the ideal function is that the input energy from foot force be proportional to the output energy as brake torque, as shown in Fig. 10.1.

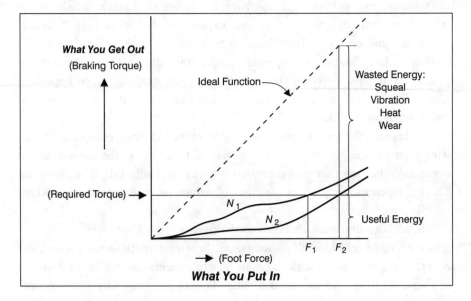

Figure 10.1 Function of a brake

In the figure, the dotted line shows the ideal situation, meaning that the input energy is totally converted into useful energy to stop the car. This is called the **ideal function** or **generic function,** and in this case, the dotted line has a slope of 45 degrees. But in reality, this never happens; rather, lines N_1 or N_2 might be the reality.

Lines N_1 and N_2 show the variation caused by customers' driving habits and conditions such as road surface, tire pressure, or the number of passengers in a car, etc. Those conditions are referred to as **noise factors.** Under different noise-factor conditions, the foot force to stop the car results in a different torque.

The input energy generated by the pedal can be divided into two parts: useful and wasteful energy. The latter is converted into undesired symptoms such as squeal, vibration, heat, wear, etc. In Fig. 10.2, if we can optimize the function in research so that Situation 1 is changed to Situation 2, the linearity of the curves is improved (i.e., the curves are straightened). With a straight line, the adjustability of input pedal force for a target torque is easily determined in the design stage, and maneuverability will be improved when we drive the car.

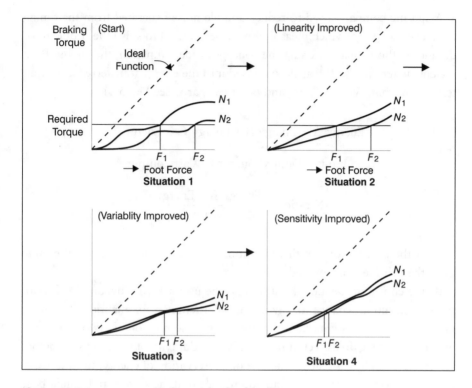

Figure 10.2 Improvement of a car brake function

When Situation 2 is improved to Situation 3, the variability of foot force to stop the car is reduced, or not affected, by driving conditions. If we can further change from Situation 3 to Situation 4, the foot force needed to obtain the required braking torque is reduced, and thus, there is a significant reduction in wasted energy—and therefore in squealing, vibration, heat, and wear. Such improvements can be accomplished by simply maximizing the SN ratio, which is defined as follows:

$$\text{SN ratio} = \frac{\text{Useful energy}}{\text{Wasteful energy}}$$

Of the four cases shown in Fig. 10.2, Situation 1 has the lowest SN ratio, Situations 2 and 3 come next, and Situation 4 has the highest SN ratio.

A specific company tried to reduce audible noise generated from the timing belt. The company, which measured noise level, tried to solve the problem for decades without success. Using the concept of ideal function, the energy from the engine (crank shaft) was decomposed into the energy transferred as output to the cam shaft, water pump, and other car parts (see Fig. 5.1).

$$\text{Energy A} = \text{Energy B} + \text{Energy C} + \text{Energy X}$$

$$\text{Input} = \text{Desired output} + \text{Waste output}$$

$$\text{SN ratio} = \frac{\text{Energy B} + \text{Energy C}}{\text{Energy X}}$$

After the optimization of this SN ratio, noise was reduced, and at the same time, the belt life was doubled.

By the choice of functional output and the use of such a dynamic SN ratio, there is a good chance of avoiding interactions. As mentioned before, interactions lack addivitity. Additivity means one plus one is two, not three or zero. What we do expect in research is the additivity of the effects of factors (or variables). Physics teaches the law of conservation of energy, the additivity of energy. Like the examples of an automobile braking system and timing belt, the functions are energy related, so there should be no interactions. Without interactions, there is additivity or consistency or reproducibility. Laboratory experiments will be reproduced, and research efficiency, improved.

10.4.5   SN Ratio

One of the most important features in Taguchi Methods is the use of the SN ratio. The SN ratio has been used in the communication industry since the turn of this century, as a means of assessing the quality of communication systems. Dr. Taguchi brought the concept into quality engineering and developed it to be the index for the quality of all kinds of products.

Conceptually, SN ratio indicates how good the quality is. In the case of dynamic SN ratio, the more a product function deviates from the ideal situation, the worse the SN ratio is. It is seen in Fig. 10.2 that Situation 1 is the worst of the four when they are compared with the ideal function, Situation 2 is better

Situation 3 is the next to the best, and Situation 4 is the best. If the SN ratios of these four cases were calculated, their magnitude would be found to increase from Situation 1 to 4 in the same order.

The advantages of using SN ratio is in its simplicity and efficiency. If either variability, linearity, or sensitivity is improved, the SN ratio increases. Thus, one index takes care of three aspects of quality. Therefore, engineers do not have to worry about variability, linearity, and sensitivity separately; they have only to try to maximize the SN ratio. That is one of the reasons why robust technology development is efficient.

10.5 ADVANTAGES OF USING ROBUST TECHNOLOGY DEVELOPMENT

There are three features in robust technology that are of great importance to R&D:

▶ Technology readiness
▶ Flexibility
▶ Reproducibility

10.5.1 Technology Readiness

Traditionally, quality problems are noticed after products are sold. In other words, quality is based on the voice of customers in the form of complaints and dissatisfaction. But by then, it is too late. Quality must be designed into the product before the product-design stage. This is possible only if the function of the product is studied.

In the development of an effective soldering process, extensive research has been done on test pieces (prior to product design) in U.S. laboratories. This is basic research methodology, which has long been a strength of U.S. firms. It has been one distinctive advantage that U.S. engineers have had over Japanese researchers, who have done most research by studying actual products. Research conducted from a mindset of ideal product function enables manufacturers to be technologically ready and able to bring new products to the market ahead of competitors. In this regard, unless we consciously decide to give up this edge, U.S. companies still have a competitive edge over many Japanese companies.

10.5.2 Flexibility

It is worth mentioning yet one more time: upstream quality is an indicator of the robustness of **a particular product**. When only a specific product is to be studied, nondynamic SN ratios are appropriate. A number of U.S. success stories based on the use of such ratios have been reported in various symposia in the past decade. This is all well and good, but there is yet a more advanced and efficient way to ensure quality, and it is through the use of robust technology development methodology and databases developed using dynamic SN Ratios.

This more advanced approach, the study of *groups or families of products* can facilitate the creation of priceless knowledge in the form of a database of proprietary design technology. From Situation 4 in Fig 10.2, it is easy to see that the output levels (applied to many products) can be much more easily adjusted through input adjustment than in Situation 1. Different outputs mean different products, including ones that differ in dimension, capacity, strength, etc.

The beauty of using dynamic SN ratios is one-shot optimization, which enables engineers to utilize the technology/knowledge database over and over without needing to repeat similar research from product to product. This means a potentially huge savings in time, workpower, and capital by eliminating the repeated reinvention of the wheel. It is an opportunity to better utilize the long-held research strengths of American engineers in the global marketplace.

Don't conduct individual product development! At least don't do so unless you have infinitely deep pockets. Let us refer again to the Aerojet Ordnance database development approach. A customer requested, for the first time, that a projectile be developed to hit a target 2000 yards downrange. Instead of developing just this specific product, future potential products were considered and a group of products with different range capabilities were developed. Recall that midstream quality is good only for a particular product, not for a group of products. By conducting research using dynamic SN ratios, adjusting the flight distance for another product becomes so easy that redundancy of research and design can be avoided.

10.5.3   Reproducibility

Given the fact that U.S. engineers are better in the above two aspects, why is there intense competition with Japanese products? The reason is that the average American engineer cannot have his or her research conclusions reproduced downstream. Most Japanese engineers study actual (but individual) products or processes; therefore, conclusions are more reproducible. (On the other hand, in the small-scale, basic research on individual test pieces, the environment is totally different from actual manufacturing conditions.) Also, until the advent of robust technology development, there was no approach for ensuring that conclusions would be reproducible downstream. Indeed, *making conclusions reproducible downstream is the key to U.S. engineers becoming more competitive.*

10.6   HOW FAR ADVANCED IS ROBUST TECHNOLOGY DEVELOPMENT?

Robust technology development was introduced several years ago, and numerous successful case studies have been reported. In Taguchi Methods' Symposia held in Japan in the past several years, most of the case studies were related to robust technology development. In March 1993, a Quality Engineering Forum was organized, and its bimonthly periodical, "Journal of Quality Engineering Forum," was published to introduce case studies in robust technology development. Today, the Forum has nearly 2000 members.

In Taiwan, Taguchi Methods was introduced on a large scale several years ago. Because dynamic SN ratios were introduced instead of nondynamic SN ratios, which are commonly used in the U.S., the case studies in their symposia are mostly related to robust technology development. There were several case studies that illustrated millions of dollars in annual savings. The areas of application include aeronautics research, electric power equipment, electric component parts, rubber, print circuit board, and even submicron research.

In the U.S., the American Supplier Institute promotes the newly introduced robust technology development approach. Since 1990, case studies on robust technology development in the fields of automotive, electronics and defense industries have been documented at ASI's Annual Taguchi Methods Symposia.

The application of robust technology development using functional quality, or dynamic SN ratio, gives solutions to all of the three aspects, namely, technology readiness, flexibility, and reproducibility. By the use of these methods, U.S. engineers can improve reproducibility, and Japanese engineers can improve both technology readiness and flexibility. So far, Japanese companies appear to be ahead in the number of applications, which will help bolster their technological capabilities. This should represent a strong concern to U.S. firms.

It is encouraging that reproducibility can be improved through the application of robust technology development. The case of Asahi Industry shows us that a company whose technological level is far behind the best in the world can become superior if the right approach is used.

Conceptually, the ideal function is easily understood. But sometimes in the research, the ideal function is incorrectly defined. Also, measurement for input/output is not always available. For example, even if the ideal function of a timing belt is properly defined, the torque may not be measurable. Such problems are strictly engineering issues, not statistical issues. This is the most difficult area in the application. Engineers must spend a lot of time discussing these issues, and that is the key to success. Consequently, development of case studies in various industries is important for the promotion of this method. Fortunately, in the past several years, the promoters of robust technology development have been successfully generating case studies in various fields. The authors hope that this new methodology will always be used to make a company more competitive.

Case Studies

11.1 INTRODUCTION

For quality improvement, it is very important to compare the traditional approach and Taguchi Methods. Traditionally, quality improvement is mostly motivated by problem solving. Root–cause analysis is important, and whatever data are measured (such as symptoms or defect rates, called responses), they are analyzed. In Taguchi Methods, it is recommended:

To get quality, don't measure quality!

This means that if we want to improve quality, do not measure the quality items we are measuring now. Instead, we should try to think about the ideal function—and use dynamic SN ratios, based on the ideal function, for analysis.

The ideal function for an engineering project differs from industry to industry, from case to case. It is not an easy task to determine the ideal function, and it usually takes hours or days of discussions. However, there are many published and successful cases that may be used as references. In this chapter, the highlights of such case studies from various industries are introduced.

All case studies in this chapter have the following common, things in unless indicated otherwise:

▶ Dynamic SN ratios are used.
▶ Zero-point proportional equation is used:

$$y = \beta M$$

where

y = output
β = constant
M= input

► Orthogonal array L_{18} is used.
► All SN ratio gains shown are results from confirmation.

11.2 MECHANICAL INDUSTRY

Case 1: NC Machining Technology Development

The NC machining process for a high-performance steel is considered one of the most difficult technologies in which to achieve a high process capability. In the study (see Reference 13) the concept of "transformability" was applied, so that the results could be used for a future family of products at Nissan Motor Company.

Components for mechanical systems such as automotive steering and power train require high strength and durability. The traditional carburizing heat-treatment process requires a heat-treatment time of ten hours. A new technology called high-frequency heat treatment needs only one minute. However, the hardness after the treatment becomes almost 30 units in Rockwell C scale. As a result, it is extremely difficult to machine, and dimensions cannot be precise.

Traditionally, actual production parts have been used to develop the machining process. Because of curvatures on the production parts, there was significant measurement error in part dimensions. Unique to this study is that test pieces were used instead of actual production parts. The dimensions of the test pieces covered the range that the machine can process. After optimization of the SN ratio, any dimension of future products could be successfully machined.

The ideal function for this case is that product dimension be proportional to programmed dimension.

As a result of the study, a gain of almost 20 db was confirmed, equivalent to about a ten-fold reduction in standard deviation of part dimensions.

Case 2: Stabilization of Injection-Molding Process for Carbon-Fiber Reinforced Plastic

In order to reduce the weight of automotive components, metal has been substituted by various types of plastic materials. In this study (see Reference 14), an injection-molding process to produce carbon-fiber-reinforced plastic (CFRP) was developed.

In the injection-molding process, quality characteristics such as reject rate, flash, or porosity were traditionally measured. In this case, the ideal function was defined as product dimension being proportional to mold dimension.

Test pieces were used in the development for the same reasons mentioned in Case 1. A gain of 2.75 db was confirmed.

Case 3: Material Development by a Spraying Process

The new materials that are composed of metals and ceramics have many interesting and useful properties in mechanical, electrical, and chemical fields. The forming process of such materials was researched (Reference 15) using a low-pressure plasma-spraying equipment that has independent metal and ceramic powder supplying devices and a plasma jet flame.

Many mechanical, electrical, and chemical properties—such as heat durability, stiffness, magnetic property, catalytic function, etc.—are required of these materials. Because the heat-related characteristics of metals and ceramics are quite different, there are many spraying conditions that must be considered, such as, ultrasonic speed, high temperature (exceeding 10,000°C), current, gas supply, and pressure, etc.

The ideal function was identified as the film thickness (or film weight) being proportional to the number of spraying times. It was also requested that the film-forming speed (β) be high.

Control factors such as the secondary gas type, power, current, spraying distance, spray gun moving speed, etc., were studied. The mixing ratio of metal and ceramic was used as the noise factor. Both the film thickness and film weight were measured as the responses. In both cases, the SN gains from estimation and from confirmation were very close to each other, indicating good reproducibility. The confirmed gains from thickness and from film weight were 15.74 and 16.73 db, respectively. It became possible to spray metal and ceramics under the same condition. It also became possible to produce film with varying material-mixing ratios.

Case 4: Technology Development of Laser Welding

The laser welding process for thin boards has been considered one of the most difficult technologies because of the variability of strength after welding (Reference 16). In the welding, laser light of several kilowatts is concentrated on a spot 0.2 to 0.5 mm in diameter. Because of the high power concentration, it is possible to obtain a welded part with a narrow width and deep penetration in a short period of time.

The quality characteristics included durability, fatigue strength, impact strength, antirust property, etc. Based on the discussion regarding the ideal function, it was concluded that welding strength ought to be proportional to the square root of weld width:

$$y = \beta \times M^{0.5}$$

The focus-point location and the clearance between the two plates were compounded as the noise factor. Good reproducibility was confirmed with a gain of 10.45 db.

Case 5: Robust Design of a Paper-Feeding Device

In paper-feeding devices for copy machines, the rate of feeding failures such as misfeed or multifeed were traditionally used in studies. In the early stage of Quality Engineering applications, the position of the paper fed by a roller was measured, and the SN ratio for a nondynamic-type, nominal-is-best (target = 0.5) characteristic had been used. Later, the concept of operating window was introduced. Based on the operating window concept, an SN ratio was successfully applied.

In this study (Reference 17), a different approach was introduced. The function of a paper feeder is to move paper to a certain position by a roller. Twelve roller-rotating angles were used as the input signal, and paper positions were measured by photo sensors as the output. The control factors included roller material, roller width, paper-inserting angle, abrasion-part material, paper-feeder pressure, and abrasion-part pressure. A gain of 3.17 db was confirmed.

Case 6: Development of a Technique for Adjusting Particle Size in a Fine Grinding Process of a Developer

The dry developer used for electrophotographic copiers and printers consists of a toner and a carrier. Various types of developers are used, depending on the application. The particle size of the developer is one of the physical properties that has a strong influence on image quality. This report describes the results of using Parameter Design for controlling particle size in the manufacturing process so that the particle-size distribution may be improved, thus achieving a better yield of desired particle size.

Size distribution typically was analyzed as classified data. As described in Chapter 6, measuring such quality characteristics is a very ineffective approach. In this study, (Reference 18), the ideal function was to have the particle-size diameter change in proportion to the consumed energy. In other words, particle size needed to be inversely proportional to grinding energy:

$$\text{Particle size} = \beta/\text{Grinding energy}$$

Grinding pressure was used to represent the amount of energy. After the optimization, uniform particle size was obtained for varying sample hardness. The particle-size distribution was greatly improved, thus eliminating the need for size adjustment, and material waste during manufacturing was also reduced.

Case 7: Evaluation of Bending Test

In strength testing of polymer material, breakage strength was most typically used as the output response. T. Shirachi (Reference 19) applied a dynamic SN ratio to evaluate strength, using material cross section as input and the breakage strength as output. His study improved the method for evaluating materials properties.

However, it would be better to evaluate the stability of displacement as load varies within the elastic range. A new analysis method was proposed (Reference 19) based on Shirachi's results, but using a load and displacement relationship.

There are two input signals. This function is defined as

$$y = \beta \frac{W}{M^*}$$

where

y = displacement
β = constant
W = load
M^* = test-piece thickness

The study concluded that it was appropriate to use the load/displacement relationship to evaluate material property within the elastic range. These results differed from those using the traditional (maximum breakage strength) approach.

Case 8: Study of Lead-free Stabilizer for Hard Polyvinyl Chloride Injection-Molding Process

In the molding process for hard polyvinyl chloride, a heat stabilizer must be used in order to prevent polymer decomposition by heat. For this purpose, a stabilizer containing lead had been used because of its excellent heat stability and low cost. Due to a revised quality standard for city water, it became necessary to develop a new, lead-free heat stabilizer to replace the one being used (Reference 20).

In the molding process, control factors such as screw rpm, stabilizer type, molding temperature, etc., were studied. To evaluate quality, two subjects were studied: manufacturing function and product function.

The ideal function for manufacturing is transformability. Here, mold dimension was used as the input and product dimension as the output. For the product function, load was considered to be the input and displacement the output. Material type was used as the noise factor for both studies. In addition, the number of shots was also used as a noise factor for the transformability study and the testing speed served as a noise factor for the strength study.

After comparing the results, it was concluded that conditions good for strength are also good for transformability. In both analyses, the effects of stabilizer type and the amount added were significant. From the confirmatory experiments, it was found that the process using lead-free material could perform as well as the process in which leaded material had been used.

Case 9: Parameter Design of Laser Welding for Lap Edge Joint Piece

Laser welding is a high energy density, low heat input process. It demands high accuracy in seam preparation and positioning, which affect the strength of welded joints. In the study (Reference 21), displacement and welding length were used as signals. Force was measured (at different displacement and length) as the output.

$$y = \beta MM^*$$

where

y = force
β = constant
M = displacement
M^* = length

Control factors included the amount of welding energy, gas type, gas pressure, laser-irradiating angle, fixing method, and fixing position. Material thickness, material type, and beam gap were compounded into a noise factor. The current condition was laid out as run no. 1. A gain of 13.22 db was confirmed. Good joint pieces were produced after the optimization.

Case 10: Optimization of Spot Welding Conditions

The products in this study (Reference 22) are used as component parts for oil switching valves, which are controlled in an on-off fashion by the electric current. The components are produced by a spot welding process.

Spot welding is a means of welding thin materials with high efficiency. Since it requires a high amount of energy input in a short period of time, the welding conditions are unstable, resulting in the need for frequent tuning. The quality of spot welding is often evaluated by destructive tests. In the welding process, appearance has been used to control quality, but it is not easy to judge quality from appearance.

The experiment was conducted using test pieces. For the evaluation of quality, it is best to measure the input/output energy relationship. In reality, however, measuring energy is often difficult; therefore, the voltage/

current relationship was measured in this experiment. After the electric characteristic was measured, the pulling strength was measured, and both types of data were analyzed to find their optimum conditions.

From the analysis of voltage/current characteristic, a gain of 14.7 decibels was confirmed, which was close to the estimated gain. On the other hand, there was poor reproducibility of the SN ratio of the strength analysis. Moreover, the confirmed strength under the optimal condition obtained from voltage/current characteristic was better than the confirmed strength under the optimum condition obtained from the strength analysis.

The results of this study were confirmed in mass production. A simple strength-test method was used for evaluation. Part of the adjustment process during production became unnecessary and consumable wear was reduced to a factor of ten. Adjustment of current also was no longer required. As a result, the number of defective welds were significantly reduced.

Case 11: Fine Grinding Process for Developer

This is a continuation study for the fine grinding process described in Case 6. This report (Reference 23) describes the analysis for improving the efficiency of a fine grinding process for a developer, using the dynamic operating window approach.

In the previous study, the ideal function was that particle size should be inversely proportional to grinding pressure. Dr. Taguchi suggested using the dynamic operating window approach, which had been applied to chemical reactions, as follows:

▶ Treat the portion with particle size larger than the upper specification limit as "unreacted," and
▶ Treat the portion with particle size smaller than the lower specification limit as "overreacted."

The data obtained in Case 6 were used for the analysis (no new experiments were run). The SN ratio and analysis method are described in Section 4.7.3.

The result of using dynamic operating window was that the particle-size distribution became symmetric. The grinding efficiency was improved compared to using the zero-point proportional equation approach.

On the other hand, particle-size adjustment became more difficult. This was the result of using the following equation:

$$y = 1 - e^{-\beta t}$$

Under the optimal condition, the fraction of both oversized and undersized particles becomes minimum, resulting in the difficulty of adjusting particle size.

Case 12: Optimizing Parameters of the NC Machine to Cut Stainless Steel

A trainee who teaches at a technological college in Brazil came to Shiga Province Industrial Technology Center (Japan) for three months. He was interested in robust design using the Taguchi Methods approach and conducted a stainless steel processing study (Reference 24). Most of the manufacturing plants in Brazil are not automated, and product quality is highly dependent on skilled labor. Therefore, the introduction of Quality Engineering methods in Brazil would have a major impact on the industries there. Test pieces were used for the processing, and a dynamic SN ratio was used.

The ideal function was established as: "Product dimension is proportional to programmed dimension." Materials SUS 304 and SUS 420J2 were used as noise-factor levels. As a result, a gain of 15.8 db was confirmed, representing a 6.2-fold reduction in standard deviation.

Case 13: Technology Development for Accelerometers

In recent years, many automotive vehicles are equipped with driving control mechanisms. The sensor attached to the control mechanism is called an accelerometer and it detects changes in acceleration when a car is accelerated, decelerated, or steered. Since this type of sensor uses electronic circuits and filling materials, the output varies a great deal due to environmental conditions such as temperature change. Consequently, the performance of the control function is also affected.

When acceleration changes, force (which is mass x acceleration) is generated and a steel ball moves inside a magnetic field. The ball's movement changes the magnetic energy, which is then transformed into an electric signal. In other words, output voltage must be proportional to acceleration.

The experiment (see Reference 25) was conducted by varying control factors such as amount and type of filling material, coil characteristics, bracket shape, resistance characteristics, etc. Temperature and deterioration were considered as noise factors. As a result, a gain of 5.5 db was confirmed.

In this case, a linear equation was used. Dr. Taguchi later recommended that a reference-point proportional equation should have been used, since there is direction (positive and negative) in acceleration.

Case 14: Optimization of the Brazing Condition for a Two-Piece Gear

Brazing, which can be used to bond a great variety of component parts, is an indispensable technique in automobile manufacturing. The technique is important in developing new, better performing products of higher value. Today, brazing is not used often because of insufficient strength of and variability in brazed pieces, although the process is very suitable for mass production. Improving the strength of brazed components would make the brazing process much more applicable in manufacturing. This is a two-piece gear brazing experiment to find a robust condition for stable and high-strength joints (Reference 26).

A good brazing process is one that does not introduce variability in strength. The brazing material penetrates the whole area, and it would be ideal for the two brazed pieces to function like a one-piece part, in this case a gear. Within the elastic range, a gear must follow Hooke's law: load and displacement are proportional. Flux supplying position, flux concentration, flux amount, pressure or contact surface smoothness, etc., were the control factors. A gain of 7.45 db was confirmed.

The following are the comments from Dr. Taguchi:

The SN ratio is calculated from the data before the test piece breaks. In many cases, the SN ratio becomes higher when the piece breaks earlier. Therefore, the elongation at the break point should also be measured, and followed with a nominal-is-best analysis. The sensitivity of elongation at the break point is also important: its target value is determined based on the objective of each application. For another approach, two SN ratios may be obtained by using

Signal M: load

Signal M^* :
$M_1^* = $ elongation within elastic range

$M_2^* = $ total elongation

as two signals.

Case 15: Robustness of Fuel Delivery Systems

An automobile's fuel delivery system must provide a consistent supply of liquid fuel in the expected operating range regardless of external or environmental conditions. The performance of a fuel delivery system can contribute to driveability issues, resulting in customer complaints. Ford Motor Company conducted a study and was able to identify the components that would yield a robust fuel delivery system (Reference 27).

Inconsistent liquid fuel at the rail may cause customer dissatisfaction by manifesting the following vehicle symptoms: difficult restart after engine-off soak, rough or rolling engine idles, and engine stumbles while cruising, accelerating, and decelerating. Insufficient liquid fuel at the fuel injector is a root cause for these symptoms being experienced by customers in the field. High temperatures in the engine, underbody, and fuel tank, as well as high volatility of the fuel lead to fuel vaporization, which may cause insufficient fuel delivery to the injectors. The high temperatures and fuel characteristics cannot be controlled or specified by engineering, so they are considered noise factors.

A new fuel system being developed targets increased fuel system robustness to the varied environmental conditions to which the vehicle is exposed. The conventional system applies battery voltage to the pump and regulates the fuel rail differential pressure via a mechanical regulator. The fuel not consumed by the engine is returned to the tank.

Instead of measuring the above-mentioned symptoms, the ideal function was defined as:

Pump efficiency: Efficiency $= (Q \times p)/(V \times I)$
System input signal: $M = V \times I$
Adjustment signal: $M^* = P$
Ideal function of system: $y = \beta \times M/M^*$
$$\text{i.e., } Q = \beta \times (V \times I)/P$$

The original design did not pass the hot-fuel handling test. During the grade-load section, the engine stalled due to insufficient fuel pressure. The optimal fuel delivery system passed the hot-fuel handling test, indicating that the optimal system provides the pressure required. The bench confirmation tests yielded a 9.1-db improvement over the original fuel delivery system. It is expected that 20% of field returns will be avoided by using the optimal fuel delivery system.

Other benefits are decreased product development time and cost. An alternate approach that was used to address this issue consisted of multiple bench studies followed by vehicle studies. That approach resulted in the same conclusion; however, it took approximately 6 months longer due to learning occurring in smaller incremental steps, and it cost an additional $25,000.

Case 16: Reduction of Chatter in a Wiper System

The function of a wiper system is to clear precipitation (rain, snow, ice, etc.) and foreign material from a windshield in order to provide a clear zone of vision in all weather conditions for the occupants. An annoying phenomenon that affects the performance of windshield wiper systems is wiper chatter. Chatter occurs when the wiper blade does not take the proper set and "skips" across the windshield during operation, potentially causing deterioration in both acoustic and wiping quality. Understanding the physics of chatter plus the wiper system is essential for designing a wiper system that is robust against noise, vibration, and manufacturing variations.

The characteristics traditionally measured to improve the quality of a wiper system are chatter, clear vision, uniformity of wiper pattern, quietness, and life.

In this study (Reference 28), the ideal function was defined as: "The actual time for a wiper to reach a fixed point on the windshield for a cycle should be the same as the theoretical time (ideal time) for which the system was designed." In the presence of the noise factors, the actual time will differ from the theoretical time. Therefore,

$$y = \beta M$$

where

y = actual time
β = constant
M = theoretrical time = 1/rpm of the motor

Control factors such as lateral rigidity of the arm, superstructure rigidity, spring force, profile geometry, rubber materials, etc., were varied. From the estimation, it was predicted that the SN ratio of the optimal condition has an approximately 10 db increase over the baseline.

Case 17: Establishment of Stamping Technology for Specific Door-Opening Area

Stamping is a process to press a piece of metal within its elastic range by two pieces of dies to form a desired shape. Defects such as crack or wrinkle are caused by the stamping conditions, the shape to stamp, material property, etc. In the stamping process for car components, the cracking of flanges occurs very frequently. The causes have been unknown in many cases.

In this study (Reference 29), instead of measuring these symptoms to find the causes of variation, the ideal function was defined as

$$y = \beta M$$

where

y = thickness change, $t_0 - t$, with t_0 being initial thickness and t being thickness after stamping
β = slope
M = intended height change

For good transformability of shape (dimensions), it is desirable to minimize the slope.

Control factors included material type, plate thickness, product angle, pressure, and some dimensions. A compounded noise factor was set using die surface smoothness, lubricating conditions, temperature, clearance, and material characteristics.

A simulation program (three-dimensional finite element method) was used instead of actual experimentation. Under the optimal condition, the gain was estimated as 3.43 db, and the actual gain from confirmation was 4.07 db.

Case 18: Improvement of an Aerocraft Material Casting Process

This study (Reference 30) was conducted to improve the precision of dimensionally critical cast components such as blades used for engines or gas turbines.

In Quality Engineering, transformability has been popularly used to evaluate and improve molding or casting processes. The ideal is not to adjust local dimensions, but to make the shrinkage of all dimensions in a piece consistent (equal). Mold dimension and product dimension are used as the input and the output, respectively, and dynamic SN ratio is used for evaluation. But such transformability is considered as being only the "objective function"; in other words, it is not the generic function. A clear example is the existence of cavities inside the cast part. A cavity causes residual stress because different positions in a part cool down at different rates. In order to observe internal structure, this study was made as a trial using the bending test as a means of evaluation.

Test pieces consist of three components with different thicknesses, and the shape of a test piece is asymmetrical. A bending test was used instead of cutting into the pieces.

Eight control factors, including material type, temperature, pressure, time, etc., were assigned to an L_{18} orthogonal array. Eighteen test pieces were prepared.

The deterioration caused by heat treatment was considered as the noise factor. The test pieces were heated to 900°C, a temperature often used in heat treatment.

A Brinell hardness tester was used for the bending test, because the test equipment can produce a linearly precise load.

The most significant point to mention about this study is that the dimensions before heating were used as a base, so that the deformation after the bending test includes changes caused by the heat treatment. In other words, the effect of heating was added to the dimensional change caused by the bending test. By doing so, the overall quality change caused by transformability and internal stress could be evaluated.

The ideal function for transformability is that dimensions before and after heat treatment must be proportional. For the bending test, the ideal function is that load and deformation must be proportional. The two sets of data were analyzed separately, and their optimum conditions and gains were calculated.

Under the optimum condition of the bending test, the gains from the bending test and from transformability were fairy close. Under the optimum condition of transformability, on the other hand, the gain of the bending test became negative. From the observation of sensitivity, under the optimum condition of transformability, the gain of the bending test became negative, too. This implies that the optimum condition of the bending test is also good for transformability. Therefore, it is more appropriate to optimize a casting process by analyzing the results from the bending test.

Case 19: Robust Design of an Automatic Document Feeder

The paper feeders used for copy machines or facsimile machines require a smooth and speedy feeding. Under the current new-product-development approach, either the design parameters are changed in a trial-and-error fashion or a huge amount of data are statistically analyzed. As a beginner in Quality Engineering, the author applied the robust design approach to a document feeder and improved the efficiency of product development (Reference 31).

The mechanism of this system is to feed the originals smoothly and continuously without letting the pickup roller pick up an individual original every time. If this objective were achieved, then feeding time reduction, a longer pickup-roller life, and lower audible noise would be expected. Instead of measuring characteristics such as time, life, or audible noise, the function of this system was defined as the feeding time being proportional to the number of pieces of originals fed to machine.

Under the optimal condition, the variation of feeding time was reduced by a factor of eight compared with the initial condition. The feeding time itself was reduced by 30%, and the number of the pickup roller operating times was reduced. As a result, audible noise was reduced, and the machine-maintenance interval was prolonged.

Case 20: Reduction in Airflow Noise of an Intercooler System

One of the methods to increase the output power of car engines is to use turbochargers (T/C) and intercoolers (I/C). Many cars designed for a high output of power are equipped with these.

The output power of an engine is determined by the amount of the mixed gas sucked into the engine cylinder. The more gas sucked in, the higher the power generated. T/C is used for "excess feeding": a method of increasing the feeding efficiency by compressing the mixed air and consequently raising the air pressure above atmospheric pressure.

When air is compressed, its temperature rises and density decreases. In order to increase power, I/C is used to cool the air. In many cases, air-cooling type of coolers are used because their simple structure is easy to manufacture and they require no maintenance.

When the airflow resistance inside the cooler is high, the cooling efficiency is reduced and audible noise is often noticed. In the traditional product-development process, the problem-solving approach has been to detect causes, measure several quality items, and take countermeasures for the individual problems.

To improve the cooling function, it is required that the airflow resistance be low and the flow rate be uniform. The engine output power varies with driving speed. The airflow changes as the accelerator is pushed down. Therefore, it is ideal that the airflow rate be proportional to the amount of air (Reference 32).

As the rpm of T/C varies under different driving conditions, it is also ideal for the airflow rate to vary proportionally to the rpm of T/C. The ideal function is therefore defined as

$$y = \beta M M^*$$

where

y = airflow speed
β = slope
M = amount of airflow
M^* = rpm of T/C

Dimensions of the cooler were varied as the control factors. A gain of 7.89 db was confirmed, which is equivalent to a 60% reduction in the variability of airflow. Under the optimal condition, the cooling capability increased by 20%, which means the engine capability increased by 2%.

With the increased cooling capability, the size of I/C can be smaller, which could reduce cost and provide more flexibility in positioning the engine room layout.

Finally, the audible noise disappeared. It must be mentioned that in the initial stage of development, audible noise was measured for analysis, but the problem could not be solved. By optimizing the ideal function, several benefits were realized.

Case 21: Parameter Design on the Green Sand Preparation for Foundry

Green sand foundry is an old casting process. Because of low cost, reusability, and easy mass production, about half of the cast products are produced by this method today. On the other hand, the binding force of green sand after mixing varies, and the quality of the casting mold may deteriorate over time, thus causing defects in the cast pieces.

Instead of using actual products and measuring defectives, test pieces were made, and the ideal function was determined (Reference 33). The ideal function was that load should be proportional to deformation.

Control factors included the mixing ratios of various raw materials, mixing time, etc. To make test pieces, sand was packed in a cylinder consisting of an upper and a lower part. The whole cylinder was pulled, and the load was measured at different amounts of deformation. The SN ratio was calculated from the load and deformation relationship.

A gain of 5.41 db was estimated, and a 4.76-db gain was obtained from confirmation. Currently, quality is evaluated using a JT tester. In this test, impact is applied to a test piece and the number of impacts before destruction is observed. The test results were:

	After mixing	1 hour after mixing
Optimal condition	64	48
Initial condition	33	16

It was confirmed that the sand mixed under the optimal condition deteriorated less than when mixed under the initial condition.

11.3 ELECTRICAL INDUSTRY

Case 22: Optimization of a Wave Soldering Process

Today, printed circuit boards of progressively higher density continue to be created. To improve quality, quality characteristics such as "bridge" or "nonsoldering" have been used. In the early stage of Quality Engineering, SN ratios of the larger-is-better type were used for bridge, while smaller-is-better type of SN ratios, were used for nonsoldering. Or, nondynamic type of operating window was used for bridge and nonsoldering combined.

In this study (Reference 34), voltage and current relationship was used as the basis for the ideal function. The relationship between current and cross-sectional area was also studied. Thus, there are two signal factors. To maximize the SN ratio of the voltage and current relationship is to study the "product function." To maximize the SN ratio of the current and cross-sectional area is to study "manufacturability." When these two SN ratios are combined into one study, both product and manufacturing functions can be optimized at the same time. It must be noted that to improve both functions, only one metric (the SN ratio of the following ideal function) was used. This is truly a simultaneous engineering approach.

$$y = \beta M M^*$$

where

y = current
β = slope
M = voltage
M^* = cross-sectional area

Four levels for voltage and three levels for cross-sectional area, a total of 12 levels, were assigned as the combined signal factor. Control factors such as flux flow, flux density, distance between solder and base plate, and flux temperature, were studied.

Under the optimal condition, an SN ratio gain of 5.4 db was estimated, and 4.99 db was achieved from the confirmation. This is equivalent to a 3.16-fold reduction in variability.

Case 23: Development of Exchange-coupled Direct-Overwrite MO Disk

Magnetooptical disks were put into the market in 1988. Since then, many kinds of technologies have been invented to expand their capacity, lower their cost, and increase their rate of data transfer. The exchanger-coupled direct-overwrite (DOW) MO disk is one of the techniques for achieving a higher transfer rate (Reference 35).

Since the structure of DOW-MO disks is complicated, the expectation is that it will be more difficult to maintain stable quality during mass-production.

The ideal function was defined as: "The length of magnetic mark is proportionally transformed to the time of light emitted from the laser." An L_{18} orthogonal array was used to assign the control factors. A combination of L_9 and L_4 orthogonal arrays were used for assigning the signal and noise factors. Some of the conditions assigned in the outer arrays were nearly the worst conditions, and there were no measurements. For these missing data, sequential approximation was used.

Since this study was the development of a new technology, there was no initial condition. Therefore, the confirmation was made by comparing the optimal condition with one near the worst condition. The gain was about 14 db.

In the past, much time was spent on studying interactions. By the application of Quality Engineering, the development time was greatly reduced.

Case 24: Robust Design and Tuning for an Equalizer

One of the important quality items for amplifiers is that the gain of frequency characteristic be flat. This is often not the case in reality, especially for amplifiers with wide ranges. The objective of this study (Reference 36) is to optimize the robustness of an equalizer used for amplifiers and find the control factors that do not affect the SN ratio but are sensitive for tuning. An equalizer is used to compensate the frequency characteristic.

In electronics, it is common for the input, the output, and the proportional constant to consist of complex numbers, with both the real and the imaginary numbers being important. In this study, using Dr. Taguchi's the analysis method for dealing with complex numbers yielded good results.

The ideal function of an equalizer is that the input voltage be proportional to the output voltage. The results showed a confirmation gain of 19.54 db, compared with the worst condition.

Case 25: Fabrication of Transparent Conductive Thin Films

Recently, the demands for flat panel displays, such as liquid crystal displays, electroluminescence, and vacuum fluorescent displays, are increasing for personal computers and word processors. The rigid requirement for the transmittance and conductance of the transparent conductive layer complicates the production conditions. In order to simplify the production process and improve productivity, attempts were made to optimize the electron beam (EB) deposition process (Reference 37).

The transparent conductive layer used for flat display devices requires good transparency and conductivity. The ideal function was determined to be

$$y = \beta MM^*$$

where

y = current
β = slope
M = film thickness
M^* = voltage

The two signal factors and the noise factor, location of base plate, were assigned to the outer array. The rpm of the base plate, amount of additive, depositing speed, etc., were assigned as control factors. A gain of 5.27 db was confirmed compared with the current condition.

Case 26: Application of Quality Engineering to a Filter Circuit

Filter circuits are used for various car audio equipment. In the past, circuit design has been tailored for individual products, which is inefficient. In this study (Reference 12), the concept of technology development was tried as a model study. Parameter Design and method of the least squares were used together in the simulation.

The SN ratio of complex number was used for the analysis. One of the calculations is explained in Section 7.3. The results of the confirmation is shown in Figure 7.8.

Case 27: Parameter Design of a Low Pass Filter Using Complex Numbers

In the design of alternating circuits, complex numbers are commonly used to describe the values of the circuit elements because amplitude and phase can be easily determined.

Root mean squares have traditionally been used when designing AC circuits. By using complex numbers in Parameter Design, the variability of both the amplitude and phase of the output can be reduced. Therefore, for a system whose input and output are expressed by sine waves, we should use complex numbers if we want to expect a better result than using root mean square. In the study (Reference 38), Parameter Design for a first-order low pass filter using complex numbers was conducted.

Cutoff frequency is an index for low pass filters. The objective function is to cut off the frequency higher than some given value. In order to reduce the variation of frequency, the input frequency has been traditionally varied to bring the output amplitude and phase closer to the theoretical curve. An assumption was made that if the frequency variability could be reduced at a certain input frequency, the variability at other frequencies could also be reduced. Therefore, in the study, the input frequency was fixed while attempts were made to improve the dynamic characteristic by varying the amplitude.

The ideal function is that input voltage be proportional to output voltage. The types of elements and the combination of RC were the control factors. Temperature variation was used as the noise factor. A 3.8-db gain was confirmed.

Case 28: Technology Development of Drain Electrode Process for Power MOSFET

A power MOSFET has been used as a reliable switching device in automobile electronics. The increasing applications of electronic systems in cars require a lower "on-resistance," the resistance when the system is in use. Normally, reduction of on-resistance is achieved by miniaturizing the unit. In this study (Reference 39), however, on-resistance was minimized through the improvement of the drain electrode process.

In the development or improvement of the electrode, quality characteristics such as the film thickness or bonding strength were observed. The generic function was defined as

$$y = \beta M$$

where

y = voltage drop
β = sensitivity
M = current

The gain was 18.01 db by estimation and 18.19 db by confirmation. An 18.19-db gain means the standard deviation of resistance was reduced by a factor of 8. Also the sensitivity under the optimal condition was reduced by 16.36 db, representing a reduction in resistance by a factor of 7.

By reducing resistance, the base plate thickness can be decreased, resulting in the miniaturizing of chips, higher productivity, and lower cost.

Case 29: Improvement of Differential Amplifier Circuit

The differential amplifier circuit is one of the most important basic circuits used in analog integrated circuits. The conventional method to design a circuit is to determine the value of an element by simulating the variation of the element at three levels (minimum, average, and maximum), but the output voltage variability cannot be reduced effectively by this method.

In this study (Reference 40), Parameter Design was conducted by assigning the circuit elements as control factors and compounding the variability of transistors as a noise factor. The ideal function is a proportional relationship between the input voltage and the output voltage. It is also ideal that the slope be equal to one. Simulation was used, and a gain of 17.78 db was confirmed, which is equivalent to a 4.5-fold reduction of manufacturing variability.

Case 30: Robust Design of a Voltage-Controlled Oscillator

In this study (Reference 41), a voltage-controlled oscillator(VCO) used in wireless communication systems was designed. During the design stage, the VCOs have been traditionally evaluated by measuring the frequency selectivity and the output power under oscillating conditions. These types of character- istics are referred to as "objective characteristics," and are not recommended in Taguchi Methods.

Instead, the basic function was evaluated in a nonoscillating condition. The DC signal from the power supply and the feedback AC signal were supplied to the transistor. These signals were put to the oscillation circuit to generate the output in the form of complex numbers. The ideal function was determined to be

$$y = \beta MM^*$$

where

y = output (complex number)
β = slope
M = DC current
M^* = AC current

The types and constants of elements were varied as the control factors. Temperature and humidity were compounded as a noise factor. After optimization, a 8.51-db gain was estimated and a 7.61-db gain was confirmed.

One of the quality characteristics required for a VCO is frequency selectivity. In the traditional approach, adjustment of frequency was done in the initial stage of design. But using the Quality Engineering approach, robustness must be accomplished first by optimizing the basic function, then it is followed by frequency adjustment. It was confirmed that good frequency adjustment could be made without affecting the basic function.

Case 31: Optimization of an Electrical Encapsulant

An encapsulant that provides electrical isolation between elements on the outer surface of a night-vision image-intensifier tube was optimized. The reliability of the image-sensor module was defined at the customer level as the ability of the device to maintain luminous gain over time. Luminous gain is the light-amplifying power of the image-sensor module.

The historic approach for improving the reliability of the product and image-sensor module was to evaluate design and process changes while exposing these devices to customer-usage environments. These evaluations were typically single factorial in nature, and the quality characteristic measured was "number of cycles" until the device's "luminous" gain degraded past a certain value or "the total percent of gain degradation." Prior to this effort (Reference 47), the change in luminous gain caused by the penetration of moisture into the module was measured. Subsequent experimentation focused on measuring leakage current using the actual sensor product, but this achieved marginal success. Finally, a coupon was developed to investigate the ideal function of the encapsulant.

The ideal function was defined as

$$y = \beta \frac{M}{M^*}$$

y = current leakage
β = sensitivity
M = applied voltaget
M^* = electrode spacing

Control factors included

Potting cylinder vacuum
Potting material ratio
Cleaning method
Chamber vacuum
Postwash dwell time
Postwash exposure
Cure time/temperature

The SN ratio of the system improved 3.8 db compared to standard conditions, and the slope was reduced from 1.373 to 0.279, or 80%.

Case 32: Robust Design of an EW Receiver

The timely detection and identification of an enemy's radar signal is critical to the success of an electronic countermeasure (ECM) mission. A project was initiated to improve the threat detection and identification capability of a generic electronic warfare (EW) swept superheterodyne receiver (Reference 48). This receiver must demonstrate robust performance in a wide range of EW conditions. To optimize robustness, the performance characteristic selected for evaluation was the receiver's probability of detecting and identifying a random radar threat versus the elapsed time of the threat in a dynamic EW environment.

In a previous study, the root mean squared elapsed time of the swept superhet receiver before intercepting a randomly selected radar threat was used for the analysis; however, it did not provide a clear indication of the receiver's dynamic performance.

The ideal function was defined as

$$P_d = 1 - e^{-\beta T}$$

where

P_d = probability of detection
β = constant
T = time

Let P_m be the probability of a miss. Then

$$P_m = 1 - P_d$$

and

$$P_m = e^{-\beta T}$$

$$y = \ln(1/P_m) = \ln\left(e^{\beta T}\right) = \beta T$$

$L_{18} \times L_{18}$ orthogonal matrices were used to assign control and noise factors. Control factors included:

> Dwell time for low probability of intercept radar (LPI) threats
> Number of cycles for LPI priority scans
> Dwell time for pulse and pulse doppler (PR) band scanning
> Additional dwell for LPI band after a threat detection
> Additional dwell for PR band after a threat detection
> Receiver threshold level

Noise factors included:

> Number of LPI threats
> Starting time of each LPI threat (first set)
> Starting time of each LPI threat (second time)
> Signal amplitude of each LPI threat
> Starting time of each PR threat (first set)
> Starting time of each PR threat (second time)
> Number of PR threats

After the optimization, a 57% reduction of elapsed time for threat detection was achieved over the current design.

11.4 CHEMICAL INDUSTRY

Case 33: Optimization of Synthesis Conditions for a Chemical Reaction

In the manufacturing of chemical products, the determination of conditions favoring synthesis reactions greatly affects quality and cost. The objective of this study (Reference 42) is to reduce reaction time, which increases productivity and reduces cost.

Traditionally, yield of product has been used as the quality characteristic. Such digital-type characteristics are not recommended in Taguchi Methods. Instead, the dynamic operating window (as illustrated in Section 4.7.3) was used to maximize the SN ratio. In the experiment, an L_9 orthogonal array was used to assign four control factors. After the optimization, the slope, β, increased 1.8 times higher than the current condition, which means the reaction time can be halved.

Case 34: Development of a Formula for Chemicals Used in Body Warmers

The heat-generating material used for body warmers consists of iron powder, activated charcoal, water, salt, and a water retainer. These materials are packed in an air-permeable inner bag, which is further enclosed in an air-tight outer bag. Recently, the demand for such body warmers has been rapidly increasing because of they are convenient to use.

However, when the ambient temperature at which a body warmer is used changes, the user may feel too warm or too cold. The user feels warm when entering a heated room or feels cold when going outside. This is because the temperature generated by the body warmer varies depending on the environmental temperature. This study (Reference 43) attempted to develop a formula that maintains a constant temperature which is not affected by environmental temperature change.

The ideal function was

$$y = \beta M M^*$$

where

y = heat generated
β = slope
M = time
M^* = amount of ingredients

The amounts of ingredients such as iron, active charcoal, salt, water retainer, etc., were assigned as the control factors. There were two noise factors: the outer-bag sealing time and the number of flannels need-ed to cover the tested unit. These were compounded into two conditions.

A gain of 3.91 db was confirmed for the SN ratio, and one of 2.56 db was confirmed for the sensitivity. Under the optimum condition, although the amount of heat-generating ingredients was 30% less than in the current condition, both maintained almost the same temperature. This is probably because the sensitivity (10log S) was improved by 2.56 db, or 1.803 in antilog value. Therefore, the amount of heat generated per unit weight increased by 1.34 (the square root of 1.803).

Case 35: Study on the Evaluation of the Friction Function of Plastic Materials and Development of a Low-Friction/Low-Wear Polyacetal Resin

Polyacetal resin is widely used to make gears for electric, electronic, or car components. Recently, the development of no-lubrication, low-noise, and low-wear material has become more and more popular.

In the study, (Reference 44), quality characteristics such as permanent deformation of the material, change in quality of the material, heat generation, vibration, or audible noise were not observed. Instead, the ideal function was identified as:

$$y = \beta M$$

where

y = friction
β = coefficient of friction
M = load

To measure friction, a friction and abrasion tester (JIS K7218-86) was available. But the equipment easily generates heat on the contact surface and requires a relatively long time for testing and test-piece preparation. Therefore, test equipment was developed for this study.

The amounts of ingredients were used as control factors. Tests were made before and after deterioration. The maximum and minimum values were observed. A gain of 4.8 db was confirmed. The life of gears made from the optimal material became 1.5 times longer than the current material's life. The heat generated due to friction of gears was reduced. Also the time needed for evaluating friction characteristic became much shorter, which resulted in shortening of the development time for the material.

Case 36: Development of a Measuring Technique for Dispersion Homogeneity and Binding Capacity of Composite Material

In the manufacturing of dry developers for copy machines and printers, it is important that colorants and charge-control agents are homogeneously dispersed and strongly bound to the binding resins.

In the manufacturing process, materials are mixed, kneaded, crushed, classified, surface-treated, and filled. Traditionally, many quality items are measured, such as ingredients after mixing, the amount of material on the surface, physical properties of the product, and various items of copied images. By measuring these characteristics, however, the performance of the upstream process such as the mixing process cannot be known until the product is obtained from the downstream process. It is time-consuming, and the evaluation is not accurate enough.

The ideal function is that materials be uniformly mixed in the mixing process and strongly bound with resin in the kneading process (Reference 45). In testing, the deformation of test pieces must be linearly proportional to the load added and also inversely proportional to the cross-sectional area.

$$y = \beta M / M^*$$

where

y = deformation
β = slope
M = load
M^* = cross-sectional area

The control factors in the mixing and the kneading processes were studied with a noise factor: the direction of mixing and kneading.
The following were the results:

▶ A gain of 9.91 db was confirmed.
▶ The resistance of the developer increased 6 times that of the current product, showing the dispersion was uniform.
▶ The charging property, fluidity, and fixing property were improved.
▶ It was estimated that the life of the developer could be 30% longer.
▶ The "image noise" problem, black and white spots on the copied image, was greatly improved.
▶ Product recovery in the crushing process was improved by 10% due to an increase in the hardness of developer.
▶ Production speed was increased by 50%.

Case 37: Optimization of an Ink Formula

There are four subsystems in a digital printer. The function of each subsystem is

▶ **Optical document scanner:** converts data to electric signals.
▶ **Thermal head:** supplies power to heating elements.

▶ **Resin film puncher:** punches holes on a thermoplastic resin film by heat.
▶ **Printer:** supplies ink to the punched film to form images on paper.

There are various quality characteristics in copy machines or printers. In the image-forming process, there are characteristics such as image concentration, dirt, resolution, tone, or uniformity of concentration, etc. However, these belong to low-level quality characteristics that are important for inspection, but are not good characteristics for quality improvement.

In the research of ink, characteristics such as permeability, stability, flow value, or flexibility have been commonly used. But the conclusions of research based on these characteristics might not be reproducible.

The objective of this study (Reference 46) was to improve printer quality through the optimization of ink formula. The generic function of ink, to transfer the image of the original to the image printed, belongs to passive-type dynamic characteristics, similar to measurement. In the printer, the last subsystem, the image on the thermoplastic resin film, consists of a number of holes (dots) of different sizes. The area of these dots is used as the input signal.

The ideal relationship would be the area of an output dot being proportional to the area of a corresponding input dot. The control factors include the conditions of carbon, surface-active agent, varnish-dispersion agent, and solvent. The aging of ink was used as a noise factor.

A gain of 4.58 db was confirmed, and the ink developed exhibited excellent quality, producing fine lines with less deterioration than evident with other inks.

Glossary

additivity a concept relating to the independence of factors. The effect of additive factors occurs in the same direction (i.e., they do not interact).

adjusting factor a signal factor used to adjust the output.

analysis of variance (ANOVA) analysis of the impacts of variances caused by factors. ANOVA is performed after the decomposition of the total sum of squares.

classified attribute the type of quality characteristic that is divided into discrete classes rather than being measured on a continuous scale.

compounding of noise factors a strategy for reducing the number of experimental runs by combining noise factors into a single output for experimentation.

confirmation experiment a follow-up experiment run under the conditions defined as optimum by a previous experiment. The confirmation experiment is intended to verify the experimental predictions.

confounding a condition in which experimental information on variables cannot be separated. The information becomes intermingled with other information.

control factor a product or process parameter whose values can be selected and controlled by the design or manufacturing engineer.

data analysis the process performed to determine the best factor levels for reducing variability and adjusting the average response toward the target value.

decomposition of variation the decomposition of collected data into the sources of variation.

degrees of freedom	the number of independent squares associated with a given factor (usually the number of factor levels minus one).
direct product design	a layout designed to determine the interaction between any control factor assigned to an orthogonal array and any noise factor assigned to the outer array.
distribution	a way of describing the output of a common-cause system variation, in which individual values are not predictable but in which the outcomes as a group form a pattern that can be described in terms of its location, spread, and shape. Location is commonly expressed by the terms of the mean or median, and spread is commonly expressed in terms of the standard deviation or the range of a sample. Shape involves many characteristics, such as symmetry and peakedness. These are often summarized by using the name of a common distribution, such as the normal, binomial, or Poisson.
downstream quality	also called customer quality, such as car noise, vibration, or product life, etc. It is the type of quality easily noticed by the customer. This is the type of quality to avoid using for quality improvement.
dummy treatment	a method used to modify an orthogonal array to accommodate a factor with fewer levels.
dynamic characteristic	a characteristic that expresses the functionality, transformation, adjustability of the output of a system or subsystem.
dynamic operating window	the gap between the total reaction rate and the side-reaction rate in chemical reactions. The greater the gap, the more desirable the result.
error sum of squares	the total of the sums of squares that are considered as residual.
expected value of a variance	the mean of an infinite number of variances estimated from collected data.
factor	a parameter or variable that may impact product or process performance.

factorial effect   the effect of a factor or an interaction or both.

fractional factorial layout   an experimental design that consists of a fraction of all factor-level combinations.

go/no-go specification   the traditional approach to quality, which states that a part, component, or assembly that lies between upper and lower specifications meets quality standards.

Hermitian matrix   in matrix A, when the element of ith column and kth row, denoted by a_{ik}, is equal to the conjugate complex number of a_{ki}, A is called the Hermitian matrix.

Hermitian form   the form using the Hermitian matrix.

hi–low table   a table showing the magnitude of effects in descending order.

indicative factor   a factor that has a technical meaning but has nothing to do with the selection of the best level.

inner array   a layout or orthogonal array for the control factors selected for experimentation or simulation.

interaction   a condition in which the impact of a factor or factors upon a quality characteristic changes depending on the level of another factor (i.e., the interdependent effect of two or more factors).

larger-is-better characteristic   the type of performance parameter that gives improved performance as the value of the parameter increases (e.g., tensile strength, power, etc.) This type of characteristic belongs to the category of quality characteristics that has infinity as the ideal value and has no negative value.

linear equation   the equation showing the case when the input/output regression line does not pass through the origin.

linearity   a measure of the straightness of a response plot. Also the extent to which a measuring instrument's response is proportional to the measured quantity.

manufacturing tolerance   the assessment of the tolerance prior to shipping. The manufacturing tolerance is usually tighter than the consumer tolerance.

mean   the average value of some variable.

mean data analysis	an analysis performed to determine the mean values of experimental or simulation runs. Also called mean effects analysis.
mean square deviation (MSD)	a measure of variability around the mean or target value.
mean square error variance	the variance considered as the error.
mean sum of squares	the sum of squares per unit degree of freedom.
measurement accuracy	the difference between the average result of a measurement with a particular instrument and the true value of the quantity being measured.
measurement error	the difference between the actual and measured value of a measured quantity.
measurement precision	the extent to which a repeated measurement gives the same result. Variations may arise from the inherent capabilities of the instrument, from changes in operating condition, etc. Also see **repeatability** and **reproducibility**.
midstream quality	also called specified quality, such as dimension or specification. This is the type of quality to avoid using for quality improvement.
noise factor	any uncontrollable factor that causes product quality to vary. There are three types of noise: (1) noise due to external causes (e.g., temperature, humidity, operator, vibration, etc.); (2) noise due to internal causes (e.g., wear, deterioration, etc.); and (3) noise due to part-to-part or product-to-product variation.
nominal-is-best characteristic	the type of performance characteristic parameter that has an attainable target or nominal value (e.g., length, voltage, etc.).
number of units	the total of the square of the coefficients in a linear equation. It is used to calculate the sum of squares.

nondynamic operating window	a gap between the maximum and the minimum functional limits. A wide gap means a more robust function.
off-line quality control	activities that use design of experiments or simulation to optimize product and process designs. These activities include system design, parameter design, and tolerance design.
omega transformation	a method of transforming the data within the range of zero to one into the data within the range of minus infinity to plus infinity.
on-line quality control	activities that occur at the manufacturing phase and include the use of the quality loss function to determine the optimum inspection interval, control limits, etc. On-line quality control is used to maintain the optimization gained through off-line quality control.
origin quality	also called functional quality. This is the type of quality used to improve the robustness of product functions.
orthogonal array	a matrix of numbers arranged in rows and columns in such a way that each pair of columns are orthogonal to each other. When used in an experiment, each row represents the state of the factors in a given experiment. Each column represents a specific factor or condition that can be changed from experiment to experiment. The array is called orthogonal because the effects of the various factors in the experimental results can be separated from each other.
outer array	a layout or orthogonal array for the noise factors selected for experimentation.
parameter design	the second of three design stages. During parameter design, the nominal values of critical dimensions and characteristics are established to optimize performance at low cost.
percent contribution	the pure sum of squares divided by the total sum of squares to express the impact of a factorial effect.

point calibration calibration of a specific point in measurement.

pooled error variance the error variance calculated by pooling the smaller factorial effects.

preliminary experiment an experiment conducted with only noise factors to determine direction and tendencies of the effect of these noise factors. The results of the preliminary experiment are used to compound noise factors.

pure (net) error sum of squares the sum of squares after adding the error terms originally included in the regular sums of squares of factorial effects.

pure (net) sum of squares the sum of squares of a factorial effect after subtracting the error portion.

quality the loss imparted by a product to society from the time the product is shipped.

quality characteristic a characteristic of a product or process that defines product or process quality. The quality characteristic measures the degree of conformity to some known standard.

quality engineering quality engineering is a series of approaches to predict and prevent the troubles or problems that might occur in the market after a product is sold and used by the customer under various environmental and applied conditions for the duration of designed product life.

quality function deployment (QFD) a term used to describe the process by which customer feedback is analyzed and results are incorporated into product design. The QFD process is often referred to as determining the "voice of the customer."

quality loss function (QLF) a parabolic approximation of the quality loss that occurs when a quality characteristic deviates from its best or target value. The QLF is expressed in monetary units: the cost of deviating from the target increases quadratically the further it moves from the target. The formula used to compute the QLF depends on the type of quality characteristic being used.

reference-point proportional equation	the equation showing the case when a signal level is used as a reference input.
repeatability	the variation in repeated measurements of a particular object with a particular instrument by a single operator.
reproducibility	the state whereby the conclusions drawn from small-scale laboratory experiments will be valid under actual manufacturing and usage conditions (i.e., consistent and desirable).
response table	a table showing level averages of factors.
response factor	the output of a system or the result of a performance.
robust technology development	an approach to maximize the functionality of a group of products at the earliest stage, such as at research-and-development stage, and to minimize overall product-development cycle time.
robustness	the condition used to describe a product or process design that functions with limited variability in spite of diverse and changing environmental conditions, wear, or, component-to-component variation. A product or process is robust when it has limited or reduced functional variation even in the presence of noise.
sensitivity	magnitude of the output per input shown by the slope of the input/output relationship.
sensitivity analysis	analysis performed to determine the mean values of experimental runs used when the means are widely dispersed.
sequential approximation	a method of providing figures to fill the open spots in an incomplete set of data to make data analysis possible.
signal factor	a factor used to adjust the output.

signal-to-noise (S/N) ratio	any of a group of special equations that are used in experimental design to find the optimum factor-level settings that will create a robust product or process. The S/N ratio originated in the communications field, in which it represented the power of the signal over the power of the noise. In Taguchi methods usage, it represents the ratio of the mean (signal) to the standard deviation (noise). The formula used to compute the S/N ratio depends on the type of quality characteristic being used.
signal-to-noise (S/N) ratio analysis	analysis performed to determine the factor levels required to reduce variability and achieve the ideal function of a characteristic.
slope calibration	calibration of slope in measurement.
smaller-is-better characteristic	the type of performance characteristic parameter that has zero as the best value (e.g., wear, deterioration, etc.). This type of characteristic belongs to the category of quality characteristics that has zero as the best value and has no negative value.
split-type analysis	a method to determine SN ratios without noise factors.
standard deviation	a measure of the spread of the process output or the spread of a sampling statistic from the process (e.g., of subgroup averages). Standard deviation is denoted by the Greek letter σ (sigma).
standard rate of mistake	the rate of mistake when type 1 and type 2 mistakes are adjusted to be equal.
standard SN ratio	the SN ratio calculated from the standard rate of mistake.
system design	the first of three design stages. During system design, scientific and engineering knowledge is applied to produce a functional prototype design. This prototype is used to define the initial settings of a product or process design characteristic.

tolerance design	the third of three design stages. Tolerance design is applied if the design is not acceptable at its optimum level following parameter design. During tolerance design, more costly materials or processes with tighter tolerances are considered.
transformation	the function of transforming the input signal, such as mold dimension or CNC machine input program, into the output, such as product dimension.
triangular table	a table containing all the information needed to locate main effects and two factor interactions. A triangular table is used for linear graph modification and the assignment of interactions.
tuning factor	a signal factor used to adjust the output.
two-step optimization	an approach used in Parameter Design by maximizing robustness (SN ratio) first, followed by adjusting sensitivity.
upstream quality	also called robust quality. This is the type of quality used to improve the robustness of a specific product.
variability	the property of exhibiting variation (i.e., changes or differences).
variance	the mean square deviation (MSD) from the mean. The sum of squares divided by the degrees of freedom.
variation	the inevitable differences among individual outputs of a process.
variation of a factor	same as the sum of squares of a factorial effect.
Youden square	incomplete Latin square.
zero-point proportional equation	the equation showing the case when the input/output regression line passes through the origin. The equation most frequently used in dynamic characteristics.

References

Note:

(1) All references are written in Japanese except the following numbers are written in English: 1, (volumes 1, 2, 3, 4, and 6), 10, 11, 13, 14, 27, 28, 47, and 48.

(2) Most of the references are cited from the *Journal of Quality Engineering Forum*, Tokyo, Japan. To avoid frequent redundancy, the journal name is abbreviated as "*JQEF*."

1. Genichi Taguchi, et al., *Quality Engineering Series*, Vol. 1: *Research and Development*, Vol. 2: *On-Line Production*, Vol. 3: *Signal-to-Noise Ratio for Quality Measurement*, Vol. 4: *Design of Experiment*, Vol. 5: *Case Studies from Japan*, Vol. 6: *Case Studies from U.S. and Europe*, Vol. 7: *Case Studies in Measurement from Japan*, Japanese Standards Association(Tokyo, Japan)/ American Supplier Institute(Dearborn, MI, U.S.A.), 1991.

2. Genichi Taguchi, *System of Experimental Design*, Unipub(New York, NY, U.S.A.)/ American Supplier Institute(Dearborn, MI, U.S.A.), 1987

3. Y. Miura and K. Ueno: "NC Machining Technology Development," American Supplier Institute Symposium, Dearborn, MI, U.S.A., 1992.

4. Yoske Goda and Takashi Furuzawa, "Parameter Design of Fine Line Patterning for IC's Fabrication," *JQEF*, Vol. 1, No. 2, Tokyo, Japan, 1993.

5. Ryoji Nakamura, "Improvement on Vacuum Fluorescent Display Material," Quality Engineering Symposium, Japanese Standards Association, Tokyo, Japan/ Central Japan Quality Control Association, Nagoya, Japan, 1993.

6. Genichi Taguchi, et al., *Quality Engineering Series*, Vol. 1, *Research and Development*, Japanese Standards Association, Tokyo, Japan/ American Supplier Institute, Dearborn, MI, U.S.A., 1991.

7. Genichi Taguchi, *Statistical Analysis*, Maruzen, Tokyo, Japan, 1972.

8. Yoshishige Kanemoto: "Stability Improvement of a Phase Advancer," *Standardization and Quality Control*, Japanese Standards Association, Vol. 47, No. 7.

9. American Supplier Institute, *Taguchi Methods Implementation Manual*, Dearborn, MI, U.S.A., 1992.

10. Nuriel Samuel and Louis Lavalle: "Application of Taguchi Methods to Friction Rated Feeder Design," American Supplier Institute Symposium, Dearborn, MI, U.S.A., 1990.

11. American Supplier Institute, *Dynamic Characteristics and Measurement System Manual*, 1990.

12. Kiyoshi Koyama and Keiji Nakao, "Application of Quality Engineering on Filter Circuit," *JQEF*, Tokyo, Japan, Vol. 3, No. 3.

13. Y. Miura and K. Ueno, "NC Machining Technology Development," American Supplier Institute Symposium, Dearborn, MI, U.S.A., 1992.

14. T. Asakawa and K. Ueno, "Stabilization of Injection Molding Process for Carbon Fiber Reinforced Plastic," American Supplier Institute Symposium, Dearborn, U.S.A., 1992.

15. K. Fujita, T. Matsunaga, and S. Horibe, "Material Development by a Spraying Process," *JQEF*, Vol. 2, No. 1, Tokyo, Japan.

16. K. Ueno and K. Mori, "Technology Development of Laser Welding," *JQEF*, Vol. 2, No. 1, Tokyo, Japan.

17. T. Nojima, H. Machida, and E. Ookawa, "Robust Design of a Paper Feeding Device," *JQEF*, Tokyo, Japan, Vol. 2, No. 2.

18. H. Shibano, T. Nishikawa, and K. Takenaka, "Development of a Technique for Adjusting Particle Size in a Fine Grinding Process of a Developer," *JQEF*, Vol. 2, No. 3, Tokyo, Japan.

19. T. Shirachi, M. Ono, K. Tuchikura, and H. Yano, "Evaluation of Bending Test," *JQEF*, Vol. 2, No. 6, Tokyo, Japan.

20. N. Goto and T. Aoki: "Study of Lead-free Stabilizer for Hard Polyvinyl Chloride Injection Molding Process," *JQEF*, Vol. 3, No. 1, Tokyo, Japan, 1993.

21. Mitsugi Fukahori, "Parameter Design of Laser Welding for Lap Edge Joint Piece," *JQEF*, Vol. 3, No. 2, Tokyo, Japan.

22. S. Kazashi and K. Kanasashi, "Optimization of Spot Welding Conditions," *JQEF*, Vol. 4, No. 2, Tokyo, Japan.

23. H. Shibano, T. Nishikawa, and K. Takenaka, "Fine Grinding Process for Developer," *JQEF*, Tokyo, Japan, Vol. 5, No. 1.

24. K. Nakayama, Julio Cesar Bento Ribeiro, K. Tsukise, T Goto, and S. Hirose, "Optimizing Parameters of the NC Machine to Cut Stainless Steel," *JQEF*, Vol. 5, No. 1, Tokyo, Japan.

25. A. Aoki, and I. Oomura, "Technology Development for Accelerometers," *JQEF*, Vol. 5, No. 3, Tokyo, Japan.

26. Akira Hashimoto, "Optimization of Brazing Condition for a Two-piece Gear," *JQEF*, Vol. 5, No. 3, Tokyo, Japan.

27. J.S. Colunga, D. Lau, J.R. Otterman, B.C. Prodin, K.W. Turner, and J.J. King, "Robustness of Fuel Delivery Systems," American Supplier Institute Symposium, Dearborn, MI, U.S.A., 1993.

28. M. Deng, D. Li, W. Szpunar, J. King, and J. Koleman, "Reduction of Chatter in a Wiper System," American Supplier Institute Symposium, Dearborn, MI, U.S.A., 1996.

29. Hiroaki Aga: "Establishment of Stamping Technology for Specific Door Opening Area," Quality Engineering Forum Symposium, Tokyo, Japan, 1995.

30. A. Obara, H. Honda, M. Aoki, and H. Yano, "Improvement of an Aerocraft Material Casing Process," Quality Engineering Forum Symposium, Tokyo, Japan, 1996.

31. Koji Takahashi, "Robust Design of an Automatic Document Feeder," Quality Engineering Forum Symposium, Tokyo, Japan, 1997.

32. H. Sano, M. Watanabe, S. Fujiwara, and K. Kurihara, "Reduction in Airflow of an Intercooler System," Quality Engineering Forum Symposium, Tokyo, Japan, 1997.

33. Y. Hori and S. Sinoda, "Parameter Design on the Green Sand Preparation for Foundry," Quality Engineering Forum Symposium, Tokyo, Japan, 1997.

34. S. Kazashi and I. Miyazaki, "Optimization of a Wave Soldering," *JQEF*, Vol. 1, No. 3, Tokyo, Japan, 1993.

35. T. Hosokawa, A. Okamuro, K. Miyata, and H. Matsumoto: "Development of Exchange-Coupled Direct-Overwrite MO Disk," *JQEF*, Vol. 2, No. 2, Tokyo, Japan.

36. Yoshishige Kanemoto, "Robust Design and Tuning for an Equalizer," *JQEF*, Vol. 2, No. 5, Tokyo, Japan.

37. Y. Nakamura, Y. Kubo, and Y. Okamoto, "Fabrication of Transparent Conductive Thin Films," *JQEF*, Vol. 3, No. 1, Tokyo, Japan.

38. Satoshi Takahashi, "Parameter Design of a Low Pass Filter Using Complex Numbers," *JQEF*, Vol. 3, No. 4, Tokyo, Japan.

39. K. Manabe, K. Yao, S. Hoshino, and A. Aoki, "Technology Development of Drain Electrode Process for Power MOSFET," *JQEF*, Vol. 4, No. 2, Tokyo, Japan.

40. M. Iwase and T. Sawataishi, "Improvement of Differential Amplifier Circuit," *JQEF*, Vol. 1, No. 3, Tokyo, Japan, 1993.

41. Fumikazu Harazono, "Robust Design of a Voltage Controlled Oscillator," *JQEF*, Vol. 3, No. 4, Tokyo, Japan.

42. Y. Mori, K. Kimura, T. Nakazima, and A. Kume, "Optimization of Synthesis Conditions of a Chemical Reaction," *JQEF*, Vol. 3, No. 1, Tokyo, Japan.

43. Hiroshi Shimoda, "Development of a Formula for Chemicals Used in Body Warmer," *JQEF*, Vol. 3, No. 6, Tokyo, Japan.

44. K. Shinohara and T. Bushimata, "Study on the Evaluation of the Friction Function of Plastic Materials and Development of a Low Friction/Low wear Polyacetal Resin," *JQEF*, Vol. 4, No. 1, Tokyo, Japan.

45. T. Nishikawa, H. Shibano, K. Takenaka, and H. Yasunaga, "Development of a Measuring Technique for Dispersion Homogeneity and Binding Capacity of Composite Material," *JQEF*, Vol. 4, No. 1, Tokyo, Japan.

46. T. Nojima, M. Koizumi, and H. Satou, "Optimization of an Ink Formula," *JQEF*, Vol.4, No. 1, Tokyo, Japan.

47. Lapthe Flora, Ron Ward, and Tim Reed, "Optimization of an Electrical Encapsulant," American Supplier Institute Symposium, Dearborn, MI, U.S.A., 1995.

48. Paul Wang, "Robust Design of an EW Receiver," American Supplier Institute Symposium, Dearborn, MI, U.S.A., 1996.

Index

Biographies

YUIN WU

Yuin Wu received a B.S. in Chemical Engineering from Cheng Kung University, taught as a professor at several institutions in Taiwan, and held senior management positions with industrial firms in Taiwan as well. Mr. Wu is an Executive Director of ASI.

Mr. Wu has long been active in quality control and improvement. He became acquainted with Dr. Taguchi in 1966 while in Japan on a study sponsored by the Taiwan goverment. Mr. Wu made some of the first English (and Chinese) translations of Dr. Taguchi's works. He is also credited with conducting the first Taguchi Methods experiments in the United States while working with private industry in California.

He has been with the American Supplier Institute (ASI), Inc. (and its predecessor, the Ford Supplier Institute) since 1982, and currently provides consultation and training in many diverse Taguchi Methods applications. He has been active as a consultant in North America as well as many countries in Europe, South America, and Asia. He has trained for the automotive, computer, and defense companies, and also mechanical, electrical, chemical, and food industries. He has written numerous publications on the subject of Taguchi Methods.

ALAN WU

Alan Wu is Vice President and Senior Consultant for ASI, and specializes in Taguchi Methods (Robust Design), Quality Function Deployment (QFD), TRIZ, and Failure Mode and Effects Analysis (FMEA). Mr. Wu was the technical engineer on the ANOVA-TM and CAPD-TM Taguchi application software programs, and has been training and consulting with manufacturing companies throughout North America, Europe, Asia, and Australia since 1985.

Mr. Wu holds a B.A. in Computer Science Mathematics from San Jose State University. Mr. Wu's association with Dr. Taguchi began through his father, Yuin Wu, who has been a close associate of Dr. Genichi Taguchi since the 1960s. After receiving his bachelor's degree, he became actively involved in learning and applying Taguchi Methods.

Over the past fifteen years, Mr. Wu has been instrumental in assisting ASI customers to apply Taguchi Methods, QFD, and TRIZ in Product Development and Manufacturing, and has a diverse range of experience in mechanical, electrical, electronic, chemical, and food industries. He has trained and consulted with such companies as: Allied Signal, Anheuser Busch, Boeing, Case Corporation, CHR Hansen, Compaq Computer Corporation, Culligan, Daimler Chrysler Corporation, Delphi Automotive Systems, E.I. Dupont, ESCO Corporation, FMC Corporation, Ford Motor Company, General Dynamics, General Electric Company, General Motors Corporation, GTE Laboratories, Hewlett-Packard, Hughes Aircraft, ITT, Kaiser Electronics, Kemet Electronics, Lockheed-Martin, LSI Logic, Melroe Ingersoll-Rand, Miller Brewing Company, Motorola, NASA, Naval Weapons Support Center, Newport News Shipbuilding, Northern Telecom, OEA Aerospace, Philips, Procter & Gamble, Ralston Purina, Seiko Epson, Storage Technology, Texas Instruments, U.S. Filter, Westinghouse, Weyerhaeuser, and many others.